Through the Lens
of Ourselves

SUNI MILLER ZMICH

Through the Lens of Ourselves

**Adoptees, Adoptive Families, and Birth Families:
Our Collective Adoption Stories**

Through the Lens of Ourselves

Adoptees, Adoptive Families, and Birth Families: Our Collective Adoption Stories

www.sunimillerzmich.com
Author Photographer: Melodie Zmich
Beach Photographer: Melissa St. James
Chief Editor: Sarah Mayor
Consultant: Gail Spector
Cover Designer: Joanne Campo © 2021 Shiitake Press
Developmental Editor: Brigitte Issel

Available in these formats:
- 978-1-7369308-0-9 (Paperback)
- 978-1-7369308-1-6 (eBook)
- 978-1-7369308-2-3 (Hardcover)

Library of Congress Control Number: 2021905881

Names and identifying details have been changed to protect the privacy of the interviewees.

Publisher's Cataloging-In-Publication Data
(Prepared by The Donohue Group, Inc.)

Names: Zmich, Suni Miller, author.
Title: Through the lens of ourselves : adoptees, adoptive families, and birth families : our collective adoption stories / Suni Miller Zmich.
Description: Rosemount, Minnesota : Shiitake Press, [2021] | Includes bibliographical references and index.
Identifiers: ISBN 9781736930809 (paperback) | ISBN 9781736930816 (ebook)
Subjects: LCSH: Adoptees--Biography. | Adoptive parents--Biography. | Birthparents--Biography. | Adoption--Psychological aspects. | Interpersonal relations. | LCGFT: Biographies.
Classification: LCC HV874.8 .Z45 2021 (print) | LCC HV874.8 (ebook) | DDC 362.7340922--dc23

Published by Shiitake Press, Rosemount, Minnesota
publish@shiitakepress.com

Through the Lens of Ourselves

Adoptees, Adoptive Families, and Birth Families: Our Collective Adoption Stories

Table of Contents

Foreword

"When we deny our stories, they define us. When we own our stories, we get to write the ending."

-Brené Brown

I am adopted.

According to my oldest daughter, I have these fleeting "Mom" thoughts. She's right, and they often occur at 2 a.m. Or sometimes they occur the second I open my eyes in the morning. I prefer to call them "epiphanies marginally worthy of solving the world's problems." And by "world," I mean my speck of existence and not the global sphere to which we are all tethered. Today I woke up and thought about the peacefulness that has blanketed me in the past few months. When I started this project, I didn't know in which direction I wanted to go or how it would end. I just felt this inexplicable need to look outside myself and hear the stories of other adoptees and those connected to them.

Anger about my adoption has been an anchor throughout my life. When I was a child, my dad called me his little chili pepper. I have chased the ability to forgive for half a century, standing on my self-righteous pedestal when others have hurt me, never hesitating to castigate or shame them. It seldom occurred to me to give a thought to their unique perspectives or anguish. Anger gave me a sense of control when my fear and sorrow tried to take the helm; stronger than my insecurities, anger kept me from despair by beating down all other emotions. I held on to it like a buoy so I wouldn't drown in depression. It served me well in that I managed to stay afloat, but it also kept me from swimming free.

Somehow, capturing everyone else's stories gave me the courage to release my rage. The sea of my own story once frightened me, but I now allow it to wash over me. Its natural buoyancy helps me float without the constant need to clutch resentment. This new awareness was an unexpected (and now welcomed) benefit of my journey. I hope that when you read the diverse rainbow of perspectives in this book, you can also find peace.

Many adoptees consider adoption as the equivalent to betrayal and loss. Divorce, death, infidelity, addiction, abuse, etc. – who hasn't attempted to pull a knife out of their own back only to find a few more to yank out? In my journey, I discovered the complication of adoption (unlike other betrayals) lies in the fact that many adoptees cannot consciously remember the perceived *treachery* because it happened shortly after birth. Yet still, they feel betrayed. In listening to this book's interviewees, many (although, not all) adoptees stumble through life, unable to identify *why* they feel a hole in their soul. The emotional eclipse is often compounded with guilt because acknowledging the sorrow would be to betray their adoptive parents. Adoptees often feel they must choose between healing themselves and maintaining loyalty to their adoptive family. Humans have proven they can overcome a wide range of emotional wreckage. The stumbling block of adoption is no different. Adoptees can also conquer their sorrow but only after acknowledging their loss and facing its origin (which was not obvious, to begin with). This book is not only about heartache; some interviewees have shared their joy in the pages that follow, which – for me – was a welcomed surprise.

Another revelation gleaned from adoptive parents (mothers in particular) was that many were afraid to admit they feel threatened by their child's tangled sense of loss. They know the love they have for their adopted child is as genuine as that of a biological parent. Some adoptive parents felt threatened when the birth mother came back into their children's lives – and sadly – in some cases, it was justified. I learned that some adoptive parents have a difficult time believing adoptees can love *both sets of parents*. In speaking with adoptees in a healthy relationship with their biological parents, I learned it is absolutely possible to love two sets of parents.

At the beginning of my writing journey, I naively thought it made sense to interview only adoptive parents and adoptees. My rationale was that the adoption story began with the child's placement in the home since the birth parents were no longer in the picture. However, I learned birth mothers also carry pain, which is intertwined with love for their children. When searching for interviewees open to discussing their experience, for every "Yes" I received, I probably received two "Noes." 100% understandable.

I hope this book speaks to the "Noes."

I have interviewed individuals about situations in which birth parents are in the picture. Those outcomes have been both positive and negative. I learned that the adoptive parents have to be deliberate when considering the best course of action regarding relationships with birth families. Every situation is unique. Regardless of the decision, adoptive parents need to acknowledge that adopted children have an undeniable pull to their birth parents – while simultaneously understanding the pull does not diminish the child's relationship to the adoptive parents. That simple acknowledgment is the first step they can take to help their child navigate their journey out of loss.

I divided this book into four main sections, with my story at the end:

1. International Adoptees (7)
2. Domestic Adoptees (8)
3. Adoptive Families (12)
4. Birth Families (7)

I have a friend who always reads the last chapter of a book first and then turns to the beginning. To save her the first-world inconvenience of having to flip to the last page, the conclusions I've learned about adoptees, adoptive parents, and birth parents are at the beginning of each section. Also note: you will see *[Tears], [Sighs], [Grins]* or *[Smiles]* in italics – those represent the interviewees' flowing emotions in *real-time* as they were telling me their stories.

I tried my best to refrain from using any verbiage that might offend someone or a group of people. Over the past year, I've had many lessons in social awareness. My "political correctness" radar has been updated, but if anything slipped through, I take full responsibility.

Every story includes advice from the interviewee. I wanted each person to feel free to express their beliefs. Their advice represents a culmination of their individual life experiences. After each person's story, I presented my thoughts – and even parts of my own journey. I believe all of our stories are woven together, and without exception, every conversation I participated in triggered a memory or an emotion already sewn into my soul's fabric.

My writing journey was propelled forward when I learned that unfortunately, a tragic component of adoption is some adoptees suffer so immeasurably that it leads them to suicide. According to a study published in the American

Academy of Pediatrics journal, adoptees are four times more likely to commit suicide than non-adoptees.[1] My friend's cousin – a young Black man who was adopted by a White couple when he was young – committed suicide after connecting with his biological family. A few years before his death, he found his biological siblings – all of whom had been raised by their biological parents. His siblings did not accept him as one of their own, calling him "White Boy." He ultimately could not reconcile their rejection with his yearning to connect with them.

My heart is still broken for my friend's cousin and his family. For a transracial adoptee, rejection is fear *realized*.

International and domestic adoptions are two very different flavors. Some of the adoption stories are about families of the same race, whereas the transracial adoption stories highlight the complexity that race adds to the ride.

I am biologically Korean. My family is White. I've always identified as White, despite what the mirror told me every day. I remember my own experiences … of my mother's Jewish family's unwavering acceptance of me, of being accepted by most members of my father's family, and of the time when my paternal grandfather told me he didn't have to accept me into the family but said that he did it anyway. I'm sure he thought he was being kind by telling me that. However, he didn't realize that it was the cruelest thing he could have said. When I was in college, I met some Korean American students who were not adopted. They invited me to some Korean Club events. They pitied me, not understanding why I lacked the fierce pride they had in being Asian. They didn't understand why I was brutally honest, and I didn't understand why Korean culture necessitated indirectness. My Jew-"ish" chutzpah intertwined with my military-brat-redneck-Christian upbringing did not dovetail with their first-generation Korean American traditions.

---

[1] Keyes, Margaret A., PhD, Stephen M. Malone, PhD, Anu Sharma, PhD, LP, William G. Iacono, PhD, and Matt McGue, PhD. "Risk of Suicide Attempt in Adopted and Nonadopted Offspring." *Pediatrics*, Oct. 2013; 132(4): 639-646. pediatrics.aappublications.org/content/132/4/639. Accessed 11 May, 2021.

My biology clashed with my environment, and I can see how my friend's cousin was devastated when his biological family did not accept him. The anguish he surely felt must have caused the spokes on his DNA to unravel, like treads on a spiral staircase splintering under life-threatening weight. When I looked at his picture on the funeral home's website, his sweet face belied what was happening internally. Neatly trimmed hair framed his smooth skin, and shapely dark eyebrows gently punctuated his kind, deep-set brown eyes. His lips were turned up slightly at the corners in a satisfied smile. The photograph of him seemed so serene ... but what shocked me the most was that he was born nearly a year after my husband and I were married. He was young enough to have been my son!

His adoptive parents must have been decimated; they adopted four Black children. I wondered how they were able to function and hoped they dipped into the well of strength they surely must have (as evidenced by navigating the adoption of Black kids in the heart of a racially homogenous Minnesota town). I wondered if they feared what the remaining three siblings were feeling. I pondered if their kids shared his tormented angst, as siblings are often linked in unforeseen ways. Is that young man waiting for them to join him in the afterlife? Does he now feel relief from his sorrow? Does he still feel sorrow, or was the freedom from his physical body enough to help him heal? I thought about my daughters and what would happen to the other if one of them ended her own life. They are connected spiritually in that separate plane detached from race and biology.

I hope he has, at last, found peace.

Struggle is often the common denominator for people connected to adoption, ranging from a nagging feeling that something is missing to *utter despondency*. Some have been able to free themselves but *only* after acknowledging the anchor of despair. In putting this book together, even working through the tough stories, I was surprised at how peacefulness gently pushed open the door to my heart. I hope this book will comfort those who find common threads in the uniqueness of our situations.

SECTION 1

Through the Lens of Domestic Adoptees

My very wise aunt read an early draft of this book. She had a 2 a.m. conversation with herself about what she had learned through the lens of the adoptees who had been interviewed for this book. When she woke up the next morning, she still remembered her thoughts and sent me an email, permitting me to print them here:

1. Adoption seems to conflict with the "natural" order of things. Though circumstances are varied, much education is needed. Potential parents need counseling before the adoption process even begins.
2. Thoughtless words can compromise good intentions on both sides. Whispering at social/familial events is a no-no. Children tend to blame themselves for bad things in their lives, and words hurt.
3. Nature vs. nurture is an argument with origins in the ancient philosophies. Realize that even when providing a "perfect" environment for an adoptee, the individual's nature (baggage – good and bad) will prevail. You can temper behaviors, but you cannot extinguish them.
4. Growing up – even as a non-adopted child is not easy. Adding adoption to the mix with all its variables can cause lifelong insecurities. Understanding these insecurities and verbalizing them can be freeing.
5. Discovering one's "real roots" can be an adventure. As in any unknown, be prepared for unintended consequences. Sometimes the knowledge can create additional issues. Try to prepare for disappointment *and* joy.
6. Having a sound support system in place is critical – one that pertains to both the various adoption issues and maintaining a healthy mental outlook.
7. When you blame your ills solely on adoption trauma, you are not taking responsibility for your life. It's how one chooses to approach conflict that determines success in overcoming this trauma.

William B. | Chief Financial Officer

Minneapolis, Minnesota
Year of Birth: 1964

As a former accounting manager, I had the privilege of running into William, a CFO, at a few business conferences. During those interactions, he was courteous, intelligent, and professional. However, when we had our interview, he was relaxed and showed a different facet of his personality. He was joyous as he eagerly told his story. The words flowed out of him like gentle rapids over boulders in a Minnesota stream. It was almost as if he was relieved. He was clearly content and spoke optimistically. His joy was infectious as I soaked up his story; it embodied what many adoptees hoped would happen to them.

William started by saying, "I've got a very weird story, actually." His adoptive parents could not have children. They adopted him when he was six months old, and his adoption was never a secret. When he was four years old, his parents adopted his 18-month-old sister. The only thing that ever bothered him about his adoption was that he didn't look like anyone in his family. However, with the lens of an optimist, he said not knowing about his biology was a good thing because his doctors would look more closely at potential medical issues. Other than that, adoption was a non-issue for him. Both of his parents have small families resulting in only a few cousins for William and his sister. His extended family never treated him any differently than the biological children in the family.

William's parents were always open to the possibility of him and his sister finding their biological parents. His sister found hers when she was around 18 years old. Unfortunately, it was a very disappointing experience. She discovered that her birth mother was involved with drugs and lived in a Texas trailer park. Growing up, William never felt the urge to find his biological parents because he had a great childhood and didn't want to "open up a can of worms." What if his biological mother had been raped?

3

What if she did drugs? What if he was a crack baby? The possibility of having a tragic backstory was enough to tamp down his curiosity. For years he refrained from searching; he didn't want to cause anyone problems. He thought if he found his biological mother, she might have to revisit hurt feelings.

Then the television show *Long Lost Family* came on.[2]

By the end of the first episode, William was hooked. Every subsequent episode he watched ended with him teary-eyed, and at times even bawling like a baby. Then he watched an episode in which a woman had been kidnapped, raped, and dragged across the country. Although she did escape her captor at a gas station, she eventually discovered she was pregnant. She decided to go through with the pregnancy but chose adoption for her newborn daughter. That episode opened William's eyes. He realized he had been short-sighted until that moment, having never thought much about his birth mother's situation early in life. Perhaps his biological mom did have a bad experience. So, despite his fear, he set off to find her.

William spat into a vial from ancestry.com, reasoning that if nothing came from the DNA testing, at least he would better understand his heritage. It had been speculated that he was French, Irish, or Swedish – but his parents didn't know for sure. Eight weeks later, he received his results, discovering he had all kinds of third cousins! He told me that everyone does and said, "It's like six degrees of Kevin Bacon." I was surprised he was related to Kevin Bacon.[3]

Apparently, everyone is.

Even though he had prepared himself not to expect anything from the results, he was disappointed when there wasn't a match to his birth parents. However, the ancestral report was interesting to William. He learned that he is 85% British – which means he is even *more* British than most people living in England. William said that many Brits are only 70% British. He shrugged

---

[2] www.tlc.com/tv-shows/long-lost-family/. Accessed 23 May 2021.
[3] Griggs, Brandon. "Kevin Bacon on 'Six Degrees' game: 'I was horrified.'" *CNN*. 12 Mar. 2014. www.cnn.com/2014/03/08/tech/web/kevin-bacon-six-degrees-sxsw. Accessed 5 May 2012.

4

and disclosed he thought it was cool – at least he knew, and then said, *"Okay, fine."*

Three months later, William was bored so he grabbed his phone and jumped on ancestry.com to check out potential matches. They found a candidate with a strong possibility of being a first cousin. He thought it was "weird" but messaged that person through the website. In his message, he asked if they knew anyone in their family that chose adoption for a child in June of 1964. He described some of his defining physical features and revealed that his original name was possibly Richard (which he had only recently learned by reading some of his adoptive legal papers). A few days later, he got a response from a woman who said she knew nobody who had given up a child but would ask around. At this point in our interview, William shrugged and said, *"Okay, fine."* He didn't expect to hear anything back from her.

A week later, the woman replied: *We are related. Give me a call.*

"Ahhhhh."

William read the message on his cell while sitting at a stop sign. He found it immensely hard to drive home because he was completely freaked out but somehow did so without getting into an accident. He told his wife, "Uhhhhh … I have a message …" He said he was shaking like a leaf when he called the woman. It turned out she was his biological cousin. Their mothers were sisters, but the rest of the family was never told about him. William discovered that he had a "crapload" of biological relatives all over the United States with cousins "up the yin yang." His biological aunt knew about him but never told her children because she thought it was her sister's story to tell.

"In all of that," William said as he smiled, "My cousin was the perfect person to get ahold of because she was a bit of a snoop." When she got his message, she called her mother and said, "I've got this weird guy on ancestry.com asking if anyone gave up a child." When she gave her mom the details, the phone was dead silent … then her mother said she had to call her back. *Click.* The aunt (of course) called her sister, William's biological mother, who lived in San Diego. She told her they might have found her son and asked if she wanted to contact him. William chuckled and said, "They didn't know me from Adam, and I didn't know them either. I could have been a psycho nut!"

William's biological mom said, "Yes," so his cousin sent him her email address and phone number. He connected through email because he didn't know how to process his feelings orally, deciding he could more fluently express them in writing. They emailed back and forth for a while. Within the timespan of those conversations, William's cousin contacted him to say that she and her mother (William's biological aunt) wanted to meet him in person. They lived only a few hours away from each other and agreed to meet at a restaurant between their homes. Again, as William was relaying his story to me, at this point he casually shrugged and said, *"Okay, fine."*

William brought his wife and son, but they didn't know who to look for. The second he walked into the restaurant, his cousin and aunt stopped "dead in their tracks." They immediately knew it was him because he looked like Grandpa.

William laughed, "That's nice – I looked like a grandpa."

The physical family resemblance was extraordinarily strong. They spent two hours at lunch. His cousin's father didn't make it to that lunch; he was skeptical about William, thinking it was a hoax. However, at another family gathering a few months later, he couldn't deny it. When he saw William walk in through the doorway, he immediately knew the biological connection was real. William met 12 to 15 relatives that day – cousins, aunts, and uncles – "which was pretty cool."

William's cousin not only introduced him to his biological family, but she also researched his biological dad. He was a college student majoring in French (who wanted to travel to France) when he met William's biological mother. She was living in her family's home on a farm. They dated, and she became pregnant. When he learned of the pregnancy, he told her, "I'm sorry, I can't do this," and walked away. He ended up marrying his female friend and confidante (who attended the same university), and he later became a French professor. Back in the 1960s, unwed mothers didn't go over well in their social circle. William's biological mother's family was prominent in the area – and they were strict churchgoers. The only way it would work was if she were to choose adoption. She lived with her sister until she gave birth to William.

With all the new information William was processing, his wife also dug into his biological roots. On the university's website, she found a picture of his biological father as a young man – matching it to a picture William had received from his biological mother. Without William knowing, his wife sent his father an email, explaining that she believed he was her husband's biological father and asked him if he wanted to connect. She told him that William did not know she was writing because she wanted to spare his feelings if there was no interest. He replied with a "yes," and William emailed him.

His biological father called him two years ago when he came to town for a Mayo Clinic medical appointment asking if William wanted to meet.

"Absolutely."

William discovered that his biological father's sister (William's biological aunt) lived five miles from where he grew up. They probably ran into each other at the grocery store. He and his biological father visited for a couple of hours. William was fascinated by their physical resemblance. His biological father had adopted two children. Unlike William's father, they were not White and, unfortunately, had rough childhoods due to racial issues.

Neither of William's birth parents had any additional biological children; his mother had step kids, and his father had adopted kids. William's son is the only biological grandchild to both.

When he tried to convince his biological mother to visit him in Minnesota, she declined because she was not "big on traveling." Instead, he went to see her in San Diego when he and his family were in California for a Disneyland vacation. He remembers driving up the driveway … knocking on the door … not being able to see through the screen – but then hearing her call out, "There's my beautiful boy!" It was strange for him to hear those words from someone he had never met. When they came face to face, she gave him a big hug. William said, "It was weird." Before then, he had heard her voice on the phone, but in that moment, he felt love for her "right out of the gate." It was strange for him to tell her how he felt – he was so grateful. Just finding her was surreal, and there are no words to express how he felt. He found contentment he didn't know was missing.

> *"There was a hole in my life that I didn't know was there. Apparently, I needed to know that."*

William feels lucky and says that he had the best possible outcome. He said, "I can't tell you how blessed I am. Many people have horrible stories. To come out this way is unbelievable." They spent the better part of the day just chatting. She told him that she had closure because he was "still kicking." She had lost her husband the year before she was reunited with William. For her, it was "a big deal" that he was still alive.

William knows he is in a very unusual situation, and it is hard for him to believe that he's "on this side of the equation." He had no regrets about spending 15 seconds spitting into a vial – none at all.

The hole that William didn't know he had throughout his life did not define him.

He has always been secure in his identity, believing his self-confidence was most likely because he is of the same race as his adoptive family. There were very few differences between him and the rest of his adoptive family. He said, "Except for my bigger nose." Until he found his biological parents, he had no clue there was something "bigger." After he got over the initial shock, he said he felt like a whole person and "gets it." He now understands the joy of knowing his background, along with the comfort of knowing he was not discarded.

Birth family reunions affect everyone differently. When William told his adoptive mom about finding his birth mother, her reaction was great – *externally*. However, he discovered later that she was struggling *internally*. She was jealous at first. She was concerned there was some other lady he called "Mom." William told her, "You've been my mom my entire life. That is not going to change. She is someone else. She has a tie, but she is not my mom. I call her 'Bio-mom.' There is a difference." He went on to tell his mom that his birth mother didn't raise him, give him values, teach him, wipe his butt or take care of him when he was sick. It has been five years since the reunion, and his adoptive mom has become more comfortable with the situation given how welcoming William's biological family has been with her. William's birth mother sends his adoptive mom letters. According to him, the interaction between the two women has been positive. He differentiated between the type of love he has for each mother:

*"The love I have for my adoptive mom is deeper. She's always been
my mom. The love I have for Bio-mom is a different kind of love.
It is not as deep, but the gratitude is immense."*

William said it was hard to express, but he imagines it must have been
excruciating for his birth mother to go through nine months of hell. He said
it still feels strange, but it is not surreal anymore. It took a couple of years to
process what he was feeling after finding his birth family. He was
"flabbergasted" initially – but "never angry." William had approached the
whole "vial thing" as a pragmatic inquiry. For William, the interesting thing
about ancestry.com is that as time goes by, more people participate, and he
sees his birth father's side continue to grow.

His birth mother's family had a split before William was in the picture. The
two sides get together independently. Members of the "second" side (not
associated with the ancestry.com cousin's side) invited him to a family
gathering so they could meet him. Relatives came in from Tennessee and
Washington. William, along with his wife and son, drove to "middle
Minnesota" and were the first to arrive at a cousin's house. They sat down
on the back porch to have a drink. When the other relatives showed up, they
stopped "dead in their tracks," just like his mother's sister and cousin did.
"You look like Grandpa!"

Grandpa.

Even though the family was split, everyone on both sides has been amiable
and welcoming. William never felt like he was putting anyone out. Their
openness is what felt surreal to William. He thinks that blood and family
resemblance made a difference and ponders whether reactions might have
been the same if he looked like a stranger. Humans naturally respond to the
familiar. Nonetheless, the acceptance he encountered grounds him, and he
feels content and very blessed.

~ Advice Through William's Lens ~

For adoptees: Don't be short-sighted about your biological roots because
you may receive closure if you find your birth parents. William had no idea
that he needed closure until he found his birth mother. He said that even if

the search results are disappointing, or you learn that something terrible happened, at least you will know your story.

"Going into it without any hopes or expectations was kind of the key."

William thinks that he probably would have been very disappointed if he had gone into his DNA search with high hopes. He remains realistic about the process, maintaining that "it doesn't hurt to look."

My Thoughts, My Lens

Listening to William reminded me that some adoptees do have joyful stories. Recently, I shared with someone that throughout the interview process for this book, I was surprised when people had positive adoption experiences.

I once struck up a conversation with a vacationing couple on a San Francisco trolley. They were overjoyed because the husband had found his birth mother, and he was going to meet her in Hawaii after their stay in San Francisco. He couldn't wait to meet her. His elation felt foreign to me – but not uncomfortable. I was happy for him, but still, I didn't quite understand what he was feeling. Our conversation was like hearing William say he didn't know "something was missing," but he is happy now that he found it. During our conversation, the man asked me if I knew my birth mother. With that familiar lurch in my chest, I told him I had unsuccessfully tried to find her. A Korean woman had helped me translate my request for information to the South Korean adoption agency. They told me that my birth records no longer existed. (I'm not sure I believe that.) When I told William about my attempt, the look of compassion on his face made me tear up – he could clearly see my clouded heart, even though I couldn't entirely understand his happiness.

Yet, at the same time, he helped to lift the shadow a bit with his infectious joy as he told his story.

It made me think about the time when my husband once innocently joked with his family that I may be older than him because I didn't know my "real" birthdate. That nagged at me for a long time – I didn't understand why I felt offended by that comment until my inquiry with the adoption agency. The Korean woman helping me said that the birthdate on my adoption papers was most likely correct – because that's standard procedure in South Korea. Hearing that bit of information was freeing, like a release valve on a pressure cooker.

Given that little bit of peace gained by knowing the validity of my birthdate, I think I agree with William's opinion that even if an adoptee's search has a negative outcome, at least he or she would *know* their history. Talking with

11

William was uplifting. He was so generous with his story; I couldn't help but allow myself to get swept up in his exuberance. I feel honored and grateful for his gift.

Andrea K. | Adoptive Services Social Worker & Counselor

Brookings, South Dakota
Year of Birth: 1975

Conversing with Andrea was like sitting down at a dinner table with a wonderful hostess who makes you feel welcome. She attentively presented her story in an easygoing manner. The week before interviewing Andrea, I had met her birth mother, Jill D. (whose story is also in this book – see the table of contents). Clearly, Andrea received the kindness gene from her. Andrea was very willing to share pieces of herself. Her experience as an adoptee and her work with adoptive families made her a compelling choice for this book. Her empathy was evident as she talked about her life and how it spilled into her chosen career: social work.

Immediately after her birth, Andrea spent the first four months in a foster home – though she was only supposed to stay there for a couple of days. The state had paperwork issues, delaying the process. Her adoptive parents could not have biological children and consequently decided to adopt. Andrea was their first child. They adopted her brother seven years later. (She and her brother are not biologically related.) The only evidence that Andrea had from her adoption was a few pieces of yellow paper on which her social worker had written, *"Mother – Pleasing personality. 5 Feet, 5 Inches – Brown hair – Weight – Nationality – Summary – Reason for adoption – Birth parents were young and didn't foresee their relationship progressing to marriage … etc., etc., etc."*

Pleasing personality.

Andrea hung on to that description for years. That was all she had. She kept the sparse words on the yellow sheets of paper close to her heart because she desperately wanted her story to make sense. After giving birth, her birth mother had written Andrea a note, saying she would always love her. She opened the door for Andrea to seek her out someday. Unfortunately, the note was lost somewhere along the way and Andrea never saw it.

As a child, Andrea often wished she knew her story or had a picture of her birth mother. When new babies were born into their extended family, they would look like "so and so." Andrea often wished she knew who she looked like, but all she had was the knowledge that her birth mother had brown hair – but then, so did everyone else in the world.

Andrea's adoptive parents were open and honest with her about her story, which was the primary reason she chose a career revolving around adoption. From an early age, her parents shared information (as appropriate). She viewed adoption as a "cool thing" and was proud of it. As she grew older, they would add to the story, explaining what adoption meant and providing her with a healthy perspective on adoption. She never felt any shame over it or sensed that anything about it was "weird" or "bad." Her parents benefitted from educating themselves before Andrea's adoption by attending training sessions and hearing horror stories of families who were not honest with their children. For example, one adoptee discovered he was not biologically related to his family – at a family reunion.

Andrea's parents took what they learned seriously and told her right away, which was unusual for adoptive parents in the 1970s. (Open communication was not promoted as much as it is now.) Her parents told her they knew her birth mother loved her and wanted her to have a great family. She remembers that their tone was open and loving. She had a healthy self-concept and felt fortunate to have her parents.

Because Andrea was shy, her mother was the one who initiated many adoption conversations. For example, when her class had to do the dreaded family tree assignment in grade school, her mother asked if that made her think about her birth parents.

Andrea's adoptive parents made it "okay" by encouraging her to think about her biological parents. Their "permission" expunged any hesitancy she had. (Adoptees often feel like they are betraying their adoptive parents simply by daring to think about their biological parents.)

Andrea always knew she would want to find her birth family one day. Before she even decided to ask her parents if they would be comfortable with her search, they preemptively told her they would support her endeavor – they offered up their "permission" first. That spirit of openness, for Andrea "*was huge.*"

When she was 20, Andrea petitioned South Dakota for her file. She wondered: *Was I really special? Does this person want to meet me? Will I be invading her life? Will I be rejected?*

Initially, she was disappointed to receive an "unidentified" generic file with no names. However, she later received an "identified" packet that included everything, which Andrea viewed as a blessing. In the packet, her birth mother, Jill, had written a note on a half sheet of pink paper. She had included some pertinent medical information, but more importantly, she wrote, "I've been thinking and praying for you for the past 19 ½ years." She had put that note in the file about six months before Andrea had started the search process. Andrea wept when she read the note.

The process was easy because they had both signed a registry. Once Andrea signed off on the registry, BAM! South Dakota sent Jill's information to her and hers to Jill. One Saturday in September of 1995, the phone rang as she was, literally mentally processing that packet. As was common in the dark ages before caller ID and cell phones, she let the answering machine get it. However, when she heard Jill's voice leaving a message, she picked up the phone.

Jill wanted to come to meet her the next day.

Sure! Oh, the myriad of details swirling around in Andrea's mind … the ones that stuck out were the funny little ones that didn't really matter. Andrea was living in an apartment, waitressing, and going to college. She thought about all of the minutiae because she was still in shock. *I have a double shift! What time will she come? How am I going to get the house cleaned?*

The next day, Andrea sat at the kitchen table, waiting for Jill to arrive. She watched as two women pulled up and parked across the street. Jill got out of the car and walked towards the apartment while her friend stayed in the car. Andrea wished she could capture that moment forever. It was hard to describe what she felt as she watched her biological mother – *the woman who gave birth to her* – walk across the street. Andrea walked outside and made her way down the apartment building stairs. At this point in the interview, as she started telling me about the scene, her eyes became misty, and her voice slowed as she described their hug. Jill held Andrea's head like she was cradling her baby. The last time Jill held Andrea was when she was a baby.

The long embrace was powerful. After they stepped back, they took a picture together.

Andrea was at a loss as to what to talk about with Jill. However, Jill had two decades of processing and anticipating that moment; so, she guided their conversation. They both sat on the couch in the same way with their toes curled under (picture an arched foot with toes scrunched over like they're clutching a straw). Andrea had been longing for that genetic connection. She often wondered: *Who do I look like? Do we have similar characteristics?* She observed Jill's mannerisms and kept looking at her. Andrea thought she had many questions but then thought perhaps she didn't … She just wanted to see Jill and take it all in. Jill tried to update her on the family relationships, about her cousins, half-siblings, and birth father. Andrea admits she doesn't remember the details of the cousins and siblings from that meeting – she was too busy taking in Jill's presence. The thing she remembers most is that they were sitting exactly alike. She was sure Jill answered her questions but didn't remember what they were. For her, it was all about the visuals. At one point, Jill asked, "Do you want to have a relationship?" *Ha, good question!* In all the time Andrea spent getting to that meeting, she had not thought about what would come after it. Well, yeah … she couldn't think of a reason to not welcome a relationship.

They kept in touch. Jill led their next steps and initiated the phone calls. They talked regularly and then met on holidays when Andrea was in town to visit her adoptive family. Jill lived a little over an hour away from Andrea's adoptive parents. Andrea was able to meet Jill's extended family, which made her feel welcome – never pressured.

Unfortunately, while Andrea's relationship was blossoming with Jill, she struggled with the relationship she had with her adoptive mom. They were coming off the typical difficult teenage chapter; Andrea was at the beginning of her college career, and they weren't "super close." The discord was hard for her adoptive mom. They were still trying to figure out their relationship when Jill came back into Andrea's life. As much as her mom had been supportive of Andrea and Jill's relationship beforehand, the situation became very intense for her once Jill became a "real person." For a long time, she didn't want to meet Jill and seemed determined to create distinct boundaries. While Andrea was sensitive to her adoptive mother's feelings, she also felt caught in the middle. Jill had so much gratitude for Andrea's adoptive mother and wanted to meet her, but Andrea's mom did not want that. They just stayed in that space for a long time. At Andrea's request – and before her wedding – her adoptive mom finally agreed to meet Jill. (Andrea didn't want their first meeting to be *at* her wedding.) The meeting was cordial, and the relationship has remained so ever since.

As an undergraduate, Andrea studied everything she could on adoption. Her degree in social work led her to a career in the adoption field. Her first job out of school was as an adoption caseworker in Chicago. She was passionate and worked with special needs adoption cases. She helped adoptive and foster care families navigate cases involving abuse and neglect. Often, they involved children with medically or behaviorally-complex issues.

When Andrea began her career, she had no idea of the harsh realities of her responsibilities. However, she quickly discovered that her job was more of a battle – learning to buck the system to get the kids what they needed. It was about advocacy and fighting the system for "difficult kids." She progressed into an assistant supervisor role, but the 24/7 crisis work burned her out. Although adoption was still her passion, she couldn't continue at that pace. Andrea went back to school to earn her master's degree so that she could have more options. After graduating, she worked for a private adoption agency in Chicago that championed the open adoption philosophy (a form of adoption in which the biological and adoptive families have access to varying degrees of each other's personal information, with the option of contact). She witnessed how infertility awakened families to adoption. Besides home studies and post-placement services, Andrea's responsibilities included preparing families to adopt both domestically and internationally through counseling and training sessions. Sadly, she also witnessed many couples back out of adoption when their families were unsupportive of international adoptions.

While training prospective adoptive families, Andrea soaked up every bit of knowledge she could find. She read many books. For her, reading about unique adoption stories was helpful in her personal quest. As a social worker, she witnessed other adoption situations firsthand. She shared her own story to address prospective adoptive parents' fears and concerns. Often parents were under the misconception that babies would not remember their adoptions, and therefore their grief wouldn't be the same as older children. However, on numerous occasions, she told those parents,

"Loss does exist because the baby in the womb was separated from the only thing she or he previously knew."

The babies sensed the loss but didn't know what to do with it. Even if the adoption reasons were valid, it would not lessen the fact that the adoption was still a significant loss – a "baby's loss" was a hard concept for new adoptive parents to understand. The intangible loss is much deeper than having a conscious memory. She advised the parents they needed to acknowledge the loss with their children as they grew older.

To prepare adoptive parents for open adoption, she would repeatedly share her story with them. She also tried to help them understand what it would be like for the birth mom to be in their lives. Her own parents had a spirit of openness, even though they had a closed adoption. She told the adoptive parents to expect communication to fall on them, as the birth parents' involvement would often fizzle out over time.

After working at the adoption agency for three years, Andrea needed to move on because she wasn't focusing on her own story; she still needed to meet her birth father. The adoptive families she worked with often brought with them grief and confusion, which allowed her little room to process her own sadness. Having the added overwhelming sense of everyone else's adoption stories in her head made her sensitive and raw about her birth father. After realizing she was still grieving his loss, she knew she desperately needed space.

[Tears.]

The confusion caught her off guard. She changed jobs and began working at a faith-based pregnancy counseling center that offered free pregnancy tests and counseling. It was a relief and break from her former job because most women who came through the center did not want to go the adoption route.

While meeting Jill worked out beautifully for Andrea, failing to deal with the grief surrounding her birth father for so many years was different. Shortly after Jill and Andrea were reunited, Jill used her small-town connections to contact Andrea's birth father. She let him know Andrea wanted to meet him. He agreed. Jill gave Andrea his address. Andrea wrote him a card, keeping it light and funny. She told him she was not looking to invade his life, but instead wrote, "Here I am – I am open to meeting you … According to Jill, I've got your big toe."

Andrea never heard from him.

The rejection upset Jill, and she called him again. He told her they just had a house fire, and he couldn't deal with meeting Andrea at that time. Initially, it didn't bother Andrea too much. She rationalized that he was just laid back. She let it go – mostly. She wondered, though.

"WELL …" [Sigh.]

Twelve years later, Andrea's adoptive mom saw a picture of an older woman in the local news and figured out it was her birth father's mother (Andrea's birth grandmother). She told Andrea that perhaps that woman was the only connection she would have to her birth father. Jill got right on it, tracked the grandmother down to a nursing home, only to discover that she had severe Alzheimer's. Her caretaker, Samantha was her daughter-in-law – the widow of Andrea's birth uncle (her birth father's brother).

Samantha wanted to represent Andrea's birth father's family, as she was very dedicated to her husband's memory and loyal to her mother-in-law. In her self-appointed role, she set up a family reunion (and included Jill), so Andrea could meet their extended family. At the reunion, Andrea met many relatives as she waited to see her birth father.

He never showed up.

Jill was furious and hurt. Andrea was devastated. While Andrea was grateful for the introductions and enjoyed meeting her cousins, she wanted to meet *him*. Samantha remained as the point person representing the family. Six months after the reunion, Andrea was taking a sick day at home (a rarity for her) when she received a letter from her birth father, Matt, which both angered and confused her. He sent three more letters. In those letters, it became apparent that he had no idea the reunion had occurred. Andrea called Jill to ask her if she was also under the impression that Matt had been invited to the reunion. She was. At this point in the interview, Andrea's voice shook with emotion.

Andrea called Samantha and asked directly, "Did you invite Matt?" Samantha answered, "No," and explained that her mother-in-law's pastor decided it would be too much for Andrea to handle.

They decided for Andrea.

Matt had been estranged from the family. They rationalized that he should be excluded due to his involvement with drugs and alcohol and his lack of involvement with his mother's care. They felt it would be too hard on Andrea because he might be a "flake." Andrea couldn't believe they thought it would be too hard for a 33-year-old adopted person! Additionally, the pastor mistakenly thought Andrea and Jill were also meeting for the first time and concluded that being introduced to both birth parents would be too overwhelming for her. Looking back, Andrea assumes that Samantha followed the pastor's lead without much thought and became busy with planning the event. At the time, Andrea was angry – their actions caused her and Jill to wrestle with immense rejection and grief, making the situation unnecessarily complicated.

Matt and Andrea eventually met in person, and it went very well, but it put her in the "awful" position of having to tell him she had already met his family. When she told him, she could see the pain in his eyes as he connected the dots. She said,

> *"It brings me to tears. This is an example of how you can't make decisions for someone else."*

She continued, "Even if it would have also been the first time that I was meeting Jill, that was MY decision." Andrea cried for a little bit at this point in the interview, then said,

"So, that was pretty crazy …"

The relationship with Andrea's birth father was complicated because other people made it complicated. He had two sons, was working through his alcohol issues, and was sober. Andrea also discovered that his wife had intercepted the card she had sent to him many years before. His wife wasn't happy about his past "love child" and was very insecure. He knew about the letter but never read it because she had hidden it from him. His past with Jill caused marriage problems for him. It wasn't until his wife passed away that he found Andrea's letter – which was a part of why he reached out to her.

Over the years, Andrea's relationship with her birth father has not been at the same emotional depth as her relationship with Jill. However, they have kept in touch, seeing each other occasionally. Mostly, it's been a laid-back relationship. He is now in good physical and mental health. Andrea said, "Simple life. Simple guy."

Conversely, Andrea and Jill have continued to nurture their wonderful relationship. Initially, Andrea had feelings of gratitude, honor, and respect for Jill. However, with time, their relationship evolved into something more; she now relates to Jill like a special aunt and addresses her by her first name. Andrea's exact feelings are hard for her to describe – she just knows they are from a separate place than the feelings she has for her adoptive mom. In hindsight, though, Andrea thinks that her adoptive mother wasn't prepared for how *she* would feel when Andrea found her birth mother. She said that the love she has for Jill is neither stronger nor weaker than the love she has for her adoptive mother. It's just *different*.

Andrea emphasized that she felt a stronger connection to her adoptive parents *after* meeting Jill. She felt more solidified in who she was and who her adoptive family was because she found the "missing piece of the puzzle" by gaining a genetic connection.

~ Advice Through Andrea's Lens ~

For adoptive parents: "It's really important that you do the grief work that you have as a parent before you take in a child (e.g., infertility). If you are still in tears on the floor, it is not fair to the child. As parents, if you still haven't resolved some of the core aspects of your own grief, you cannot be tuned into their grief. My mom DID. She spent several years working through it. She was able to put her attention on me. She was able to initiate adoption-related conversations and let me know it was safe." Andrea also said that sending messages of safety to children is huge. [Adoptive] parents should not be threatened by birth mothers. [They] should let their children know that they can safely talk about their adoptions. If their children don't want to discuss their adoptions, that's okay, but let them know it would be totally normal to think about their birth parents. If the children are shy, they will need a little prompting to go to the more sensitive places. Parents need to be able to tune in to their children.

<u>For adoptees:</u> "Permit yourself to feel how you feel. Every story is unique. It is not going to be the same. This is your story. Feel the way you feel. If you're feeling sad, that's okay. Get the support you need. If you don't feel the same way as someone else, that's okay. There is not a right or wrong way to progress. Explore those emotions and do not sweep them under the rug – maybe you'll find out you're okay. It is tough to connect the dots. It's hard. It's very difficult to go there. It's worth it. There are so many layers."

My Thoughts, My Lens

When Andrea described how her social work did not allow her space to examine her own adoption, it resonated with me, bringing me back to a brief time when my career was in social services – right after graduating with a bachelor's degree in psychology. I worked at a children's home in Virginia, which required me to live and sleep for three days at a time with the children and teenagers placed there. There were several permanent resident houses on the campus, but I worked in the girl's emergency care house with short-term residents. The kids coming through my house were mostly in transition and likely at the height of their volatile situations. I was terrible at my job; I didn't have the emotional armor required for longevity in that type of position. As a new adult myself (only a few years older than some residents), I couldn't reconcile my emotions with the rage that many of the kids spewed. They were *hurting*. Most of them were so far down the path of bitterness due to betrayal and abuse that they lashed out at every living thing that came near them. Many had direct memories of one or both of their biological parents and had to live with the pain resulting from what they perceived to be parental rejection – either voluntarily or involuntarily. The disconnect between their brains and hearts resulted in chasms that seemed too deep to bridge.

While their stories broke my heart and scared me, I operated from a safe distance of sympathy, not empathy. To empathize would have meant that I had to *share* their pain – and I couldn't do it. It wasn't until recently that I realized I couldn't work with them effectively because doing so would have been like looking in a mirror. I could help meet their physical needs (food, clothing, and shelter), but I couldn't meet their emotional needs because I was hiding from my own. I didn't have space for anyone else because I had not yet processed my own feelings about my adoption. When I think about those kiddos now, I pray that they are no longer drowning – or at least are in the process of working their way to the surface. While everyone's timeline is different, I now know it is possible to rise up. I hope that their healing came about sooner than later.

I took a long break from thinking about adoption. That detour spanned a few decades. Meanwhile, I became an accountant (*eye roll*). In a colossal overreaction to the emotionally debilitating career in social services, I did a complete 180 by going back to school to get a master's degree in the most emotionless career I could find. Paradoxically, I found comfort in numbers … the order and categorization soothed my brain. To me, there is something reassuring about the cadence of patterns, balance, and spreadsheets. When your debits equal your credits, your books are closed, and your monthly financial statements are finalized; it's like winning the lottery. I know. I am a ridiculous nerd. But despite my efforts to bury myself in work instead of my rage, I found I could only ignore my past for a few more decades.

You know that quiet voice that whispers to you when you first wake up in that fuzzy space between sleep and full consciousness – where your dreams and reality collide?

I would sometimes hear those little nudges to examine my adoption. Nevertheless, just like Andrea, I allowed my career to fill my life with anything but *me*. Even when I took a break from accounting to be a stay-at-home mom when my girls were little, I focused on my kids and not myself. However, by finally taking the step to examine my feelings, the pain that once held me prisoner has slowly melted away.

Listening to the interviewees in this book catalyzed my healing.

It is foreign (but not uncomfortable) to experience this new peace, which was not previously within my reality.

Jack S. | Digital Marketing Specialist

Jacksonville, Florida
Year of Birth: 1985

I met Jack when he was a toddler. He was charmingly goofy with a sideways self-effacing sense of humor. His sleek blonde hair made him look younger than he was. He made me laugh with his cynical one-liners and cringe at his self-vandalizing behaviors. But when Jack genuinely laughed, he couldn't hide his boyish core. He was a bit of an enigma, a kind soul wrapped around exasperation due to his demons. His complexity emerged as I watched him grow out of his innocence and turn down the dark, twisted path of the emotionally directionless – full of drugs, depression, mental illness, self-destructive behaviors, and – most of all – anger.

I related. Completely.

While I did not go down the extreme paths to the extent he did – at times, I was tempted by the allure of destructive activities promising to help me forget that, like Jack, I never wholly belonged to a *community*. Jack's downward spiraling was hypnotic – like watching an inverted tornado in slow motion.

We initially agreed to one phone call – he didn't want a face-to-face meeting, but we ended up speaking twice. Given the depth of emotions we explored, I can see why he wanted to be heard yet unseen. Five months after our second conversation, he passed away in his sleep (at only 34 years old) because his heart finally broke. He had been living at home with his adoptive parents, trying desperately to get back on his feet, working long hours to save enough money to get his own place. When I spoke with his devastated adoptive father, he hoarsely said that Jack couldn't escape his biology. (Jack's biological father had a quadruple bypass in his 30s.) Because of his health history, his physical heart literally could not stand up to the years of self-inflicted abuse – even though his emotional heart was on the mend during our interview. The ironically cruel part about Jack's death was that for years his parents expected him to die of a drug overdose or in a reckless car accident – not in the safety of his bed.

Jack started our conversation by saying, "About my biological parents – I have a little bit of resentment around this issue. There are laws in place for a reason. I had a closed adoption." When Jack was in his mid-twenties, at the height of his paranoia (brought on by mental illness), his biological father, Joe, hired a private investigator to find him. Joe was dating Jack's biological mother, Jennifer, after they had been apart for many years. Jack was conceived when she was 16, and his biological father was 18. They called him on Christmas Day and told him he was their Christmas present. Jack cynically replied, "I'm Jewish. I don't celebrate Christmas." They were living within an hour's driving distance from Jack, and he agreed to drive to their town to meet them for breakfast. Meeting them was awkward. For Jack, the most unnerving part was that he looked so much like them. He described it like an "uncanny valley effect." The more information he received, the more he felt like he was simulating them. Jack felt like his genetic identity was suddenly forced on him.

Before Jack had time to process what had happened at that breakfast meeting, Joe threw together a reunion party to introduce him to about 50 biological family members representing three generations. The gathering was tough on Jack for two reasons: his social anxiety and the lack of time to prepare himself mentally. In contrast, Joe had the advantage of over 20 years to process his feelings. He told everyone at the party that when his father (Jack's biological grandfather) had learned about Jennifer's pregnancy, he said he would pay for one or the other: the baby or college – Joe's choice.

Joe loudly announced that going to college was the right choice …

Joe's self-justified proclamation crushed Jack. Even though his thoughtless actions had *everything* to do with Jack, they also had *nothing* to do with Jack. Joe came from a wealthy family owning a well-known international business; they value their privacy. However, Jack resented that they did not respect his privacy when they disregarded the closed adoption agreement and hired a private investigator to find him.

Two weeks after the party, Jack moved to Israel. Because Jack's adoptive family is Jewish, he went to Israel via an all-expense-paid "birthright program" in which 18 to 32-year-old Jewish people could visit and work.

Those programs are designed to persuade Jewish young adults to become citizens.[4] Jack had a wildly vast range of experiences in Israel – from studying to working, to getting his heart broken, to descending into mental trauma because a waiter in a nearby hotel went on a shooting rampage. When he first moved there, he had to create a new support system from scratch. Many of his friends were in the military, and – as anyone associated with a military community can attest – they were a tight-knit family. The bonus for Jack was that it instantly doubled the size of his family. But when the hotel shooting happened, it traumatized him so much he moved back to the U.S., losing that support system.

Despite the mentally-destructive experiences in Israel, Jack still considered joining a synagogue because it offered him community. His yearning for a sense of community had been passed down through his biological mother's family. Coincidentally, while not Jewish, Jennifer's family lives next to each other on 10 acres. Three generations of families live on the same property – with chickens and small gardens. Jack said their living situation was similar to the kibbutz communities that exist in Israel:

> **Kibbutz** *[ki-**boots**, -**boots**]* *Noun, plural* **kib·but·zim**
> *[ki-boot-**seem**]. (In Israel) a community settlement, usually
> agricultural, organized under collectivist principles.*[5]

Modern kibbutzim are private cooperative communities with a wide range of industries, not just farming. As a side note, Jack boyishly laughed when he said he became familiar with actress Gal Gadot's kibbutz in Israel.[6] He was pleased that Wonder Woman had a community, too. Jack liked that his birth mother's "kibbutz" respected his privacy (unlike his biological father's family). According to Jack, she is a sweet southern belle, and he wished her the best.

Jack has endured several rejections in his life. The initial rejection occurred when he was given up for adoption. The next occurred as a young child. Jack always had trouble making friends because he was a nerdy, glasses-wearing, Jewish, bisexual kid. In the 1990s. In the South. Growing up, he

---

[4] www.birthrightisrael.com/about-us. Accessed 5 Mar. 2021.
[5] www.dictionary.com/browse/kibbutz?s=t. Accessed 5 Oct. 2020.
[6] en.wikipedia.org/wiki/Gal_Gadot. Accessed 12 May 2021.

had only two "friends" – both were children of his parents' friends – and one was a bully who beat him. The Florida rednecks were unrelentingly cruel to him throughout his childhood.

His adoption and sexual identity were intertwined with his personal identity, both playing a significant role in Jack's attempt to find his identity within a community. When his fellow middle-schoolers discovered he was bisexual, the bullies tortured him. Jack became suicidal and protected himself by wearing Goth outfits to fit in with that crowd. Unfortunately, he had to ditch the dark trench coat when it became too dangerous after the Columbine shootings. His next phase was to hang out with stoners; they were more accepting.

I asked Jack why he thought we, as adoptees, love others more than ourselves. He paused and slowly let out a somber breath, "We are getting really deep." He thought that maybe to blend in more, we try harder to do those things for other people at the expense of our own health and sanity. He said,

"We keep putting our hopes in other people's baskets."

As a pre-teen, the next rejection happened when Jack's adoptive grandmother stopped talking to him about anything of substance. The silence hurt him deeply, and he was unable to understand why that happened. His closest guess was that she identified better with younger kids. Jack has a cousin (also adopted) and said that helped offset his grandmother's rejection – a little bit.

The next rejection came when Jack confronted his biological father, questioning his intentions for contacting him. Jack suspected Joe wasn't interested in getting to know him but was more interested in giving that appearance to help solidify his rekindled relationship with Jennifer. Jack told him as much (in coarse words), and Joe immediately cut off ties. Not long after that, Joe's relatives stopped talking to Jack, too. He continued to converse with Jennifer sporadically. Some talks were normal, some were unhealthy.

In college, Jack was aimless, and it didn't occur to him to call his adoptive parents. As an only child, he discovered that his friends were his family. I asked Jack, "Do you hate humans at times?" He gave a sad laugh, "Yeah, but now I pity them more than hate." He elaborated,

*"Part of my downfall is the introspection – I love people – but wish
I could fix them ... I think everyone is broken."*

Jack was sensitive to conflict and did not handle high-stress environments
well. At times, he depended entirely on other people for his self-esteem. In
his opinion, social support networks were necessary, and he was jealous of
people who had them. Eliminating toxic people in his life left him with no
friends, which was hurtful and liberating at the same time.

I asked Jack if he could give me examples of positive and negative behaviors
that stemmed from his adoption. He replied, "I don't see positive or
negative behaviors because I don't see that duality." The decisions he made
in the past were because he was seeking validation. *"I've got stuff I regret, but
all of those things made me who I am today."*

Adoption is one of a few factors that formed his identity. In his opinion, he
was dealt a lousy hand in some ways but got lucky in others. It didn't make
him better or worse than anyone else; it's just that many decisions he made
were due to his feelings of alienation stemming from his adoption.

~ Advice Through Jack's Lens ~

For adoptive parents: "Give a shit." Jack said if he were an adoptive parent,
he would try to be there for his child and wouldn't be judgmental. He said
he felt like his parents didn't try to understand what he was into. He did
acknowledge that his adoptive parents were there for him to the best of their
ability. They gave him a very comfortable and loving home. They provided
a safe place for him, paid for endless therapy sessions, and sent him to rehab.
But despite their efforts, he was determined to travel down the tangled path
of self-destruction and regret.

When Jack was in second grade, the school counselor told his parents he
was a deeply troubled child. Jack resented that, saying he was just angry
because he had no friends and didn't feel like he belonged. Looking back,
he believed his parents and counselor should have asked him *what* was
wrong, or even *if* something was wrong, instead of presuming that he had
mental health problems. He wished his parents had resources in the 1990s
(like the internet) because they could have connected with others
experiencing similar situations.

After surviving childhood, his teenage years, and his 20s, Jack was weary by the time he agreed to this interview at 34 years old – yet was earnestly trying to improve his life. When he died in his sleep, I think he finally collapsed from the weight of a lifetime of rejections. Right after our second interview, I had written the following paragraph:

> *"Today, Jack is currently on a good path and is in a healthy relationship. He is picking up the pieces of his past and taking supplemental IT certification courses. I told him that I thought he would be a good father if he ever decided to navigate those waters because he <u>understands</u> pain and would be able to help his kids through the lens of first-hand experience. Underneath the armor of aloofness is a warmhearted, approachable, intelligent, and kind human. I am lucky to have him in my life."*

Rest in peace, Jack. I hope you successfully navigated the river of the afterlife and are looking forward to seeing me as much as I am looking forward to seeing you again someday.

My Thoughts, My Lens

I understand Jack's yearning for *community*. Although Jack did not experience racism, he felt alienated from a young age. Every time I experience racism, I am reminded that I also do not belong to a community by birth.

When my kids were young, I felt like I was part of a community for a period spanning about five years but was crushed when I had to walk away. My husband and I were part of a group of friends I thought we would have forever. Our community included six other families and most of us were not super close with our own extended families. We naturally formed a comfortable group of friends. Just like Jack, I depended on my friends for my self-esteem. I felt like I had the brothers, sisters, nieces, and nephews I had always yearned for as an only child. Our kids went to the same schools; we had happy hours, game nights, dinner parties, outings, and trips. I thought I had found community, believing that our kids would grow up together (and even thought a few might marry each other).

My hopes were eviscerated when I discovered that at least one spouse in five out of the six families liked to tell N-word jokes behind my back (the sixth family did not actively participate but was complicit). It was like a sport to them. They would get on a roll to see who could tell the nastiest joke. Before I witnessed it myself, I had no idea they were doing that because they kept it away from me, knowing I couldn't abide racism. Everyone in the group was White except for a man who was mixed Black/White – and me. He explained that he used the N-word to take away its power. *That* I understand – I was around when rappers started that trend in the 1990s to deflate its power by taking their word back.

What I couldn't understand was why he encouraged our White friends to do the same.

I called them out, but they refused to take any responsibility, accusing me of over-reacting. One woman told me it was just that we had different opinions … and they should be allowed theirs. I thought it was a horrific thing to take a stand on (i.e., their right to "freedom of speech" by engaging in racist jokes) – and was devastated they wanted to keep their dehumanizing jokes more than they wanted my friendship. For a few days, I was unable to stop crying – so I put on my jogging shoes and ran to slap myself silent. Typically, I jog like a turtle, but that time, I was flying. As I plowed through the neighborhood and into the next, I cried for six miles straight. By the time I got to mile seven, I was so exhausted and nauseated that the physical tears no longer flowed (but the internal ones still stung my soul). For the next few months, my friends wanted to sweep it under the rug and continued to invite us to the usual events. But my husband and I decided that we couldn't teach our daughters to accept racism passively. Ultimately, with my husband's support, I cut off ties to my chosen community.

At the time, my extreme emotional reaction didn't make sense to me (I am not Black). But in retrospect, I've concluded that I couldn't stop crying because being adopted had made me ultra-sensitive to being an outsider (both racially and socially) anywhere I lived. I've never lived in an Asian community (except as an infant). To witness their flippant and cruel callousness aimed at another race was a personal affront.

Looking back, it is clear that losing my chosen family was equally as devastating as losing my birth family. But the second time, the loss was *my* choice. I used to actively wish they would all come down with a year-long bout of incapacitating fiery diarrhea. Perhaps one day I will finally step over into the space of *unconditional* forgiveness, but for now, it's a win for me – that I no longer fervently hope that karma finds them and smites them down.

With butt boils.

I still feel a little sting in writing this, but it's not nearly as distressing as it was for several years after our fight. I recently had a dream in which one of the couples apologized and we were hanging out like we did before everything blew up. Perhaps my subconscious has let go of my anger sooner than my conscious brain – which is a relief. (I wasn't sure if I had the capacity to completely move on.) I will get there.

It is difficult when families or communities disagree on emotionally charged issues. My parents and I differ on some social issues; I try to steer our conversations away from politics. But I will never un-choose them like I did my friends. Admittedly, it has to be challenging for my parents, too. I can be hard on people and have yet to learn how to let others "save face" (as demonstrated in my story above). That concept makes sense in a practical way but befuddles me from an execution standpoint.

When Jack had to leave his community in Israel (returning to the U.S. as an "only child"), the pain was as crushing as that of his adoption.

I'm sure it was hard for Jack's parents to raise him, just as I'm sure that it was hard for my parents to raise me. My father has told me I was an only child because he was content with just one kid. I think he might have been trying to spare my feelings. I'm not sure I believe him (no offense, Dad). With my adoption separation issues and attention-mongering, I know I was a challenge. If I had to raise myself, I most likely would have stopped at one kid, too. I once read,

> *"Some adoptive children need as much attention as a newborn ... parenting an adopted child can be the equivalent of parenting three (biological) children (depending, of course, on the child's history and current struggles)."*[7]

If adoptive parents would equip themselves upfront with the knowledge of adoptee trauma, they might find mental space for more children. Jack's parents were at a disadvantage as the breadth of adoption literature and support communities had yet to appear when he was young. Many more adoptive resources and communities are available now. I recently spoke with an adoptive parent who said that he and his wife were required to attend a three-day transracial adoption seminar before adopting their children from South Korea.

Ignoring problems is never the answer; facing them as a family and working through the associated pain is the only way to approach adoption. As the years go by, the social stigma and shame associated with adoption have begun to melt away because influential adoption researchers have surfaced. As members of the adoption community, we need to stop ignoring our feelings, hoping they will suddenly cease to exist. Instead, we should take

---

[7] Crenshaw, Shirley as quoted by Rachel Garlinghouse. *Come Rain or Shine, A White Parent's Guide to Adopting and Parenting Black Children.* CreateSpace, 2013, p. 187.

advantage of this opening and work to build up our families through research, knowledge, and love. I know that's what Jack would have wanted.

Nathan A. | Civil Engineer

Minneapolis, Minnesota
Year of Birth: 1960

When Nathan and I spoke, he reminded me of a geode with a gruff exterior and a sparkly interior. It was easy to see that the years had softened the craggy edges – common to many engineers – as he learned to embrace his emotions. (I believe I can say this with confidence: I am married to a salty engineer and love his rough edges very much.) Nathan was very organized, methodical, grounded, selfless, and seemed to balance practicality with spirituality.

The concept of adoption didn't sink in with Nathan until he was in the second grade. His adoptive parents, Henry and Molly, never hid it from him or his adoptive sister, Joy H. (whose story is in the next chapter of this book). She was adopted first. When she was 20 months old, their parents let her "pick out" her baby brother, Nathan. There were no hidden agendas or misunderstandings regarding their adoptions. As they grew, Nathan thought their family appeared to make sense from a physiological standpoint. His father and sister were over 6 feet tall – his mother was on the petite side – and Nathan split the difference between their parents' heights. They were all White, so, in Nathan's mind, they looked biologically related. (In contrast, his sister did not feel like she looked like their family.)

Nathan felt loved by his family and grandparents. His extended family was relatively small. His dad, Henry, was an only child, and his mom, Molly had only one brother. Unfortunately, a few bullies in the family would say crude things at family gatherings, inquiring about Henry and Molly's "bastard children." From a practical standpoint, the comments didn't bother Nathan, but he felt bad for his mother because they hurt her. (Unlike him, those types of comments deeply hurt his sister.) The small size of their nuclear family made them close. His childhood is full of fond memories of family camping and adventures at the lake with his parents and aunt and uncle (who didn't have children). Nathan and his sister were the only grandchildren in their small family: "the only game in town."

As a young child, Nathan has no poignant memories about his adoption. He had the knowledge but didn't really care … or care to understand the difference, describing himself as a Labrador puppy … stupid and happy. When he was a teenager, his adoptive mother told him his birth mother's last name, and that she had been a student at the local university. Still, Nathan was content to remain in a happy state of ignorance and did not pursue his birth family. From a practical standpoint, he had a nice childhood – ample food, clothing, and shelter. His father wasn't around much during Nathan's childhood because of his work habits. Growing up in the depression, Nathan's father embraced the Dale Carnegie philosophy, and started working as a pre-teen because his family had little money. As an adult, when he wasn't working at his regular job, he would do something else on the side to generate income. He was frugal and very successful, but because he enjoyed working and followed a "pick yourself up by the bootstraps" philosophy, he was often absent from home. At the end of his career, he slowed down a bit, spent some time with Nathan, and attended a few of Nathan's high-school sporting events. However, it was Nathan's mother who was involved in the majority of his activities. (Per Nathan's estimation, time spent was 80/20, Molly vs. Henry.) Although she had a career, she committed much of her time to her children. She was a Girl Scout leader and took Nathan with her troop on camping trips when his father wasn't around. Nathan was happy to participate and spend time with his sister and mother. The girl scout camping trips fulfilled his love of the outdoors.

Nathan has fond memories of his family's summers at a northern Minnesota lake. Over the years, his family slowly developed their property. They started with a small travel trailer and outhouse, which necessitated retrieving water from a neighbor's well. Every few years, they would add an improvement; first came a better outhouse, then electricity, and then a well. In a few more years they bought a bigger trailer – and yet a few more years later – a telephone … technology would jump up a notch every so often. Idyllic summers of fishing and berry-picking afforded Nathan a lot of outdoor freedom.

At 17, he met his future wife, Renae. She asked questions about his adoption, but he still was not interested enough to pursue his birth family. In his late twenties, Nathan's interest level in his adoption scaled up when his youngest daughter – at age four – was diagnosed with an autoimmune disease. Her diagnosis was life-changing for everyone in his family. He looked through his adoption paperwork for hints of medical issues and even called the adoption agency to see if he could get his medical records, but they were not available. He started a passive adoption search, which entailed supplying his current address, email, telephone number, and a few sentences about himself to the agency. If his birth family decided to look for him, his information would be available. This differed from an active search which required more cost and effort. Unfortunately, there were no hits on his passive search.

Ever the methodical engineer, Nathan said three specific factors converged in his life that influenced him to change his birth family search from passive to active. First, his parents had both passed away, eliminating his fear of conflict with them. Second, his sister's birth mother had found her, and their reunion had a positive outcome. Third, his kids, now in their late teens and early twenties, began asking about his genealogy. They were curious to know things like, "Why do I look like this? Why are my feet this big? Who am I related to?" They were bringing up issues he was also naturally curious about as a child but had never taken action to resolve.

Now that he had the motivation, he stopped passively waiting for someone to contact him. The search process was painless. He contacted the agency, wrote a check, had a phone interview and then a face-to-face interview with an agency social worker. The social worker provided coaching and resources to support Nathan in developing a relationship with his birth mother. During the process, the agency asked him to write a letter to his birth mother to explain the reasons for his search. Even though the process was emotional, it went smoothly because the adoption agency led him through the steps. Nathan felt it was very beneficial to have the agency involved. Additionally, his faith played a large part in his journey. He described it as receiving "little nudges to stay on the path ... little things that pushed him in a direction that made sense."

For Nathan, the emotional part of his search included writing the first letter about himself. It was an introspective process that took him four drafts to complete. He wrote a one-page summary about himself based on example questions from the adoption agency. Who am I? How would I describe myself? Am I mad at my birth mother? (He was not.) Did adoption affect me? Those questions were designed to encourage understanding and to begin to build the foundation for a future relationship. It was a surreal challenge for Nathan as he described his childhood and who he was as an adult. The details were sufficient to let his birth family know he had a normal/happy/stable middle-class upbringing, which included specifics about his education and career, belief structures, and volunteer activities. He let his birth mother know he was an advocate for adoption because he felt it worked out well for him. (And when his own children were considering adoption, he encouraged them.) In the letter, he described his wife, children, grandchildren (two of which are adopted), and he included one photograph.

Nathan didn't want to be disappointed, so he set his expectations low, and the adoption agency helped him to be realistic. Nathan learned he had two birth certificates: one for the live birth (which was sealed), and a second one that listed Henry and Molly as Nathan's parents. He would *not* receive information about his birth father because legal paternity never had been established. (i.e., His birth father was not on the original birth certificate and was therefore considered an "alleged" father.) Working to buffer what could happen, the agency gave him website links and articles to help him prepare for the potential downsides of the search process. The agency also prepared him for a response of rejection – his birth mother could potentially say she didn't want to have any contact.

Staff members at the agency had current information on his birth mother. They explained that a series of three letters would be sent to see if she was interested. The first letter was generic without letterhead. It read something like, *"Dear Jean, we have information about your family from the period around 1960. Please contact us at this address or telephone number if you would like additional information."* The justification was that they were fishing for interest. If they did not receive a response, the assumption was either his birth mother had passed away, or she didn't want to respond. The next step would be to send a second letter – more of a teaser that would include his birth month – but still not on letterhead. If the agency did not receive a response to the second letter, they would send a detailed third letter about Nathan on the adoption agency's letterhead.

The agency did not have to send the second and third letters.

Jean responded within two weeks. The agency contacted Nathan to get his permission to go forward with the process. He permitted them to send his photograph and the letter he wrote about himself. The adoption agency acted as a clearinghouse and sent the letter anonymously. Jean wrote a similar letter to what Nathan had written to her and sent a photograph of herself and her husband, John (Nathan's stepdad). When he looked at her picture, his first thought was, "Crap! I don't look anything like that woman."

That hurt.

Nathan thought he would see himself in the photograph. Over the years, his sister fed his fantasy of looking like his biological family. She would say things like, "There's this guy I saw at work, he's gotta be related to you! He looks like you, and talks like you." Like many adoptees, Nathan wanted to have a physical connection with somebody somewhere, and those thoughts had dominated his thinking for so long that he was greatly disappointed when he didn't see his physical likeness in Jean.

They continued to write about a half dozen letters back and forth. He learned she was retired from a teaching and research position at a state university, and he had a half-sister, Sara. Jean sent him more photographs, each letter becoming a little more intimate. One picture was of Jean's father (Nathan's grandfather), and the noticeable similarities to his appearance wowed Nathan – physical build, jawline, hairline; those resemblances made him feel so much more connected to Jean. In her letters, she presented her life and history. One reason she gave for choosing adoption was that her father passed away when she was 14 years old, and she didn't want her baby growing up without a father as she did. The other reason she gave was that it would have been difficult for her as a college student to raise a child properly.

When Nathan read her explanation, he said he felt relieved. He said, "It sounded thoughtful and practical." Knowing he was loved, and not simply abandoned made him comfortable with her decision.

Nathan assumed she lived in Minneapolis. As she sent clues about her life and lifestyle, he would try to put those pieces together in a Minnesota setting. He thought that they lived within half an hour of each other – but was wrong; she lived on the West Coast. The series of letters culminated in their exchange of email addresses, phone numbers, and the decision to stop having the adoption agency as a clearinghouse forwarding their letters. The agency coordinated a meeting between Nathan, Jean, and her husband, John. Jean and Nathan met for an hour, with the agency's coordinator sitting in the meeting for the first few minutes. John joined them after that, and at the end of the meeting, the three of them went to lunch.

Nathan's first *thought* when he saw Jean was, "You're really tall." He didn't expect that. Nathan expected that she would have a similar stature to his adoptive mother, Molly. Nathan's first *emotion* when he saw Jean was joy. The second *emotion* was relief.

He was relieved that they connected, believing it meant closure for Jean, and their new relationship was heading in the right direction. Beginning in his early 20s, true to engineering form, Nathan methodically lived his life, setting small incremental life goals for himself as a husband and a parent:

1. He and Renae were able to conceive and have a son (his grandfather's wish to secure the family name's longevity): Life goal, check. "*I can die a happy man.*"

2. His kids graduated from high school: Life goal, check. "*I can die a happy man.*"

3. His kids attended college and graduated: Life goal, check. "*I can die a happy man.*"

4. A few of his kids got married: Life goal, check. "*I can die a happy man.*"

5. Grandkids came along: Life goal, check. "*I can die a happy man.*"

When Jean came into his life and he understood her decisions, he felt he helped *her* to receive closure by contributing to fill the gap in her life. (She had told him that she felt bad each year when his birthday rolled around.) She no longer has to feel that way. "*I can die a happy man.*"

Their relationship has felt "natural" to Nathan in recent years. On his first trip to visit Jean, he was cloistered at her home. Once they got to know each other, Nathan was "let out in public." At that point Nathan was "on display" and the barriers were removed. He went to Jean's former university office, walked around the campus, went to the local grocery store, and even attended church with her where she introduced him to the rector and some of her friends (which was a big step). He wasn't sure if his 80-year-old mother could show up at her church with a long-lost son and "out" herself to everyone – but she did. It was amazing to him that she could admit he existed, take him by the hand, and walk him through her church without shame. On her first visit to Minnesota, Jean joined Nathan and his wife at their church where he introduced her as "his mom." Their church friends already knew his adoption story. Having Jean with him at church felt "nice."

The success of their relationship has been in part due to the counsel of Nathan's adoptive sister, Joy. She offered the wisdom of her own birth family experience as Nathan's journey with his biological family progressed. Nathan and Jean have seen each other six times during a four-year span. Nathan and his wife have flown to see Jean and her husband, and vice versa. He has met Jean's close friends in and around St. Paul. They have been together for Christmas. Nathan learned that he and Jean have a shared interest in community service. (She volunteers with seniors, and he is involved with a prison ministry.) Coincidentally, both of his mothers had common interests such as the love of the outdoors, hiking, and photography. Nathan's kids pointed out that the women even decorated their homes in a similar fashion. When he started calling Jean "Mom," it was a huge step.

Nathan and his biological half-sister, Sara, also started a relationship. (He is ten years older than her.) She has visited Minnesota and met all 32 members of his extended family at a Fourth of July cookout – which was gutsy, in Nathan's opinion. She loves hiking, the outdoors, gardening, and has many animals. When he started calling Sara his "little sister," it brought a new level of intimacy to their relationship. He has listened to her wisdom and advice when navigating his relationship with Jean.

Nathan is looking forward to continuing his relationship with Sara, Jean, and John. At this point in the interview, he pulled out his phone and proudly announced that he had exchanged 89 text messages with Sara and 359 with Jean! Nathan's kids and grandkids have also benefitted from having a relationship with Jean and John. They write letters and email each other independently from Nathan.

At first, Nathan was highly sensitive to the fact that his children are Jean's only grandkids. He didn't want his sister, Sara, to feel like his Minnesota family was superseding her biological family role. He brought up the prodigal son biblical parable, knowing that Sara supported Jean and John for 49 years, not wanting her to feel like he was trying to rush in and take her place. He worried about sharing that fear with her because if it ended up that she felt that way, it would have saddened him. However, he took the risk, and they had a fruitful conversation, which ended well.

The slow, methodical, measured approach all parties took to forming their new relationships has served them well. Each of them needed time to process their own elements of curiosity, guilt or shame, one step at a time. Nathan felt guilty for not contacting Jean sooner, wondering how their lives would have been different if he hadn't waited until his adopted parents had passed away. Jean had to process her decision (and perhaps shame) of not keeping Nathan. He wants her to heal, and said,

> "I'm fine. She needs to know that things turned out well. The fact that I was adopted has made a difference in my life. But the difference was not a negative experience. She should not feel guilty or ashamed because she made a good decision."

As Nathan and Jean slowly built their relationship, Nathan became more comfortable as "nuggets" of family information came in from Jean. She gave him documents with a family genealogy going back to the first and second-generation immigrants. It comforted him to learn his grandfather was also a civil engineer working for a state Department of Transportation. Jean filled Nathan in on the family history when she and John visited him in Minnesota. She gave him a tour of her old neighborhood, telling him stories of her childhood in St. Paul. She showed him the house where she grew up, her old elementary school, her uncle's former home, the street where she rode her bicycle, and the family burial plots at two local cemeteries. At one cemetery, Nathan was kicking the grass around some headstones and found his adoptive mother's family gravesites; his uncles, aunts, and grandparents were less than 100 feet away from Jean's family! Making those connections made the genealogical history of his biological family feel real. Nathan said that at some point, he and Jean could have said, "Okay, we met. That's it." However, she drew him into the family by connecting to St. Paul … and for him, it was so strong – there was no turning back. He would like his kids to take the same tour with Jean at some point. However, if she cannot do so, he could recreate it because he has the maps and genealogy information – he's determined to that keep piece of their biological history alive.

Nathan is looking forward to the future. There have been some surreal moments for which he was unprepared – at times, he unexpectedly would feel the need to hold Jean's hand or want to talk to her. He wonders if it's because he misses his adoptive mother, Molly. There are times he yearns to see Molly, too. He said that his new connection to Jean had caused a longing he had not felt before. It scares him and catches him off guard, but he can still process it. He said, "Life is too short to be a jerk all the time … haha …"

~ Advice Through Nathan's Lens ~

For adoptive parents: "Get ready to have your hearts broken. Your children will experience pain in their lives, and as parents, you'll experience it with them. Adoption gives you one more level of potential pain … the potential for unanswered questions and unquenchable heartache is real." Nathan and Renae have two adopted grandkids. According to Nathan, they are still young and haven't had to face those hurdles yet. Unlike Nathan and Joy, there is no denying that they are not biologically related because they are of a different race than the rest of the family. They understand the concept of adoption and are just starting to build their own awareness of their adoption journeys. They understand that Jean is Nathan's birth mother – they have a similar birth mother/adoptive parent relationship in their lives. Nathan and Renae are highly cognizant and sensitive to the fact that their grandkids must deal with racial issues as they become older.

For adoptees: "If it makes sense, if you feel the 'nudge,' try to connect with your birth family, but take it slow and be respectful. Have others with you on the journey … make sure you have trusted advisors."

For birth parents: "That's a tough one … if the decision has left a hole in your life or in your heart, then work to fill that hole if the opportunity presents itself – whether that's accepting the longing, or seeking closure (or some other fancy word), if there's a gap, then strive to fill that gap."

The whole process of getting older, having kids and grandkids, becoming connected with his birth mother, and having an even better relationship with his wife has been good for Nathan. In his words, "It's been good. 'Good-plus!'"

[Grin.]

My Thoughts, My Lens

Nathan is a wonderful human. While he does not have the direct experience of being a member of a diverse racial and ethnic background, his first-hand knowledge of being adopted will certainly help his grandkids navigate that base layer of their adoption experience.

Nathan's positive reunion with his birth family is what many adoptees crave; I find it encouraging. Reaching a "natural" state of interaction with his birth mother has to have been sublime. I love that he has two sisters (one adopted and one biological) and feels close to both. I'm happy for him – that he chose to go after a relationship with his biological family. Had he given up at any point, he would have missed out on a fulfilling experience – one that circled back for him positively and inclusively.

Joy H. | Retired Court Reporter

Minneapolis, Minnesota
Year of Birth: 1958

When meeting Joy, it felt like I had met a kindred spirit. We both like to flip over issues and examine them, again and again. And again. She was like a weary world traveler who had finally put down her suitcase ... gentle and amiable but tired. To retreat from the world and *breathe*, she had recently moved to a small town in Michigan (population: 1,500 people) off the shores of Lake Huron – with no cable or hi-speed internet. She was willing to share her journey of longing to belong. Her aura exuded a melodic inner sadness. When she talked about finding her birth family, it made sense to her, but the sorrowful cadence of her childhood steps continued to march on.

With other family members, Joy was generous with her time and friendship. In my observation, she gave and gave and gave ... she became everyone else's person, but to this day, she still struggles to live for herself. Her adoptive parents modeled a giving spirit (of time and money) to both Joy and her brother – often to the detriment of their own financial comfort. Joy's adoption experience deeply contrasts with how her younger brother's life unfolded (Nathan A. – whose story is in the preceding chapter of this book).

Joy always knew she and Nathan were adopted. One of their favorite bedtime stories was about her picking him out when she was 18 months old. Her parents wanted to make her brother's adoption special; it was their way of including her in the process. Joy knew her parents loved her deeply, although adoption was not looked upon favorably back in the 1950s. The first real memory Joy had of adoption was of her aunt commenting to her parents she and her brother "were not *really* theirs."

[Tears.] "Sorry."

Looking back, Joy now understands that comment was a reflection of her existing self-doubt – making her wonder, "What is wrong with me?" As a child, she did not make the direct connection between her relative's comment and her feelings of doubt. In contrast, insensitive remarks did not affect her brother in the same way. She described it like a low-grade headache that constantly bothered her, but it didn't prevent her from functioning. Her aunt had exacerbated the feeling of "difference" that was already there. She often searched for similar physical traits with her adoptive family but ultimately concluded she did not look like her parents or brother (whereas he thought they looked like a "natural" biological family). She also felt isolated from groups at school and had only one good friend at a time. That feeling of separation is still with her today – she still longs for inclusion. Her mom and dad never made her feel that way directly – she was clearly loved, but in her mind, she *belonged* nowhere. Additionally, she wrestled with knowing that her parents would have had their own child if they could have, making her their second choice. Most of her life was full of disillusionment. She said,

> *"Adoption is not bad. You ingest these things, and they become who you are until you really look at them – and they're so much a part of you. You can't get rid of it. I'm 61. I'm still working on it."*

One memory that still stings for Joy is when one of the neighborhood girls cruelly teased her about being adopted. When she went home crying, her mom responded she needed to tell that girl, "My parents got to pick me, and your parents had to take what they got." Joy followed her mother's advice. It shut that girl up and *she* went home crying.

[Smile.]

As Joy grew into her family role, she became her mother's best friend and her dad's confidante. She thinks that was why she had only one good friend at a time. Her mother participated in everything Joy did; she was the Girl Scout leader, the room mother, and the Sunday School teacher. Everywhere Joy went, her mother participated fully. When Joy was young, they worked in coloring books and did homework together.

I asked Joy if she wanted her mom to do those things with her. She replied, "Sigh …Yeah, I probably did." Her mother was Joy's secure refuge, but it was interlaced with the desire to strike out independently. After thinking about it, Joy said, "My answers may be about my personality, rather than the dynamics of adoption … and yet the dynamics could be like that because of the adoption."

I asked her if she meant something like the chicken or egg, to which she replied, "Exactly. I maintain that the chicken was first." As we continued to talk, it seemed her lack of self-esteem stemmed from a combination of her circumstance and genetics. She never felt petite or cute – and always felt like everyone was staring at her. Reaching her full height of 6 feet in the fifth grade deterred her from participating in activities. She quit ballet lessons because she overheard her teacher remark that she was too tall. Her height led her adoptive mother to dress her in "old lady clothes" that would fit her. Joy hated the outfits which led to tension between them. Once, in middle school, her mother slapped her, and Joy slapped her back. That incident marked the reversal of their roles. Joy became her mother's parent, and she felt further isolated from her peers. When she reached high school, her friends moved on without her. Many instances of rejection by various people led Joy to retreat. However, over time she regretted giving up and not trying alternate activities, wishing she had not been so daunted by the perceived rejection and lack of self-esteem.

Joy said she also had an odd relationship with her dad because she was also his confidante. She reluctantly admitted that her impression was he liked her more than he liked her mom. When he passed away, she found an unfinished letter to her revealing that he both loved her as a daughter and was *in love with her*. Joy had always suspected that because of her adoption, he could justify how he felt about her. She said, "Kinda weird. Very strange. Never icky. Some icky." She and her dad were good friends and had many fruitful talks. However, there were many incidents that – when added up – were definitely off-color. One of her dad's favorite memories was of them holding hands and walking in town when she was 10. A drunk guy stumbled out of a bar and leered at Joy. He told her father he was lucky to have her as his *partner*. Her dad never acted on those "under-the-surface" feelings, but she always wondered if they existed because she was adopted and not biologically related to him. She adored him but still struggles with the memories. When she adds up all of the separate incidents, she concludes that her suspicions were probably not wrong.

I asked Joy if her mom picked up on her dad's secret feelings. She replied, "Yes. So, what I did was 'be less than' all of the time." If her dad ever praised her, she would keep it to herself because she could tell how those compliments affected her mom, and she stopped doing most things she loved to avoid hurting her. Although Joy's father showered her with praise about her gifted musical and singing abilities when she was young, he later dissuaded her from pursuing those activities as a career, encouraging her to choose a more utilitarian pursuit. Other than getting good grades in school, Joy tried not to stand out, wanting to be special in *nothing*. She didn't play sports, quit dance lessons, dressed poorly, and became the family's peacekeeper by staying home routinely, making herself small. Joy now regrets pushing down her natural interests. She said, "The 'not natural' way of feeling was amplified."

In reflecting on her relationship with her adoptive parents, Joy developed an interest in the belief that the soul already exists before coming back to earth; humans pick their parents and situation according to what they still need to learn. Joy wondered if she and her brother picked her parents because they desperately needed children. She said, "We filled that need." She talked about her deep fascination with The Urantia Book, a work offering a spiritual perspective on questions such as *"What is the meaning of life?"* or *"Is there a purpose for my suffering"* or *"How can we achieve lasting world peace?"*[8] It makes sense to me that Joy would be drawn to philosophy with such spiritual depth, given her childhood longing to be made whole.

Over the years, Joy never felt the need to actively search for her birth family – but her mom often said she would try to help her find her birth parents after Joy turned 18. Her mom even told her and Nathan the names of their birth mothers, in case they wanted to initiate the search. Although Joy felt her mother was very supportive, she chose not to search – she didn't want to hurt her adoptive parents.

Joy continued into adulthood with little conscious thought about her birth family. She and her first husband shared a duplex with her parents. In hindsight, Joy realizes the significance of sharing a roof with them. On one Wednesday in 1990, when she and her husband were at work, her dad was

---

[8] www.urantia.org/learn-about-urantia-book. Accessed 2 Oct. 2020.

at their place, answered the phone, and took a message from the adoption agency. They wanted Joy to call them. He was very excited because he thought Joy and her husband were adopting a child. Joy returned the call the next day (on Thursday). Her birth mother, Rae, had left a letter requesting any form of contact that Joy would allow.

No problem.

Joy called her on Friday. She discovered Rae was married to a judge and lived only three miles away! On Saturday, Joy was at their house.

> *"It was like we had always known each other … no big 'Omigosh.'"*

Joy believes they were both probably too dazed to have that big "aha thing." Everything was perfect. It was like they had seen each other the week before. Rae had the exact kind of house that Joy would have lived in. It was Christmastime, and Joy felt like she was stepping into a harmonious melodic scene, as though she had always been there – Christmas carols, decorations, coffee, and maple caramel rolls baking in the oven. Neither Rae nor Joy cried, but Rae's husband did! After about an hour, he pointed out that they did everything alike – gestures, tone, inflections, and speech. They even sat the same way in their chairs. And even though they didn't resemble each other physically (Rae was 8 inches shorter than Joy), they had many of the same habits that could only be explained genetically.

Rae had moved to Minnesota from Michigan to give birth. When Joy learned Rae was a concert pianist and accountant, her chosen profession of a stenographer (court reporter) made sense. Both professions require a highly attuned kinesthetic sense – a stenographer's craft is similar to a pianist's ability to sight-read music. Stenographers convert what they hear into a phonetic language and then edit it back into the written word. Over the years, Joy often thought about returning to playing the piano but never had because she was too self-conscious. She would soon discover that in addition to their mannerisms and talents, they also had similar personalities.

In reuniting with her birth mother, at 31 years old, Joy felt she had found her place. She and Rae became very close. Within the first few years of their reunion, Joy met many of her biological relatives – she had cousins scattered across the country. As they got to know each other, Joy learned that Rae mentally struggled after giving birth. Rae was so traumatized by the circumstances of Joy's birth that she didn't have any other children. She and Joy's birth father mutually decided not to marry, understanding their relationship was a fling (they were both in love with someone else). Rae's mother (Joy's birth grandmother) lost her job over her "promiscuous horrible child." In the late 1950s, her daughter was considered a tramp for having a baby out of wedlock. Rae was vilified. Sadly, she married the first man who came along willing to marry her – and he acted like he was doing her a favor. He treated her like a "fallen woman" for religious reasons. She had a nervous breakdown ten years later, ended up in a sanitarium, and had an elective hysterectomy.

When Joy was 55 years old, Rae became sick and Joy stayed with her, finding more pieces of her life's puzzle. At the same time, Rae's husband had Parkinson's Disease and was deteriorating. Joy took care of them both. Living with her mother for the first time went a long way to solidifying their closeness. Staying together in the same house was wonderful for Joy. *"You really get to know somebody when you live with them. You get to know yourself as well."* Joy already knew she and Rae had similar personalities, and that knowledge was strengthened during that time. Joy realized that she spent many years suppressing who she really was by learning how to conform to her adoptive parents' personalities. She felt like her adoptive brother did everything right, but she didn't. Even so, she wasn't sure if the two of them were ever accepted by their extended adoptive family. She wonders if her doubt is because they were adopted or if *she* were to blame because maybe she gave off certain vibes, that is – that she wasn't *really* a relative.

Eight years after meeting Rae, Joy decided it was time to meet her birth father. She enlisted the help of her friend, a U.S. Marshall, to locate him. When a lawyer friend made the first contact, her birth father agreed to meet her. She went to Michigan to meet him. When they met, she was surprised to discover that he still had the letter from Rae describing Joy's weight, length, etc. Equally surprising was that along with the letter, Rae had sent a bill for her medical expenses.

He paid it.

Meeting her birth father was strange for Joy – she discovered she was tall like him, and even though she did not want to admit it, looked exactly like him. He was a successful CEO, and his appearance was very important to him. He wanted to tell her things about his life that one would tell a new acquaintance, not a daughter. She characterized their relationship that followed as "interesting" because initially she didn't like him all that well, describing him as self-centered and opinionated. "Stuff" and success meant more to him than anything else. He cheated on his wife for years, in his words, "Because I could." Joy said she learned that Rae was just a "piece of ass" to him. However, she and her birth father stuck with it and continued to work on their relationship. She has grown to love him as her birth father. They now have "something" more than a friendship – but not a parental relationship. He has mellowed out now that he is an older man.

Joy feels that she immediately developed a connection with her birth father's two daughters (Joy's half-sisters). While they do not have their father's build like she does, they all look alike. She didn't know how important family resemblance was to her until *that* moment ... but evidently, it was. In describing meeting her biological sisters for the first time, Joy said,

"I felt a subtle internal click. Wow, I actually look like someone."

Joy enthusiastically talked about her sisters. They are on opposite ends of the personality spectrum, and Joy is somewhere in between (resembling her birth mother). Her oldest sister was a fun and rebellious free spirit, a 1960s-child throwback. She rejected their father's money as a badge of honor. He forbade her to play with her poor friends because he equated being poor with being "bad" – a move that launched her crusade of proving him wrong. Joy understood her sister; they connected spiritually.

Joy's youngest sister was very goal-oriented and extremely smart. She was successful and owned her own businesses. According to Joy, all three sisters have their dad's good and bad traits: strong business acumen, intelligence, functioning alcoholism, lack of hobbies, promiscuity, and tendency to be critical of others. Even so, she is "endlessly grateful" to find them. Joy and her middle sister talk every day. They both claim each other as their "person." They have grown close over the last few years and both dream that one day they will live together.

Joy's sisters are now her best friends; they are her life. Having the vantage point of being raised by someone else, Joy dug into what she would and wouldn't want to be like if her birth parents had raised her. She said, "My adoptive parents were much better for my personality. God knew what he was doing when he placed me into that situation, aside from the fact that neither one of my sisters would even exist, had my birth mother married my birth father."

Prior to meeting her birth family, Joy spent a few decades wondering if they would reject her. She is now on the other side and no longer has that fear. Before she was reunited with her them, her *adoptive* father's fear had always been that she would reject them. He did not want to lose her, admitting he was afraid her birth family would be more attractive than theirs because they might have more "pizazz." In the years leading up to meeting her birth family, Joy always had to reassure him, describing it as an ongoing battle. She recalled her adoptive father never disciplined her because he was so afraid that she would run away. However, he relaxed after meeting her birth father. Joy believes that temporarily living at home at that time helped allay his fear. Nothing had changed – her father could see she didn't abandon them.

In contrast, Joy's adoptive mother accepted her relationship with her birth family immediately. Initially, the interactions between the two families were filled with underlying tension. However, in the early 1990s, Joy took over holiday celebrations, inviting both sets of parents, during which her two "mothers" became more comfortable with each other. Joy came down with a serious health issue, which motivated her two mothers to follow through with previous promises to have lunch together. From that point they forged a new positive relationship.

Joy's adoptive parents have since passed away. However, she still avoids directly addressing either of her birth parents as "Mom" or "Dad." She will call them by their first names to other people (except with her sisters, in which case she will say "our dad."). She said,

> *"Calling my birth father 'Dad' feels presumptuous. It implies an intimacy that I don't have. I don't want to tread on my sisters' right to that name … Calling Rae 'Mom' makes us both uncomfortable."*

Another piece of Joy's puzzle fell into place when she learned she was half Polish. The knowledge of their heritage connected her to her sisters. It appears the adoption agency may have lied about her background in her paperwork due to the prevailing prejudice against Poles in the late 1950s. She grew up thinking she was Swedish and German. She now thinks it's funny that she took five years of German in school only to discover that she had no German lineage. (Although she does acknowledge the possibility that historically Polish and German geographical boundaries were blurred.)

Since moving to Michigan, Joy has eaten more kielbasa (Polish sausage) in the past few years than over her entire life. Her newfound heritage has given her an excuse to eat the sausage she loved her whole life – but avoided because it is full of fat. Joy also talked about her birth father's family Christmas tradition of making pierogis (think: flat half-moon shaped ravioli boiled and sautéed in butter). There are many different varieties, but their family prefers the farmer cheese and egg combo. Farmer cheese is similar to feta in texture but milder in taste. Joy noted the traditional pierogi potato and sweet cheese fillings are compelling, but regardless, all varieties *must* be topped with sour cream. Joy's heart-attack dumplings have even been incorporated into her Italian meals.

Traditions can be learned. But Joy fiercely believes personality traits are genetic – *not* learned, as evidenced by 30 years of her birth family interactions. She comingled her birth father and sister's Polish traditions with her birth mother's personality traits. In doing so, she was able to add a new chapter to her life's story which includes the harmony and "Joy" that she yearned for as a child.

~ Advice Through Joy's Lens ~

<u>For adoptive parents:</u> "Adoption should not be hidden from the children. They should always know. Try not to make your adoptive children your reflection. If their 'natural' genetic traits or tendencies aren't like yours, it doesn't mean they're bad. Many things that I would have done in life are not things my [adoptive] parents would have done."

<u>For adoptees:</u> "I had a great experience [finding my birth family]. I will never regret looking, but [your birth parents] are not your mom and dad." Joy encourages everyone to find their birth parents but not to expect anything because everyone's situation is different. "It's not rejection if they don't want to meet you – because they don't know you. You have no idea of what they came through or went through or why they do what they do. I've had such a good experience that I recommend it because it's good to know who you

are, your background, and where you came from. Be true to yourself. Be who you really are, not somebody else because your [adoptive] parents wanted you to be that way. Trust that you will know who that is. Don't be afraid to be that person despite the family you are in."

My Thoughts, My Lens

Joy's delight over her newly discovered Polish cuisine that came along with the family who welcomed her "back to the table" amused me. As she continues to nurture the relationship with her birth family, I hope she finds the self-worth she longed for throughout her life.

I understand why Polish food makes Joy feel like she found a piece of her puzzle. Watching my family eat pierogis and other Polish food is a joyous event (my husband is Polish). Going to a local Polish lunch counter releases the little boy in him. I recently made a large batch of the heart-attack pierogi dumplings from scratch. You'd think I had made him a plate of edible gold coins. My husband and daughters raved about them, which is funny because my cooking – while solid – is no culinary feat!

Given my family's reaction, it's hard to dispute that food is somehow cooked into our DNA. My obsession with Korean food proves it. I agree with Joy that food "likes" and "dislikes" are genetic. It's that intangible and comforting feeling of knowing you "belong" that brings you back to the table over and over again. Food connects Joy to the roots she did not have as a child. Her life differed markedly from her younger brother's adoption experience, as he did not feel the pressure to conform to his family, having an idyllic childhood.

However, Joy's parents tried to make her "in their reflection" for most of her life, which compelled her to withdraw from the music she loved. When she said that, I remembered a time in elementary school when my mother bought me a beautiful ancestry book. She wanted me to catalog our family's history by interviewing and documenting the reflections of our family members. I started the project but abandoned it after a few interviews. As a child, I wasn't able to articulate why I resented the gesture; I know my mother meant well because I was HER child. However, neither of us realized that I felt like a fraud beneath all of the layers. As a child, I felt like what I wrote in the ancestry book was about someone else's family and not *my* history.

My mom once told me that she wished her mother (my adoptive grandmother) had traveled to South Korea with her. She wanted to share her adoption experience. She had that biological connection with her mother. The ancestry book was her way of passing along the gift of those familial bonds, but I was a child and unable to appreciate the gesture. I now feel guilty about having those feelings because my family has been kind, generous, and supportive over the years.

I recently had a dream. My mother, Miriam, my beloved grandmother, and all of my Jewish relatives were present. We had gathered to meet a relative we never knew existed. She was wearing a polka dot red dress and even looked like my mother's relatives. As I welcomed her, I introduced myself to the woman by saying, "I'm Miriam's daughter." I think my subconscious knows I belong to the family that adopted me. My conscious mind has struggled over the years to separate the nagging feeling that I am a product of a "forced fitting." I suppose it will always be there. But like Joy, as the decades come and go, it is more of a ballad than a discordant symphony.

Alex B. | U.S. Air Force Captain

Minot, North Dakota
Year of Birth: 1994

Alex charmed me immediately by eloquently presenting herself with the wisdom of a 100-year-old sage. I thoroughly enjoyed talking with her. I respected her philosophical approach to life as she described her aspirations, which require discipline and restraint. She has taken charge of her life and displayed zero evidence of wallowing in sadness about her adoption. She described working through the challenges of being half White, half Chinese, and gay in North Dakota, a state very much insulated from ethnic and social diversity. Had I been born 25 years later under different circumstances, I am 100% certain that I would want her to be my friend.

First, Alex's parents adopted her older sister. When they were going through the adoption process a second time, the North Dakota adoption agency presented Alex as a potential fit, with a caveat classifying her as "special needs." Alex's parents were hesitant to adopt her because of the classification until they discovered "special needs" meant that Alex was half White and half Chinese. I asked Alex if she was offended by the classification. She answered, "Not really. It's North Dakota. What do I expect?" She reasoned, there were very few races other than White in North Dakota, so of course, she was "special." She said that prospective parents would have to consider taking on a completely different culture, and this was the only way they could classify a baby that was not *completely* White. The adoptive parents would have to understand – *that* is their kid, and they must deal with everything that "comes down the pike."

She clarified, "I'm *NOT* saying it's *right.*"

Alex picks her battles. Her philosophy is that being overly sensitive about labels and adoption – or all of the things that make her different – would just make her even more of a target, allowing people to "pick at her weaknesses." She lives by the principle that she has to be the best

59

representative of her community – whether it is the adoption community, the gay community, or the Asian community. She said,

> *"I want to be the best data point I can be because I might be the only data point that someone ever meets."*

Alex's parents and sister are White. Her mom's story – Anna B. – is told in the Adoptive Families section of this book (see the table of contents). Unlike Alex, her sister never felt like an outsider; she always felt she belonged in their community. Alex thinks her sister had it easier because she looked like their parents. Her sister's children look like they biologically belong to the family. Alex was never exposed to Chinese culture in North Dakota and feels "short-changed" because Asian culture is so much more disciplined, which she felt would have benefited her.

Growing up in a very White, Midwestern Catholic town was "both good and bad" for Alex. She respects the iconic, humble, hard-working, Midwest culture and carries some sweet memories about Midwesterners. However, the bad slightly outweighs the good because she is gay, which she describes as her "otherness." When she was younger, she experienced some depression but was not suicidal. What helped her work through her depression was her natural strong-willed personality. Being Asian was also a differentiator growing up in the Midwest. Alex felt she missed out on the shared genetic aspect, but issues emerging from her ethnicity didn't affect her as much as the obstacles that came with being gay. She said,

> *"Being adopted is more a novelty … like a quirk, almost."*

At times, people become confused. At a parent-teacher conference, her teacher once asked, "So … is her dad Asian?" Coworkers have asked Alex about the "lovely White family" in her photographs. She shrugged, laughed, and said that anyone who has met her family loves them. When considering the nature vs. nurture debate, the "nurture" from her family is evident. The "nature" struggle occurs during times like medical visits or school projects. During her elementary school's ancestry project, Alex felt like she was making one for someone else's family.

Alex's friends get angry about her adoption for her, but she is over that anger. She reasons, "Others will react to your pain in the way you react to it." She understands that most people can't even imagine what it would be like to be adopted because they are close to their families. They cannot fathom not looking like their parents and siblings – or not having the same mannerisms or commonalities. She believes it's reasonable for them to feel sorry for her when they see she lacks that basic human comfort. Alex does acknowledge some adoptees may not feel accepted by their adoptive families because they lack the strong bond that biological children often have.

Alex laughed as she talked about the annoying events she endured growing up. Her grandmother once scrubbed her arms raw because she thought her elbows were dirty. Asians have darker elbows and knees (insert visual of me slapping my forehead). On another occasion, when Alex turned 18, she went with her sister and mom for a two-hour road trip to Bismarck to get tattoos (mom's treat). Alex forgot her ID, but they assumed it would be okay because they were with their mom, who could sign off on the procedure. HOWEVER, the tattoo employees did not believe Alex was her daughter. They assumed Alex's mom was trying to get away with getting a tattoo for her daughter and her "daughter's friend." They find it funny now. Alex said it took her a long time to conclude that,

"Being adopted adds extra steps to my life."

For Alex, being adopted wasn't as internally polarizing as being gay. People in her life have grown accustomed to her being adopted and do not "see" it when she is with her family. However, she said, "Strangers can see that I am gay." Her sexuality put her on the extreme edge of being an outsider. However, her adoptive parents – to their credit – tried to figure it out. Alex often pondered whether they wondered, "Would this be happening if they had biological children?" When Alex was growing up, her mom wasn't as accepting of her "otherness" as she is now. It was a growing process for the entire family. It took her parents approximately ten years to become comfortable with her being gay.

As we continued our conversation, it was obvious Alex loves and respects her adoptive mother. She said she was fortunate to have her for a mom and that she is a very sweet lady. Growing up, her mom was one of those people who kept everything extremely organized. She made calendars with their pictures and would write all of the events on them – complete with color-coding. Every day was jam-packed in a "very, very organized fashion." Alex believes that she would not have gotten the same opportunities with a single mother if she had stayed with her 19-year-old college student birth mother.

She feels "super lucky" with parents who were willing to put in the time, effort, and money.

Alex has discovered that having a sense of humor opens up conversations. She believes if a person is offended by someone or something, it means that person indeed respects the offender's opinion or perspective. So many people get bullied by allowing themselves to be hurt. Alex wants the LGBTQ community to know themselves well enough to protect and defend themselves.

> *"Be a good representative of your community in public. Deal with your issues with a therapist … If you aren't trying to represent all of us well, then you're hurting yourself, too. If you know things you won't change for anyone else, then everything else can change around you, and you still know who you are."*

However, Alex did say, if your parents are mistreating you, get out of there and find people who will support you. When she grew up, she didn't have internet platforms to find herself. Instead, she had to rely on pop culture. We talked about a Queer Eye episode in which Bobby Berk shared that he was adopted. When he came out to his parents, they disowned him. I told Alex when I watched that episode, it broke my heart. Alex said, "Yeah. It happens." Her friends heard rumors that her parents had disowned her (they hadn't). She thinks it was probably because of who her parents were. For many Catholics, being gay is a sin – a Deal-Breaker. Alex is an atheist and wonders if it is because of how the church mistreated her. She said,

> *"The way that people use scripture to demonize the LGBTQ community and tout moral superiority causes a lot of harm to many children. The beliefs are ingrained in you as something you should be ashamed of, and that accepting who you are inherently makes you a bad person. I felt this was degrading my self-esteem. So, I grew up and realized everything I was told about morality through the church was very backward. I didn't want to hate myself for who I loved. I decided early on that I wouldn't allow people to treat me like that anymore based on religion or otherwise."*

After moving out to be on her own, Alex never felt the need to go back to church because she has found her own sense of purpose. She does appreciate that some people find purpose and community in religion, but she could not find that community for herself.

For Alex, the "weirdest part" of being adopted was that she wasn't sure if she could share her "otherness" with her dad's extended Catholic family. She was 15 years old when she came out. Alex knew she was gay at 5, but it took her until she was a teenager to finally accept herself (a common misconception is that you can't *know* until puberty). She thinks her parents knew for a while but were just hoping it would go away. They would have been content to avoid it for the "rest of time." Alex admits she was not that "super strong person in high school" who bravely sat their parents down to come out. It wasn't until she got her first girlfriend when her mom confronted her.

At this point in the interview, Alex grinned.

She confirmed her mom's suspicions.

Her mom ordered, "You're not wearing a tux to prom ... and don't tell anyone!"

Alex has garnered wisdom by looking through the lens of her parents. She said that her parents just didn't want her to make life difficult for herself. Her family life was a combo of a little bit "let's sweep it under the rug" and a little bit "tumultuous." Alex is very open-minded and genuinely considers her parents' perspective. They grew up in the 1960s, 70s, and 80s. (The AIDS crisis happened right in the middle of the 80s.) Gay people were being murdered, dying, couldn't get jobs, and couldn't find places to live. "The history of the HIV and AIDS epidemic began in illness, fear, and death as the world faced a new and unknown virus ... In June 1982, a group of cases among gay men in Southern California suggested that the cause of the immune deficiency was sexual, and the syndrome was initially called gay-related immune deficiency (or GRID)."[9] She realized her parents were afraid for her – and their reputation. She said the interactions she had with her adoptive parents about her "otherness" could happen in a birth family, too.

---

[9] "History of HIV and AIDS Overview." www.avert.org/professionals/history-hiv-aids/overview. Accessed 3 Sep. 2020.

She admits she was not thankful for her parents as a teenager, but she now feels grateful as an adult.

Alex's parents were instrumental in helping her to develop a successful military career. They gave her the tools to get into the U.S. Air Force Academy in Colorado Springs. Her parents sent her to leadership seminars, prepared her for interviewing, and taught her to manage her time and money. They sacrificed and supported her (and her sister) with their extracurricular activities and sports by showing up for everything. Their mantra was, "Go all in or not at all." At the Academy, she was immersed in a conservative and disciplined culture. In some ways, growing up in North Dakota prepared her for being an outsider at the Academy.

Alex earned a full scholarship to the Academy, and while there, she met her future fiancé. Her parents were still struggling a little with her "otherness." She took charge of her situation and told her parents, "I have a girlfriend. I love her. You can try to understand me, or you can lose a daughter. I have a job and free school, so I don't ever have to come home again. I have people here who will take me in. I don't need you." She felt she had to give them an ultimatum and said, "You know the Midwest: they were hoping it was not going to be brought up. They hoped it would go away." Her parents bravely decided to fly Alex's girlfriend home with her for Christmas. Her mother has since come around. She accepts Alex is gay and is excited about the upcoming marriage. Her dad recently passed away. Alex said that because his relatives are traditional Catholics, it is hard to know where they stand. She knows that she does not fit in with some of them.

Alex has the confidence to acknowledge that she hasn't ever wholly "fit in" anywhere over her lifetime. She said, "If I wanted to fit in, I picked the wrong profession." She has participated in military panels in public speaking forums to educate her colleagues on what it is like to be gay. Talking about her sexuality "has been an interesting ride." When asked if her talks were received well, she replied, "No one was dumb enough to NOT receive it well."

[Smirk.]

She suspects she has been passed over for a few promotions because she is gay.

Through the Lens of Ourselves

Additionally, she had instances in which she was "punished weirdly in suspect ways." Mostly it was about her haircut. It was entirely within regulations, but there were two complaints about it to the inspector general. As a result, she had to explain to her boss why she was a so-called "troublemaker." She said it was odd, but there was not much she could do about it.

Alex has learned to control her emotions with the help of good mentors and her parents. She does not hold a grudge against her parents about their fears but instead chooses to appreciate the skills she learned about leadership and education from them. As a child, she didn't know their entire story; her parents grew up in an era of prejudice and recrimination, an era of terror for gay people. Her parents' fear of her sexuality was a fear for her own safety.

Alex is now at a point where she has the confidence to move forward without the weight of her past. When she was three days old, her biological mom wrote her a letter and told her to contact her when she was old enough and ready. She said she would love to talk. Just a few weeks before our interview, Alex contacted her biological mother, having found her information the previous year through a series of events that began with Ancestry.com. The DNA test matched Alex to a biological first cousin and a last name – her biological mother's maiden name. It was easy to connect the dots, as Alex already knew her biological mom's first name; she found a LinkedIn profile and then searched for her on Facebook. Even though she had the information for a while, Alex said she "only recently decided to go for it." Part of the reason she waited was that her adoptive dad's health was declining, and she did not want to put pressure or stress on her adoptive mom. Her lovely mom already carried the guilt of taking care of her ailing husband and not having enough time for her daughters. The other reason Alex took a while to decide to find her birth mom was that she had been rejected by some of her adoptive extended family members. Finding herself "outside" of her family made her realize she didn't want to put that same pressure on her birth family.

The communication between the two women has been going well. Alex's biological mom apologized for not being her mom but was proud of the parents she had chosen for Alex. Alex's biological dad's family's situation was complicated because he is full Chinese – his family can never know that Alex exists. It would be unforgivable. Alex has accepted that. She is at peace

65

with it because the need to connect with her birth mother had always been much stronger than the need to find her birth father (which is common for adoptees).

Her biological mom got married a few years ago and has 12-year-old twin daughters – Alex's half-sisters (twins run in their family). They plan to meet in person soon. As I watched Alex talk about her birth mother, it was clear the biological connection comforted her because her eyes glistened when she said that if she had children, she would most likely have twins, too.

Over her life, Alex tried "fitting in" with her family, her North Dakota town, and the military community. And when those efforts didn't completely work out, she discovered that she could "be her own person." Now that she has the confidence of truly knowing herself, she is ready to meet her biological mother. She understands why trying to fit in is a pull for some people because she has felt that same emptiness. However, she has decided not to let depression hold her down. "Depression is unnecessary." She feels that if had she let depression hold her back, it would have proven she wasn't good enough, and she *refuses* to let it happen. The "special needs" status that the North Dakota agency assigned to her at the beginning of her life no longer applies. It is her tenacity and courage that makes her "special."

~ Advice Through Alex's Lens ~

For adoptees: "Find mentors and people you respect. Take the good things [your parents] have taught you and make your own family. Find your own community. Be your own person. Build your own career. They can feel successful, and you can feel independent. Taking that set of skills from that environment will give you more perspective on who they are. When you're inside, it's hard to see it. READ. Read about people who are like yourself."

"Find your own path. If the people that adopted you aren't those you respect, then find others. That's true for people who aren't adopted, too. Just feeling like the outsider is the biggest issue we all face."

Alex said being adopted is a gift, but it depends on the family that adopts you. Sometimes it is the "luck of the draw." She jokes with her parents that they bought and paid for her. "If you don't like it, you bought it." Alex believes that adoption is not for everyone because some people do it for the wrong reasons. She finished with, "However, figure out who you are for yourself. Remember, you're not alone."

My Thoughts, My Lens

Initially, I was jolted when I first heard that Alex's adoption agency in North Dakota considered her "special needs" due to her ethnicity. She had a great attitude about it, though. Her ability to "use her powers for good" as an agent of change proves – indeed – how *special* she is. She intends to write a book to help the LGBTQ community. I have no doubt it will be a best-seller!

At an adoption conference I attended, an adoptive father and physician addressed adoptive "special needs" in a presentation about the history of adoption, outlining it in "three waves."

The first wave of American Adoptions (between 1910-1970) was confined to rigid racial boundaries. "Children defined as having *special needs* were considered unadoptable." The presenter said historically, children were classified as "special needs" if they were abused, neglected, handicapped, older children, sibling groups, or children of color.[10]

During the second wave (between 1970-2000), international and special needs adoptions more than quadrupled. Two of the reasons were: (1) Fewer White American children were available for adoption due to an increase in abortions after Roe V. Wade in 1973, and (2) a rise in awareness of positive outcomes in special needs adoption cases.

With the third wave of adoption (at the beginning of the 21st century) came the recognition that all prospective adoptees had special needs due to toxic stress. The presenter said, "Virtually all children now available for adoption have special needs." He showed slides of data from studies that indicate

---

[10] Dana Johnson, MD, PhD. "The Role of Pre-placement Medical Review in Contemporary Adoptions: Setting Expectations, Assessing a Child's Needs and Supporting Successful Family Formation." *Virtual National Adoption Conference,* NCFAconference.org, 23-25 Jun. 2020.

when babies have no one to comfort them, it alters how their genes are modulated.[11]

Sherrie Eldridge answered the question, "Won't my child feel labeled and judged if I tell her that she has special needs arising from adoption loss?" She addressed parents who thought it was cruel and defeating to label their children that way:

> "Let me assure you that just the opposite is true. It is a paradox, for the concept of special needs brings with it comfort and a feeling of being understood. It is like salve on a wound. Many adoptees try to convince themselves and others that they have no special needs. They are masters at keeping that vulnerable place within themselves concealed. However, beneath the surface there is often depression. Rage. Bewilderment. Confusion about identity. Fear of loss. Shame. Lack of direction. Lack of emotional stamina. Low stress tolerance. Floating anxiety."[12]

I found Eldridge's perspective to be thought-provoking. After learning how the special needs classification was intended, I realized that it's just an unfortunate and clumsy word choice to describe individuals from non-White backgrounds. Alex's pragmatic view on her special needs status reflects her confidence in *knowing* who she is. And *that's* special.

---

[11] Shonkoff, Jack P., Garner, Andrew S. "The Lifelong Effects of Early Childhood Adversity and Toxic Stress." *Pediatrics,* Jan. 2012, 129(1), e232-e246. pediatrics.aappublications.org/content/129/1/e232. Accessed 11 May 2021.

[12] Eldridge, Sherrie. *Twenty Things Adopted Kids Wish Their Adoptive Parents Knew.* Bantam Dell, a division of Random House, Inc., 1999, p. 37.

Edward W. | Architect

Gary, Indiana
Year of Birth: 1963

As our conversation unfolded and Edward recounted his climb out of depression, I couldn't help but hear echoes of his internal combat fatigue. He artfully talked about his feelings, and was emotionally intelligent and admirably unapologetic for his sorrow. I appreciated his honesty and willingness to share his struggles with depression and expose his past sense of hopelessness and disconnection. These days, he is in the process of pulling off his mental muzzle; he has reached a level of self-awareness necessary to move forward.

Edward's parents adopted the Brady Bunch (three boys and three girls). When they were 40 years old, they had a biological seventh child. After the youngest child's arrival, his parents told the adoption agency to stop calling them. The siblings tease their youngest sister for being "the oddball."

[Smile.]

Edward is the second oldest sibling in his family. His adoptive mother is of French and Irish descent, and his father is full Italian. Both parents were college-educated, Catholic, and very loving. Edward grew up in Gary, Indiana, when it was vibrant (before the White Flight of the 1970s). It makes him laugh to see people's reactions when he tells them that he's from "Scary Gary." Back in the 1960s, many unwed mothers would go there to give birth. Others may have given birth in another part of the country, but the adoption agencies would put "Gary, Indiana" on the birth certificates to hide their identities.

At the time of Edward's birth, his future adoptive grandparents were foster parents. They would care for newborns on a temporary basis until an adoptive family could be found. Edward was one of many newborns without adoptive placement – and scheduled for foster care. When he was still in the hospital right after his birth, his future grandfather was also at the same hospital, gravely ill and unable to take one of the newborns in the nursery (who were also scheduled for foster care). Knowing this, upon visiting her father-in-law in the hospital, Edward's future adoptive mother visited the nursery. As she tells the story, she fell in love with one of the newborn babies, who had dark curly hair like her father-in-law. She hatched a plan, deciding she and her husband would adopt this new baby boy (they had already adopted a girl). This boy would be her father-in-law's first male grandchild. Edward's mother happened to be a nurse. To cheer her father-in-law up, she came to the hospital dressed in her nurse's uniform, snuck into the nursery, "kidnapped" Edward, and brought him to his future grandfather's room. She presented Edward to his grandfather, announcing that Edward would be his namesake. Edward's father later told him he never saw Edward's grandfather smile so wide.

[Smile.]

Open adoptions were not an option in 1963. Edward later learned from his adoptive mother that his birth mother contacted the agency several times over many months after his adoption, trying to get him back. However, in the 1960s, once the papers were signed, the adoptions were irreversible. He feels "really sad about that." He has little information about her other than she was in her late 20s or early 30s and of French descent. Edward has thought about trying to find her but doesn't want to "eff" with her mind by just popping into her life. *"Here I am ..."* *[his voice trailed off]*. He did say, though, that if he ever met his birth mother, he would tell her, "Thank you. You made the right decision." Two of Edward's sisters have found their biological parents through the adoption agency. One of them has an ongoing relationship with her stepsiblings.

Edward never contacted the agency, although one of his sisters encouraged him to do so. His internal dialog has flipped back and forth countless times. He thought he would be "freaking somebody out" if he commenced a search. He has vacillated between thinking he might go through with it and thinking that meeting somebody who "abandoned" him wouldn't be in his best interest. He has also considered that it might not be in his birth mother's best interest either. He has struggled with wanting to be considerate – because she did try to get him back. Other times, he has thought, "Would it help me not be as unsure as I am? Maybe."

Despite his internal debate, he always lands on the fact that his parents have been *his* parents since he was two days old. He said,

> *"I sense a lack of connection. Is it just the human condition? It could be greater because I never had a relative that was related to my blood. I can pass as an Italian. Big nose and black hair. My temperament is volatile and demonstrative like my father. Do I have this lack of connectivity to human beings because that's the human condition or because I don't have blood relatives?"*

Edward and his adoptive parents have a very loving relationship. To him, they are his "real parents." They created a home in which adoption was normalized for *all* of their kids. He remembers going to court for two of his siblings' adoptions. The same judge had presided over all six adoptions. Both times, he greeted Edward's mother with, "So nice to see you again, Mrs. W." Edward remembers being proud of their adoptions and thought it was a "cool thing." He also remembers explaining adoption to his siblings. They all look very different physically and have seven distinctly different personalities.

Edward has always felt disconnected from other people, including the extended family; he's never been able to explain it. He wonders if everyone has that same feeling or if it's just him because he's adopted. For example, he doesn't look like his brother (who is younger by 11 months). They both took DNA tests; his brother is pure German, blonde-haired, 6 feet 2 inches and 350 pounds. Edward is dark-haired – of mostly French and Eastern European descent – mixed with a little Italian, Irish, English, Dutch, and even 1 percent Afghan. For fun, when they were growing up, Edward and his brother would play along with confused people as they tried to find any physical resemblance between them. Since they were so close in age, as children, they fought like cats-and-dogs (and boys) but get along well now as adults. Edward wonders if the physical differences contributed to his feelings of disconnection. Even though he does not feel close to his extended family, Edward maintains, "Family keeps you humble. You gotta love them, even if you don't get along."

Edward became an architect because he has an artistic sense of needing *to control, organize, form his world around him, and create space to connect to things.* Yet, his architectural style is one of disconnection. While he likes to confront and solve problems, he admits he avoids emotional problems because he doesn't know which emotions are influenced by his adoption and which are influenced by his personality. He has struggled his entire life, wondering if it was due to external factors, internal predisposition, or something as simple as just being human. He said that his search for connection was the "proverbial trying to find myself."

Although at times, it is difficult for him to flesh out whether there are multiple origins to his struggles, he definitely attributes his fear of abandonment, rejection, and lack of belonging to his adoption.

Through his search, Edward has concluded that his feelings of separation were not physical because he resembles his biological parents. However, at the same time, he wonders if he uses their physical similarities as justification – questioning if he ever imprinted (the psychology principle of bonding at a young age). He had told his sons they are his only blood relatives … and has apologized to them for their big noses.

Edward not only feels a disconnection with others but also feels a disconnection to *himself*.

For years, he felt like his own head wasn't connected to his body. He often had to *force* himself to move. He would have to consciously think about the act of moving, having an overwhelming sense of "not being within himself."

However, at 57 years old, Edward feels he is finally getting his act together. He now strives to feel a wholeness and connection within himself. He has started breathing exercises to feel his "physical vessel" more – and accepts himself within it. By sorting through his "personality preprogramming," he knows he can consciously evolve.

> *"I was an angry grumpy young man but don't have to be an older grumpy man. Smoking was one of those things I did to feel attached … because you bring it into your lungs and you feel … you have that oral sensation, and it was a way to say I exist."*

When Edward quit smoking over a year ago, he gained clarity. Looking back at his smoking years, he realizes that he couldn't get far away from it enough to gain perspective. Additionally, as a "reformed Catholic," Edward used to feel guilty and ashamed for being alive. The message he learned from the church was, "If you're not Jesus Christ, you're the Devil … yes, you're a total [eff] up, but so is everyone else. I don't know if that's because I'm adopted … and don't know if the smoking was because of my need for connection … maybe my whole existence is an adoption story." As he was actively quitting, he had both physical and psychological withdrawals, but it was cathartic when he finally quit for good because he had to live *within* the anxiety of his craving.

> *"To ride the wave of craving, instead of resisting the wave: it was a riptide."*

Edward learned that he had to let the wave take over – and eventually, each wave *would* end. After a while, the waves became less overwhelming. Through quitting smoking and changing up his depression medication, he returned to the physical vessel of his body and no longer feels like he is "floating."

These days, Edward has a better understanding of his existence and is easier on himself.

~ Advice Through Edward's Lens ~

For adoptive parents: "My parents did the best they could. They weren't perfect. I know I'm not a perfect parent. They cared for us the best they could and treated us as their children. There was no favoritism. There's only so much attention to go around. Try to limit the size of your family. Limit the number of kids you adopt or understand that kids need attention. The big ones need attention, too."

For adoptees: "Everyone has their own story. Believe in yourself, I suppose. I'm working on it. Even if other people don't believe in you, you gotta believe in yourself."

My Thoughts, My Lens

Edward is currently working on bettering himself emotionally and physically. For example, he rides his bike a "gazillion miles a day." He joked, saying he has reduced his "pregnancy weight" from second trimester to first trimester. Now that he has looked directly at his emotional pain and moved past the "riptide," he is looking forward to his future. I respect his determination. He embodies the work of the renowned author, Brené Brown, who said,

> *"If we can learn how to feel our way through these experiences and own our stories of struggle, we can write our own brave endings."*[13]

Go get 'em, Edward.

---

[13] Brown, Brené, PhD, LMSW. *Rising Strong*. Spiegel & Grau, an imprint of Random House, a division of Penguin Random House LLC, 2015, p. xx.

Kelly S. | Nursing Assistant

St. Paul, Minnesota
Year of Birth: 1967

Kelly's house is located by a river in the woods, and she was outside during our first phone conversation. As we progressed, I could hear the comfortable "silence" of the woods surrounding her. She was uncomplicated, matter-of-fact, and relaxed as she described her uneventful adoptive childhood.

Our second meeting via video chat was much different. Kelly seemed a little shell-shocked. As a nursing assistant, she works the night shift at a nursing home, and in between our two calls, Kelly's "natural" sense of family was blown up when she discovered that an interim patient under her care was her *biological grandmother.*

Kelly's daughter had found a biological first cousin through a 23andME.com DNA test. Armed with an unusual last name, Google, and Facebook, Kelly and her daughter saw that they were related to Kelly's patient, Mary. The cousin verified that Mary was Kelly's biological grandmother. Because Kelly worked the night shift, she didn't know Mary on a deep level. However, she did think Mary was pleasantly friendly and "pretty cool." She kept her discovery to herself because the nursing home rules dictated nurses were not allowed to take care of family members. Even though Kelly didn't know Mary as a relative growing up, she wasn't sure how it would play into the nursing home's rules. After a few weeks, Mary went to live with her son, still unaware that Kelly is her biological granddaughter.

After Mary moved out of the nursing home, the cousin connected Kelly with her biological mother, Susan, through Facebook. At the time of our interview, they hadn't yet met in person. Susan had battled colon cancer and was still very careful about meeting face to face due to COVID-19 safety precautions. Cancer is prevalent in her biological family; Susan lost two of her siblings to the disease. Kelly acknowledged cancer is serious but emphasized that the practical upside to connecting with Susan was learning about her own medical history.

Kelly was relieved to learn Susan's story; she hadn't become pregnant as a result of rape or molestation. At 17, Susan didn't know she was pregnant until she was three months along. She was in a new relationship, and timing didn't allow her to be sure whether Kelly belonged to her ex-boyfriend or her current boyfriend. Kelly also learned that Mary (the grandmother) had been very cruel to Susan. When Susan was young, she overheard Mary telling the neighbors she would never have had Susan if it weren't for the cheap WWII condoms. When Mary learned of Susan's pregnancy, she offered no emotional support. Instead, she dropped Susan off at a home for unwed mothers in St. Paul, which was known as "Watermelon Hill." When they said goodbye, she told Susan she needed to come home "alone" after the baby was born, or she shouldn't bother coming home at all.

Susan did return home without her baby to find that Mary had calculated the adoption cost. She told Susan she wouldn't have to pay the money back if she agreed to move out the day she graduated from high school – and she had to agree to pay for her own wedding. Learning about the heartless ultimatum was the first time Kelly felt any significant emotion about her adoption. She said, "The hair stood up on my arms."

For now, Kelly prefers messaging with Susan on Facebook. She is not comfortable talking to people, hating the awkward silences that often occur. By communicating online, she can reread her conversations. Susan gave her an ancestry report with family history dating to the 1800s and her family photograph collection. Susan joked with Kelly she was glad to give it to her before she "croaked" – her other family members would not have to deal with getting rid of her possessions. Kelly is relieved that she and Susan had to delay their face-to-face meeting, as it gave her time to process her adoption story and sort through the ancestry family information. Coincidentally, many of Kelly's ancestors have the same names as her own children. For Kelly, learning they shared a naming history was surprising yet "very interesting." Kelly also discovered that she has many biological relatives living close by. Her biological grandparents own a cabin near her home and have even shopped at her neighborhood grocery store. The proximity feels "crazy" to her – but not uncomfortable.

At this point in their relationship, Kelly feels compassion for Susan. She does not feel a mother-daughter connection but leaves room for it to change when they meet face to face. She likes her, though, and feels she is kind. They have many things in common: the same hairstyle, the same penchant for working night shifts, and the same love of cats (even though they both have cat allergies).

Kelly learned that Susan had no other biological children but has taken in less fortunate girls. One of them even calls her "Mom" on Facebook. Kelly likes Susan's sense of humor and laughed when she said that neither of them had much luck in the relationship department. Susan has joked with her, "Don't worry about it. It could be hereditary. It's not your fault. We are both creep magnets."

Kelly asked Susan if she would have kept her if her circumstances had been different. Susan took a while to respond but finally admitted that she probably still would have chosen adoption. She told Kelly it was actually a blessing she was adopted, given how abusive her mother (Mary, Kelly's grandmother) was. Susan's foster daughter told her on more than one occasion that if Mary were her mother, she would have killed herself a long time ago. Susan tried to give Kelly a realistic insight into what things were like in the 1960s. She had no support from her family and worked in a laundromat, unable to care for a child as a single mother.

In contrast, Kelly's adoptive family was always very supportive. When Kelly became pregnant at 17, her parents loved and supported her. It crushed her dad, but he still helped her. Kelly did not have to struggle to keep her son. She had housing, daycare, and a job. Kelly believes, "Family support is everything."

Even though Kelly is adopted, she feels like an integral part of her adoptive family. She was treated no differently than her siblings. If her parents had not told her about her adoption, she most likely would have never known. Her parents already had two older biological sons when they adopted her, and after Kelly, they had another daughter biologically.

As a child, Kelly did not want for anything and had an uncomplicated life. She had good parents and said that it was "awesome" being raised by them. Having siblings contributed to her happiness. She never felt she was "missing something" from her life. She is grateful for her "tightly knit family."

Whenever she brought up her adoption to her parents, they would reassure her, telling her she was chosen, and they picked her specifically. They always addressed her doubts. Kelly talked about how many adoptees bristle at hearing they were "chosen" because they feel like they were the last option (after "natural" pregnancy, infertility treatments, etc.). She thought that perhaps she feels differently because her parents were able to have more biological children. They *specifically* chose her as their own before having one more baby. Kelly was genuinely surprised that other adoptees have negative feelings; she had always assumed other adoptees shared her positive experience.

Given Kelly's positive upbringing, she balances her adoptive parents' feelings with her own. She does not plan on telling them about her being in contact with her biological mother, knowing it would hurt them deeply. When she was a teenager, she asked her parents about her own medical history, which deeply hurt their feelings. Kelly admitted that it was probably in the delivery of her question – not the question itself – as she used the phrase "my real parents" and thinks she was probably demanding (as teenagers often are). But because her parents were so crushed, she decided that she would never bring up the topic of her biological family again.

And she will never tell them about Susan.

Kelly said, "Until my daughter spat into a cup [for DNA testing], being adopted simply was not an issue for me." But now that she has to acknowledge her reality, she's grateful she has the time to cautiously process her feelings before meeting Susan.

~ Advice Through Kelly's Lens ~

For adoptees: "Be grateful for what God has given you. Many kids spend their lives in foster care."

For adoptive parents: "Treat your adoptive kids equally and the same. Don't make them feel they are your third choice."

My Thoughts, My Lens

Kelly's story is an encouraging example of how adoption can be harmonious. Children do not choose their parents, but when the adoptive family unit is healthy and embracing, children emerge unscarred – as Kelly did.

I suppose the same could be said for biological families.

Many prospective adoptive parents are frightened by adoption horror stories, though clearly, *not every story is punctuated by trauma.*

Some adoptive childhood experiences are folded into normalcy, much like Kelly's experience. For most of her life, adoption was not central to her existence; instead, it was a peripheral detail. Similarly, my daughter once told me she often forgets that her grandmother (my mom) is not biologically related to her. My adoption is not an overarching factor in my kids' lives, which is how I want it to be.

My husband grew up in an unstable household with biological parents. It still affects him, as he continually strives to have a "normal" family life. His emotional scars are now guardrails that guide his decisions. If he had grown up with a stable family (like Kelly's), then perhaps he could have emerged unscarred, too.

Some *adoptive* families are loving. Some are abusive.

Some *biological* families are loving. Some are abusive.

I sometimes wonder about the powers of the Universe when it comes to matching children with their parents. In my opinion, it can be a crapshoot. We have no control over who our parents are – some people win the family lottery, and some are punched in the groin. My husband's philosophical approach to life is an unlikely combination of Existentialism and Christianity. He likes to think that God wants to see how we play the cards we have been dealt.

I like it.

Personally, I found it reassuring that Kelly's story proves successful adoptions do exist. Surely, her blessed childhood will be her anchor as she learns to navigate her new relationship with Susan.

SECTION 2

Through the Lens of International Adoptees

Domestic adoptees (of the same ethnic group as their adoptive parents) often deeply feel the magnetic draw of their biological roots. Growing up in a transracial family adds another layer of complexity to the adoption experience. International adoptees (of a different ethnic group than their adoptive parents) also feel the same genetic pull as domestic adoptees, but their lens is magnified in a different way because their physical appearance is a frequent reminder of the missing biological connection. Unfortunately, race is usually a measuring stick of self-worth, and for some transracial adoptees, it is the *only* assessment.

Throughout my life, my original culture often summoned me – luring me with incessantly loud whispers. For decades, I attempted to fit into my adoptive family's culture. However, ultimately, I could not turn down the mitochondrial invitation.

In my observation, even when adoptees have rejected their original cultures, they could not completely turn away from them. Biology somehow hums quietly – yet deafeningly, seducing us with food, art, literature, and music.

Jason M. | Information System Security Officer

Kyongsangnam-Do, South Korea
Year of Birth: 1985

Jason struck me as a trustworthy, patriotic, and an all-American good guy. He was very engaging when he talked about navigating adoption challenges by using the lessons he learned from his parents and his military experience. The first time I spoke with Jason on the phone, it was very brief (we would schedule a longer conversation later). In that short four-minute call, it was clear he embraced loyalty. He quickly pointed out how accomplished his two adopted siblings with disabilities were. One went to the University of Virginia and is now an architect. The other has a master's degree from Georgetown. The intense pride he had for his siblings was undeniable, kind of like a winning high school football coach giving a speech about his players at the end-of-season banquet.

When we had our second video call, the first thing that Jason said was,

"A piece is missing, but I don't know how to get it back."

Jason said that having a twin brother has helped him navigate his feelings about adoption. His adoptive parents had one biological son and then adopted his sister from South Korea. Jason and his twin were also born in South Korea, but their sister is *not* biologically related to them. His parents always knew that they wanted to have a large family, and to expedite another adoption process after adopting Jason's sister, they agreed to take children with disabilities. Because Jason's twin has cerebral palsy, he was available for adoption quicker than children without disabilities. Not wanting to separate the twins, Jason's parents took both boys. When Jason's older adoptive brother learned that their parents were adopting him, he was very excited because he thought Jason would teach him karate. Jason now appreciates the innocence his older brother had as a young child. He remembers times when his older brother stuck up for him when they were kids. Now that they are adults, Jason values his brother's fierce loyalty.

85

As they grew up, Jason and his twin brother went in opposite directions in every way possible – choices, interests, and activities. But even though they are very different, Jason is grateful for the bond he has with his twin. When his sister gave birth to her daughter, she said that meant she finally had a true blood family member. Until that point, Jason had never given much thought to familial blood. But when Jason had his daughter, he realized there was truth to what his sister felt. His sister and her daughter are *"legitimately"* attached, just as he and his daughter are. When Jason's daughter was born, he bought her the book <u>Sadako and the Thousand Paper Cranes</u> (by Eleanor Coerr) and put it on her shelf to read as she grew older. He pulled the book out and showed me its cover. It is a wonderful historical novel written for children about the courage of a young woman in Japan. Jason compared his own feelings about adoption to how he feels about his daughter, saying he could never put her up for adoption. Ultimately, she will not have the internal struggle he had. She will never wonder whether her parents wanted her. His daughter helps to fill in the gaps of his loneliness.

Jason's father, mother, oldest brother, and wife are White. However, since his sister and twin brother are Korean, he grew up accustomed to having siblings of the same race. Although Jason does feel like something is missing, he acknowledges that he probably had an easier time than other adoptees without someone of the same race in his or her family. Even so, he and his adopted siblings have very different experiences and views of adoption. His twin brother is artistic, highly sensitive, and in tune with his own emotions; therefore, he is impacted significantly by racism. Jason is athletic, has thicker skin, and is less impacted by bigotry.

Jason's parents tried to shelter their children from racism. However, despite their efforts, its punch toppled the three siblings in very different ways. Jason's siblings were much more reactionary to racist events than he was. He said, "Actions speak louder than words." He lets incidents "run off his back" and has gotten a better response from the "perpetrators." He said, "For example, imagine you're sitting in a restaurant, and someone makes a comment. If you act a fool, you are validating what they are saying." Ironically, Jason thinks that the *most* racist individuals he has encountered were other Asians from fully Asian families in high school. They told Jason he was not a "true Asian" or that he was a "whitewashed Asian." He didn't have Asian friends growing up. He shrugged as he said, "They were mean to me." Historically, many Koreans culturally viewed international adoption as a shameful circumstance to be shunned. For a while – to protect his feelings – Jason would jokingly say shocking things about Korea or Koreans. He compared the approach to war, having to demonize your opponent. He dealt with his feelings by demonizing his birth parents.

> *"It's easier to build up a wall and hate somebody than to honestly take a step back and think they truly did it because they loved you. The tragedy of that is now I have a wonderful life. A life [my birth mother] would never have expected. I owe it to her, and she'll never see what happened."*

He pushed down his thoughts in high school, ignoring those feelings that gave him "shivers and chills." Jason decided that he'd "add some color" to the team if he joined any group.

When the siblings were younger, social perception of their transracial family bothered Jason's mother. If, for instance, they were in public with only their father, people assumed he was married to an Asian woman. If, on the other hand, the kids were in public with their mom, people wouldn't believe they were her kids.

Jason acknowledges that his family's racial differences must have bothered him on a deeper level and admits he was a difficult kid for his parents to raise. When accompanying his siblings to their numerous medical appointments, he rebelled and often acted up. He had a quick temper and constantly devalued himself. As a child, he often cried because of his many difficult questions surrounding his adoption, but his parents did not sugarcoat their answers. They told him they didn't know, and therefore, they would not guess. He always had a sinking feeling that his biological parents didn't want him. Looking back, Jason applauds his adoptive parents for handling it that way.

Jason's rebellious phase continued into high school; he had to graduate online because he moved out of his parents' house the day that he turned 18. Jason laughed and said, "Then I found out I needed money." He picked up a graveyard shift at a server host company to support himself.

Today, Jason is very different than he was as a child. He learned self-control after he graduated high school and joined the Army. His decision to enlist was influenced by the stories he heard over the years from his father about being a JAG officer in the Marines. Military camaraderie was attractive to him, helping him fill in the "missing piece" he felt as a child and teenager. He completed basic training at Fort Benning. Then he advanced to Infantry and Airborne school, landing him in the 25th Infantry division. His first 15-month tour was in Alaska, and he was later transferred to Iraq at the height of the conflict in the early 2000s. Jason's fellow soldiers became like siblings to him.

Familial blood doesn't matter in the military; brotherly bonds are created from a different kind of blood.

Some of the soldiers Jason knew have gone on to do amazing things in the civilian world. One of his roommates in Iraq was one of the most racist individuals Jason had ever met, but Jason won him over. By the end of the tour, he wanted to be roommates with Jason when they moved stateside – and Jason was only one of three soldiers invited to his wedding. Even someone predestined to wear racist blinders could not resist Jason's gregarious and loyal personality. During his tour of duty, Jason was cross-trained as a combat lifesaver and tended to most casualties. His team leader was the 3000th person killed in Iraq, and it was a big news story in the United States. At the end of the tour, only four original members of Jason's squad returned.

Being a combat lifesaver was a logical step for Jason because he learned to practice selflessness from his parents. It helped him shift his focus away from the loneliness of adoption. Although he grew up in a 10,000 square-foot home with an indoor pool, his parents actively presented their kids with opportunities to consider less fortunate people. One year, when his family went to the NYC Macy's Thanksgiving parade, they stayed in a swanky hotel. His parents asked for the leftover bread, divided it among the siblings, and directed each to give it to the homeless people.

Fast forward a decade. In Iraq, a missile narrowly missed Jason, landing unexploded near his team. The Army brought in the explosives team to diffuse the missile. When Jason was pulling guard, an Iraqi family of farmers brought bread to the American soldiers. That humble act bewildered Jason because the family had nothing – their kids had no pants, yet they shared what little they had with the soldiers. Jason concluded,

"So how can I feel bad about my situation?"

The children in Iraq were not accustomed to seeing many Asians and would call him Jackie Chan. Jason said, "It's funny because it shows that inherently, people are going to assume [that] because you look a certain way, you are going to be affiliated with certain things. But the most Asian thing about me is that I love rice." The tour in Iraq profoundly affected Jason. When he came home on mid-tour leave, he learned how much his military service affected his family. He realized that *all* of his actions affected someone else.

He realized he was *not* alone.

In that moment, appreciation for his adoptive family commenced. The life-changing combat experience made him realize he had been a "pain in the ass" to his parents. He said, "They deserve the title of *'the parents.'*" His parents were very loving, and Jason joked that if they had beaten him (they didn't), he would have understood.

> *"I really do have a lot. I really am lucky and fortunate. To be honest, the reason I went into the military was to suffer. To earn the life [that] I had been given – to know some hardship. An affluent family adopted me, and I didn't do anything to earn it. Basically, I hit the lottery. It was easy for me to take all of my anger and just fight anything I could, any chance I could."*

After Jason's tour in Iraq, he and his father took a trip to France. Jason has fond memories of touring WWII sites because of their shared interest in military history. While they were there, Jason saw stereotypical Japanese tourists, and it occurred to him he could not fit in with a group of "true Asians." He would not fit in with people from Korea. Or France. Or Japan. Instead, Jason concluded that he fits in with racially diverse groups.

At this point in the conversation, Jason paused, removed his patriotic camouflage baseball cap (with an American flag patch stitched on the front), rubbed the top of his head, and slowly said, "Loneliness. I don't want to downplay those feelings, because what's going on in someone's head is not trivial. When it comes to me and my feelings to fit in, I don't care about it. Is it because of the things I have gone through? Or is it because I have hated that feeling so much? I've pushed it to the back of my head." I asked him if the feelings of loneliness were still there.

[Sigh.]

"Yeah ... but if I am going to cry, it has to be about something terrible. I am not going to waste my tears. My sadness — I trivialize because of the things I have seen."

Jason went on to say that not addressing loneliness isn't a good thing, but it *is* hard for him to look at it. He thinks other people have suffered so much more than he has, and therefore he would rather spend his energy on other facets of life. Jason waffles back and forth about finding his birth mother. He feels like wanting to know his backstory is selfish. He said,

"The problem I have, though: no matter what I do, there's guilt. There is not a bone in my body that doubts who my parents are. Regardless of how loving an adoptive parent could be, there is always going to be a portion that an adoptee will never be able to escape unless they have closure [from knowing] ultimately that they were unwanted."

Jason's parents support his birth family search. His mother gave him all of his adoption records, and he believes his mom and dad would be thrilled if he found his birth parents. However, he struggles with not knowing if they gave him up for loving reasons or due to tragic circumstances. He believes he would rather know the truth one way or another. However, what stops him is that he may not get his "Disney" ending.

"No matter how much I want to find out who I came from, I always end up looking back and saying, 'Why?' The people in my life have been wonderful and caring, providing me with everything I needed and way more. So, that makes me feel bad. Millions of kids go to bed hungry. What do I have to be sad about?"

If he found his birth parents, he would want to discover *who* they are. In doing so, it would be like figuring out who he is on a fundamental primal level. However, he feels he has come to terms with his adoption "enough" to move past it, being happy to bring perspective and color to others in his life.

~ Advice Through Jason's Lens ~

For adoptees: "Don't assume the worst. Rather than considering the potentially negative reasons you were adopted, maybe it's best to assume it was done for a loving reason." Jason continued to explain that if you assume your parents were addicted to drugs or your mom was raped, you can spin that into thinking you weren't wanted. But the opposite could be true, too. He suggested that perhaps they loved you very much but couldn't take care of you financially; perhaps they loved you enough to want to give you the best possible life. Jason said, "And you should make the most of that sacrifice."

For adoptive parents: "Accept that your children are now American. I am an American. I don't know anything but being American. My parents tried to show us traditional Korean things, [but] they were always super 'whitewashed.' I didn't need a whitewashed version of Korean traditions. I didn't need the traditional Asian bowl haircut. It was hilarious."

My Thoughts, My Lens

As we were wrapping up our conversation, Jason was curious about what I had seen with other adoptees. I told him that in my observation, those who were not accepted by their extended adoptive families or who did not fit in socially seemed angrier or lonelier than those who were fully accepted by their families. He could see my point.

Jason = Cool + Approachable + Unreserved + Open-minded.

We jumped right into his feelings in the first sentence of our conversation. His charismatic personality made our conversation flow easily. Jason's natural ability to draw people to him was the fuel he needed to integrate with his military comrades successfully. The lessons he learned from his parents shaped his perspective on his adoption experience and how he interacts with the world. I'm sure that has served him well over the years as he deftly handled prejudice and carefully navigated around the "piece of him that is missing." I love his approach of adding color to any team or group he joins.

In doing my research for this book, I attended an online conference on adoption. During one discussion, a social worker shook with emotion as she talked about an instance in which a lawyer shamed prospective adoptive parents for not wanting to adopt outside their race. She was *pissed* at the lawyer. In the group chat, I posted that I thought we should work towards normalizing public perception of transracial families. Another participant replied to my post and said that social workers have to give their clients what they want.

Agreed.

Of course, we should not shame people who know their boundaries and are not mentally equipped to take on the challenges that come with transracial adoptions.

The adoption road is *not* for the timid. *Adoption comes with a consequence.*

I respect people who are self-aware enough to know their limits. However, by normalizing the perception of transracial families through education and exposure, the probability increases for prospective parents (who might not have otherwise been introduced to the idea) to take a second glance at different-race adoptees.

Not to downplay the loneliness that comes with transracial adoptions – I like to think that creating transracial families is like making a grilled cheese sandwich. Sometimes I like to swap out the American cheese for muenster and add a sprinkle of nutmeg. It's *still* a delectable ooey-gooey grilled cheese sandwich.

Muenster grilled cheese is the Jason-approach-to-life: adding a different flavor.

Now, *that's* delicious.

Nicholas L. | Labor Market Analyst

Kalfa, Greece
Year of Birth: 1954

In all my interviewing experience, Nicholas's story is unique in that adoption trauma does not exist in his world. He reminded me of the tranquil surface of a lake at daybreak in July, his smile the sun's reflection on the water. By the time we finished our 2 ½ hour interview, my cheeks hurt from smiling. He was content and very positive. I found it interesting that he used the word "Mom" interchangeably for both his birth mother and adoptive mother. It seemed like it didn't even occur to him to be negative about adoption. When Nicholas mentioned that other people had a hard time with being adopted, he acknowledged the concept – but didn't *understand* it. We are all products of our past experiences, and his life was obviously fulfilling, an outcome that all adoptive parents want for their children. He surprised me when he said he had an emotionally unencumbered life.

Nicholas always knew he was adopted. His American family moved from Massachusetts to Virginia when he was in the third grade, but he was born in rural Greece in 1954. As a toddler, he was passed around in foster care but does not remember it and barely has a memory of coming to America. His adoptive parents couldn't find an American child and were asked if they would accept a foreign adoptee. They agreed. They wanted an infant, but they were given a choice between three toddlers when an infant wasn't available. The first child they chose became ill and couldn't pass the medical exams. Nicholas was second on the list, passed the exams, and made it to the United States when he was two years and nine months old. He vaguely remembers being a little scared and was not able to speak English. His relatives said he was standoffish at first and that he really liked bread. His parents would find bread tucked away in many places. He adjusted well and lived a normal American life. He has a hazy memory of being at the family Christmas party where some of his American cousins asked him where his mom and dad were – saying, "Not *them*, but your 'real mom and dad.'" While many adoptees struggle with the "real parent" label, it was never a big deal to Nicholas. As he grew up, he occasionally wondered if he might have any blood relatives but never had to search because the legwork had already been completed.

In 2007 and 2008, Nicholas received a couple of letters with vague inquiries about his identity and thought it was a scam. He threw them in the top drawer of his dresser, mentally filing it away as "interesting." On a Tuesday evening in 2008, he got a call from a woman at The International Social Service (ISS) who explained that he had relatives in Greece looking for him. Nicholas was skeptical, but they continued to have a back-and-forth email exchange. During that period, Nicholas did some investigating on his own. He felt relieved when he was able to verify ISS was indeed a legitimate non-profit organization that connected birth family members. They sent him two photographs that removed all lingering doubt: his original passport photograph and a Christmas picture of him as a toddler in America that his adoptive mother had sent to ISS to let them know how he was doing.

ISS sent Nicholas a big package that contained translated letters from his brother, sister, and mother. They also included a series of pictures of his Greek family. Nicholas said it was truly amazing. He said, I kinda opened it and stared …" For a long time.

His brother and sister wrote, "Now we can be a family – as we were always meant to be." They also told him that they could have been a family sooner had they known he existed earlier. Their mom couldn't rest until they found him.

They even offered to take DNA tests because they knew he had been skeptical. The most moving part of the package was the letter from his mother. She wrote, "I can die in peace if I can see you." *How do you react to that?*

Before they made the trip to Greece, Nicholas and his mother corresponded via letters. In one of her letters, she wanted to know if he could forgive her. He wrote back, "There's nothing to forgive!" He told her that because she gave him up, his American parents had a child they wanted. He had a happy and successful life in America and has no regrets. The only thing he lost was time with his Greek family (but the upside was that they made up for it since their reunion).

In December 2008, Nicholas made the long trip to Greece with his wife and two kids; he needed the emotional support from his family. Before they left for the trip, his wife created a photo album of Nicholas's life, and they brought it with them to Greece. The book looked similar to a high school yearbook – except that it was a multi-yearbook of his life. (He later discovered that it was a big hit with his family – they shared with everyone.) Nicholas and his family arrived at the Athens airport on December 17th, the same day he had arrived in America 50 years before. They stayed in Athens for a few days to acclimate and get over their jetlag before meeting the family. Workers from ISS met them at the hotel to prepare him for what was to come. They filled him in on Greek customs and on details they had about his family. He learned it wasn't unusual for reunions not to go well. The ISS representatives told him about another adoptee from Holland who found the visit to be too overwhelming when she met her family – she left the country after only three days. Nicholas and his family stayed and hoped for a positive outcome … in his words, "Roll with the punches – not that there were any punches."

On the third day, his brother, sister, and an entourage of relatives made the drive from the coastal town of Patras, where his sister and her husband lived. The purpose of their trip was to pick him up and to bring him back to meet his mother. Nicholas and his family were waiting in the lobby and could see the parade through the windows. He felt amused watching them descend on the hotel, but he became emotional when they met face to face. All of the relatives hugged and kissed him on both cheeks, but because only a few cousins spoke English, Nicholas felt a bit of uncertainty. Nonetheless, he brushed aside his discomfort, and off they went for a 3-hour-drive … with no idea of where they were going.

Nicholas and company wandered into his sister and her husband's apartment. They called in his 80-year-old mom from the back room. Her tiny frame was clothed entirely in black, topped with a headscarf that crowned her dark eyebrows. (Black was the traditional dress for Greek widows.) The moment was surreal for Nicholas. This little old lady came up and grabbed him. She was crying to the point where it literally scared her granddaughters. They had never seen her so overcome with emotion. Nicholas wasn't quite sure how he should feel at that moment because of her reaction. He hugged her back and patted her on the shoulder. Growing up with New Englander parents, Nicholas was much more reserved than his birth mother. But in the next few hours, he allowed her warmth to embrace him. Nicholas's 13-year-old niece did most of the translating because she was taking English in school. Nicholas's wife took many pictures of his mom just holding his hand and him holding hers. Frequently, she would reach up, pull his face down, and pat his face, saying, "My child, my child" – almost as if she couldn't believe he was really there.

During our interview, Nicholas showed me the photographs of their reunion. It was evident that he took his American vitamins because he towered over his mother. He stands at 5 feet 10 inches, and his mother didn't even come up to his shoulders. He was also much taller than his brother and sister. He said he could look down at the parts in their hair. Nicholas didn't get to meet his father because he had passed away years before the visit. The pictures continued, and Nicholas's wife captured their son and daughter with his nieces. His mother was overjoyed to have all of her grandchildren together. Nicholas spent three weeks of "culture by immersion" in Greece. He said, "That blew me away. My family couldn't have been more gracious. It was easy to warm up to that." Previously, Nicholas and his wife traveled to Europe and had a taste of other cultures. However, he said it was not the same as being in someone's home. They stayed in his sister's 2-bedroom, 1-bathroom apartment (because the relatives insisted the local hotel was not acceptable). Nicholas and his wife slept in his sister and brother-in-law's bed while his kids slept in his nieces' beds. Even his 80-year-old mother slept in the living room. He felt bad, but that's just how it was done. The family had clearly articulated to ISS that Nicholas needed to accept their hospitality. *"Family takes care of family. Period."*

During their stay, they took a trip to Kalfa, his tiny birth village. Nicholas, his family, his brother, and his mother stayed in a house borrowed from one of their cousins. While there, he learned about the family sheep business. He was welcomed into the fold; when his brother showed Nicholas the family's Kalfa property, he told Nicholas that the land belonged to him, too. While there, Nicholas learned that he was related to almost everyone in Kalfa.

All 300 residents.

Over several days, a multitude of relatives came to visit his mother's long-lost son. His mother was one of five children, and his father was one of five brothers. One relative drew a family tree for him that had many branches. Many relatives told Nicholas that he looked exactly like his deceased uncle

– they even had the same gait. When he saw his uncle's picture as a young man, there was no denying the family ties. The relatives brought him gifts, as was the custom. Nicholas felt like a rock star because everyone in the village had heard about him. His mom was like a grandma to everyone, and when they learned that she had found her son, they all had to meet him. Greeks tend to stay up late at night. Lunch is at 2 p.m., and continental dinners are at 8 or 9 p.m. Nicholas found the social interactions to be fascinating. One evening at 10, a group of young relatives in their 20s came to meet Nicholas. His kids got out of bed to meet them. The older Greek relatives knew maybe 50 English words from watching TV, so the younger family members would translate. Nicholas said the culture was very similar to what was portrayed in the movie – *My Big Fat Greek Wedding.* He said, "I had cousins coming out of my pockets." They were very loud and expressive. Nicholas learned that his dad had a very strong presence and tended to be very dominant. He even got to see a video clip of his deceased birth father. His mother's side of the family was more laid back. His Greek family would chatter away as Nicholas and his family absorbed the new foods and customs.

During their visit, it was clear his mother was frustrated by the language barrier – she had so much to tell him. Therefore, his sister arranged to have an English teacher come by to translate their mother's story. When he arrived, Nicholas's mother requested that everyone leave (except for Nicholas's wife). She wanted privacy to share her story (and not through the 13-year-old niece). Nicholas sat down with her, his wife, and the teacher. At one point, during the interpretation, Nicholas's wife turned to him and said,

"She wants to hear that you forgive her."

Nicholas told his mother,

"If you feel there's anything I need to forgive you for – I do. Freely."

From that moment forward, their visit was a "love-fest." It was as though his mother's burden instantly disappeared. Hearing her story and getting to know her perspective gave Nicholas a deeper understanding of his adoption. Nicholas's mother and father were distantly related. His father lost his parents at an early age and had to raise his brothers. His mother (along with other women in the village) would come by to help this "distant relative," and somewhere along the way, she became pregnant. However, they were not mature enough to get married. An unmarried pregnant woman was a BIG DEAL in the 1950s. They lived in a small village, and everyone knew that she was pregnant. She was more than frowned upon; she was ostracized. Nicholas's birth father was not ready to marry her because he felt like he needed more time to take care of his siblings. Nicholas was baptized when he turned a year old. In keeping with Greek tradition, his name was announced at that time. Three of his cousins were also named Nicholas, which granted him access to the "Nick Club."

Nicholas = Νικόλαος.

Because of the social estrangement, his mother was under extreme pressure to "give Nicholas up and get on with her life." Nicholas's godmother tried to help his mother raise him for a while; however, his mother was so repeatedly scorned and rejected by the village that she gave in to the pressure. Because Kalfa was in the mountains with no paved roads, his mother, her brother and his friend traveled by donkey to drop him off at the orphanage in Patras.

She regretted her decision for 50 years.

Ten years after his mother dropped him off at the orphanage, Nicholas's parents got married, had a son right away, and then had a daughter five years later. During that time, he said, "Everyone knew everyone's business." Around 2000, someone from the village slipped up and said something about Nicholas in front of his brother. His brother was stunned and directly questioned his mother. She confirmed it and shared the details of her secret lifelong regret. She told him she was to the point of giving up hope of ever finding him. So, Nicholas's brother and sister made it their mission to find him.

At this point in the interview, Nicholas's voice grew shaky as he said that he was trying not to cry. He said that when his brother and sister were growing up, they would often witness their mom's anguish as she cried and wailed, "Oh, my, my child, my child!" They never understood why she was crying. When they found out about Nicholas, her actions made sense. The revelation made them determined to find him.

It took eight years.

As was customary, Nicholas and his mother exchanged gifts. Nicholas had brought Virginia wine and fairy crosses made from a mineral found only in Virginia and one other place in the world. His mother gave his family stunning jewelry. He told the translator he felt like the prodigal son in the Bible – the son who intruded in the family after being away for a long time. He felt like his brother and sister had always been there for his mom and that he just barged back in. However, his siblings lovingly disagreed and were very gracious, as were all of his cousins and relatives. The villagers told him that was the happiest they had ever seen his mother.

Nicholas bonded with his brother and sister during his three-week visit. They worked around the language barrier with Greek-English dictionaries, watched TV shows with subtitles, and played a lot of card games. He and his brother also played with fire at the barbeque pit. Because he was living with them, Nicholas had much more of an opportunity to get to *know* them.

When his sister dropped him off at the airport in Athens, Nicholas said it was emotional leaving them. His sister asked him if he felt more at home in America or Greece. He hugged her and said,

"Wherever my family is, that's where I'm at home."

Nicholas was able to visit his mother twice before she passed away in 2010. Since then, he and his wife have continued to return to Greece. One trip was over Greek Orthodox Easter, during which the village of 300 became a village of 500 because former residents (who now live elsewhere) returned home for the holidays. The local church has a long chanting "high service," complete with incense and robes. Nicholas described it as "Catholicism on steroids." At midnight, the church goes dark. The priest comes out from behind a screen with a candle, and they pass the light of Christ to everyone holding candles. Because everyone from the village cannot fit into the church, the oldest member of the family may go to the service to receive the light of Christ to bring back to their families. It is an honor to receive the flame. Usually, his brother represented the family, but he deferred to Nicholas because he was the eldest. Not wanting to intrude, Nicholas told his brother it was not his intention to insert himself because he had not been there over the years. However, his brother graciously said it was the right thing to do and insisted that Nicholas attend the service.

Nicholas and his family learned about the Greek food culture over their numerous trips. Meals were very orderly with linens. Plastic utensils and paper plates were never used. Outdoor rotisseries with whole lambs cooking for hours on a spit were the norm on holidays. They ate calamari, octopus, and Nicholas's favorite – lemon chicken soup. His sister introduced him to crispy pancakes fried in olive oil and gyros with fresh-cut French fries stuffed inside the wrap. He learned that he shouldn't put his hands on his lap at the dinner table. His nieces giggled at him when he did so ... in Greece, you need to place your hands *on* the table.

Nicholas learned that Greeks do not eat a big breakfast. When he requested toast for breakfast, he discovered that Greek toast is very different from American toast. His niece brought him two grilled cheese sandwiches. Nicholas chuckled and said it was just like the scene in *My Big Fat Greek Wedding* when they talked about how plain toast without marmalade was barbaric. He also learned that the entire country of Greece would stop functioning if they could not have coffee. Greek coffee is prepared by boiling the water on a Bunsen burner. However, to make Nicholas feel at home, his sister bought an American drip coffee maker for his visits. When they traveled to the village, she would haul it along with them to make sure Nicholas had his American coffee. He was touched by how far out of her way she went to make him feel comfortable. Nicholas also learned that Greek men do not step foot in the kitchen. He tried to help, but his sister kicked him out! When she broke her arm, her husband had to help with the domestic chores but drew the line at hanging up the laundry on the clothesline during the daytime – he waited until it was nighttime so that no one would see him.

Nicholas's brother and cousins took him and his family to places Greeks went on vacation, away from the touristy spots. On a cold day, they took him and his son to Ancient Olympia. The stadium was in ruins, with marble everywhere. His brother challenged them to a race at a long starting block. As they were sprinting, his son's hat came off, and he got distracted with it. Nicholas now tells everyone he got to run at Olympia – and won!

After many years of visiting Greece, Nicholas and his wife wanted to return the favor of hosting, so they arranged for his nieces to visit them in America when the girls were 15 and 20. They spent five weeks touring the Mid-Atlantic states. They introduced the girls to Nicholas's adoptive sister. The goal was to show them that America was not full of drug dealers and shootings like they saw in the movies. They introduced them to American cuisine: BBQ, southern pulled pork, tacos, Chinese takeout, and hamburgers. However, the girls enjoyed learning how to make chocolate chip cookies the most. At the end of the visit, Nicholas and his wife sent their nieces back to Greece with measuring cups and recipes. Nicholas's sister was shocked that they wanted to cook. In *her* kitchen.

In Nicholas's mind, his adoptive parents are his parents. They never learned about Nicholas's birth family because they had passed away before he went to Greece for the first time. His father's sister said she didn't think his adoptive mom would have embraced a reunion with his birth family, though. Nicholas believes the idea of having to share him would have been difficult for her. Initially, when Nicholas's adoptive sister learned that his biological family found him, she was fine with the news – but a little chilly. Not hostile. Just a bit cool. She said, "Now you're going to forget about us." However, when she met Nicholas's nieces during their visit to America, she was stunned at their family resemblance; the matching prominent dimpled Greek chins were undeniable. *"She got it."* Nicholas said,

"You can't run away from genetics."

When Nicholas was growing up, he never felt like something was missing, never had an identity crisis, or a burning desire to find his biological parents. While he views his life through the lens of positivity, he does understand that other adoptees are often unfulfilled. When he hears stories of people who are crushed upon discovering they are adopted, he can't directly relate. He is grateful that his family came looking for him; because of their efforts, his life expanded, and his birth family enriched the focus of his life.

~ Advice Through Nicholas's Lens ~

For adoptive parents: "The whole idea of letting children know [they are adopted] from the start is a good idea. There is less mystery or stigma. Don't be threatened."

For adoptees: "Hopefully, you had a normal upbringing. If your adoptive parents hid [your adoption] from you, understand they thought it was the best thing to do because they didn't want you to be hurt. If you're interested in finding your birth parents, it can be rewarding, but you have to be open to whatever the experience is going to be. Sometimes, I imagine, [finding them] is not [rewarding]. I more completely understand my mother's sacrifice and how it affected her life."

My Thoughts, My Lens

Because Nicholas referred to the movie *My Big Fat Greek Wedding* several times, I fired up Amazon Prime and rented it. It had been well over a decade since I had watched it on a VHS tape. It was a great visual for getting a feel for Nicholas's colorful family. I cracked up when Toula said, "Nice Greek girls are supposed to do three things in life: marry Greek boys, make Greek babies and feed everyone until the day we die." Nicholas said that the younger Greek generation of women is slowly changing those norms, but the households are still traditional in his small village. Many scenes in the movie were entertaining: the grandmother dressed in black from head to toe, the whole lamb over the spit, the mountains of potatoes, the parade of relatives, the dry toast, and the references to a thousand relatives named "Nick." It was like one of the Nicks was talking directly to Nicholas when he quoted Dear Abby:

> *"Don't let your past dictate who you are, but let it be a part of who you will become."*

Getting a cinematic feel for what Nicholas discovered in real life was a joy. No wonder he grinned during the entire interview.

However, I suppose if I am honest, I was also a little jealous. I would love to discover that I had a huge family with open arms ready to feed me authentic food from my birth country. And that's not to take an inch away from his happiness ... his story is delightfully savory and one that many adoptees wish they could have. It was a blast learning how he discovered his ethnic roots and about the loyal family that came looking for him.

While Nicholas is grateful for his life, he did acknowledge that other Greek orphans did not have the blessed life he has had. He directed me to a few articles about Greek orphans:

In 1996, The New York Times published an article detailing several stories of illegal Greek adoptions. The babies were stolen, records were falsified, lies were told to both the adoptive and birth parents, and officials were indicted. It is estimated that at least 2,000 children were stolen and sold on the black market. "And while the institutions in those cities are considered well-run today, suspicions run high that they operated a baby-selling racket from the 1930s to the 1970s."[14]

In 1996, Los Angeles Times published an article corroborating The New York Times article. When the article was written, *The Association for the Investigation and Uncovering of Evidence of Adopted Children* had already helped 200 people find their birth families. 75% of those orphans were adopted illegally.[15]

75%!

While some adoptees were sent to unfit families, some, like Nicholas, had happy adoptive lives.

In reading the articles, what struck me most was that between the layers of atrocity were blankets of joy. One adoptee learned that her mother had died a year after her birth, but she found her Greek extended family, and 100 of those relatives held a big celebration for her in her mother's village. Although the article was written a long time ago in 1996, the adoptees' yearning to know the truth of their heritage was echoed in the recent conversations I've had with many adoptees.

To have knowledge and understanding is the "ask" – *even* if the knowledge doesn't end with a celebration of 100 people … *even* if the knowledge is so horrifying that it decimates the soul. I see why many adoptees are willing to take that risk.

---

[14] Bonner, Raymond. "Tales of Stolen Babies and Lost Identities; A Greek Scandal Echoes in New York." *The New York Times*, 13 Apr. 1996, www.nytimes.com/1996/04/13/nyregion/tales-of-stolen-babies-and-lost-identities-a-greek-scandal-echoes-in-new-york.html. Accessed 14 Jul. 2020.
[15] Konstandaras, Nikos. "Greek Americans Fear They May Have Been Black-Market Babies." *Los Angeles Times,* 29 Sep. 1996, www.latimes.com/archives/la-xpm-1996-09-29-mn-48657-story.html. Accessed 14 Jul. 2020.

John H. | Middle School Teacher

Daegu, South Korea
Year of Birth: 1976

Passionate. Funny. Selfless. John reminded me of a determined pinball shooting back and forth between the bumpers in a controlled frenzy – while never timing out. I was impressed by his strong sense of self and his unwavering empathy for others. He was extremely likable, had a wonderful sense of humor, and an impressive memory bank. Because of his compassion and goodhearted demeanor, I would bet that he's the type of person most people wished they had for a brother. As a teacher, he was earnest about his job, willing to take on the responsibility of being one of the few POC (Person of Color) representatives in his school district.

As an Asian American (with Norwegian and Dutch European American parents), John's adoption status was never questioned because he obviously looked different than his parents. They could not have biological children and adopted him when he was six months old. They told him about his adoption at a very young age, and he was their only child. Over the years, John and his parents *never* discussed his birth parents. The subject was not brought up in any way by his parents, and he never wanted to ask.

> *"I think part of me at some level realized it would make my parents very upset, maybe? That was pretty intuitive, for whatever reason."*

He remembers people inquiring about his birth parents. When he was growing up, talk shows like Jerry Springer, Ricky Lake, and Montel Williams were the rage. They often featured birth family reunions. He felt a sense of aloneness in his complete lack of curiosity regarding his birth family. He thinks our society tells him that he *should* want to know who his birth parents are. American culture and the media have bombarded him with the opposite view of what he feels. He has zero desire to find out, and *not* because he is ashamed. He is very proud of his Korean background. He lives by the mantra that his adoptive parents *are* his parents, so why would he need to find his birth parents? He never had questions such as, *"Who am I?"* or *"Who are my parents?"* He knows many adopted people feel differently than he does and attributes that to the strong sense of self he developed at a very young age.

John's mother gave him his file of adoption papers when he was approximately 40 years old. He put them away in a fireproof box in his closet before looking at them. The documents felt sterile, as they factually listed numbers, details, and names. John learned he was left in a marketplace in South Korea. It sounded like his birth mother just abandoned him and took off. He said, "Finding out about that – I think that at that time, I feel like different emotions went through me. I felt sorry for my birth mother at one point. Things were rough for her. I wasn't angry, um … uh, I think I feel lucky. Ha-ha. I could have died." In John's mind, his parents were the people who raised him. When he discovered how he became an orphan, he still had no desire to learn his history; it solidified his already existing sense of detachment. John said there were two options to consider. He said,

> *"It would be presumptuous for me to say that she did it because she knew she couldn't take care of me, that she knew maybe I would end up in a better place. The alternative option would be that she just wanted to get rid of her burden. Either way, it reaffirmed my decision of having that not be a part of who I am."*

Growing up with his parents was hard, and John was unsure if it was due to being adopted or other factors. His parents were challenging people to connect with emotionally, but they were very loving in their own way and wanted the best for him. They tried their hardest, and for that, John is grateful. To keep him connected to Korean heritage, his parents sent him to a Korean camp (based in Minnesota) for two summers. He remembers having a traditional sparkly bright-colored Korean formal wear outfit. The camp teachers taught the kids about Korean food, language, literature, martial arts, and dance. John has very few memories as a young child but remembers that the camp was a positive experience. His mother had a Korean cookbook she used to cook up dishes of love for many years. Symbolically, she recently gave it to John's girlfriend, who also enjoys cooking Korean food for him (and he loves to eat mountains of it). The book is proudly displayed on a stand in their kitchen. During our interview,

John retrieved it and showed it to me. It was well-loved and worn, with discolored aged pages and splattered food stains of comfort. The index tabs were notated in both English and Korean, much like John's existence. Korean food was a way for his mother to link John and his girlfriend together.

Another thing that John's parents did to keep him in touch with his heritage was to incorporate part of his Korean name when they adopted him. John is extremely appreciative that they named him John Min Park Hansen. John attended a teacher workshop in which the participants were asked to share the importance of their names. After reflection, the significance of the backstory of his own name spoke to him. It included both his Korean and Norwegian ancestry. On paper, John Hansen is Norwegian – but John Min Park Hansen is also Korean.

He no longer goes by "John" but prefers to be called *Hansen*. His ex-wife (and people he knew before his divorce) called him John, and therefore, symbolically, "John" is a part of his life that he no longer celebrates. (Although, it doesn't upset him that his lifelong buddies and mom still call him *John*.) Currently, he is known as *Hansen* to his students and coworkers. His girlfriend calls him Hansen. The workshop's takeaway was that his name represents so many levels of who he is as a person. Adopted. Asian. Norwegian. Divorced. He recreated the workshop with his students. When he shared his own story with them, he created an empathetic platform for them to talk about who they were. The workshop was meaningful to his students, too.

Growing up, Hansen was immersed in a White culture. Most of his friends and family were White; therefore, he naturally felt like he was White, too. It became second nature to him. However, there were a few occasions where he would be reminded that he was *not* White. In early elementary school, little kids would make fun of him with the "classic slanty-eye thing." On another occasion, he remembers being in a grocery store when a younger kid blurted out (without malice), "Look, Mommy, a Chinese boy." Hansen was neither mad nor sad about the incident – it just was a jarring "ping" to his self-awareness.

"Still … this exterior shell of me that is not conforming to the norm of honestly what I feel inside. Those moments tend to catch

me off guard. On a daily basis, I don't think about [not being White]."

Hansen took a lighthearted approach to his ethnicity. When he was a kid, he teased his best friend's little sister by telling her that he was Norwegian. She was young and couldn't figure out the difference. In the seventh grade, his family moved from his childhood home several hours away to northern Minnesota, where he met his lifelong friends. When he and his friends discussed People of Color, they told him it was natural for him to be with them. Their strong connection has remained intact to this day; they still see each other on a regular basis. *They* are his family. He was one of three Asian students out of a graduating high school class of 600 students. However, Hansen was not friends with the two other Asian students. They were not adopted and came from fully Asian households.

At this point in the interview, Hansen paused. He then visibly cringed when he remembered that he failed to stick up for one of the other Asian students who was being bullied. Hansen felt sorry for him but purposely distanced himself. He now wishes he had been more compassionate and would have risen to the challenge. The other Asian kid was the stereotypical "Hollywood Asian" student required to have a straight A record. Studying was his mantra, whereas Hansen was the class clown – an extrovert – and socializing was his priority.

Hansen's support base was not his family – it was his friends. Conversely, he had a disconnect with his parents growing up. (His mother is now a widow.) He is unsure of the reason for the disconnect and speculates it's because he's adopted or an only child. Or neither. He has stronger connections with his friends because of how his parents negatively modeled what family meant to them. Hansen said it would devastate his mother to hear him say that because it is the opposite for her. He said, "I am the light of her day. I will always be that little boy in her mind."

His parents struggled when he was growing up. Hansen's grandfather (his mother's father) passed away when his mom was very young. His grandmother was a single mother raising three children. Over the years, he was privy to the toxic stereotypical Minnesota passive-aggressive relationships of his mother's family. (Minnesotan agricultural heritage pervades the state's culture: i.e., don't piss off your neighbor because you might need them someday. However, in an effort to avoid conflict, many

Minnesotans often experience "leakage" in the form of passive-aggressiveness.) Hansen's family was very respectful on the surface and face to face. However, they were "back-stabby" in private. That decidedly molded Hansen's perception of how members within a family unit relate to one another.

Hansen thinks the root of his disconnect most likely was his family's dynamics but leaves space (if he is wrong) that the disconnect was really about his adoption – stuck in his subconscious. Holidays were very destructive and a source of childhood pain because of his family's toxic relationship. He prefers to have quiet celebrations instead of big family events for holidays. Both his ex-wife and current girlfriend have tight-knit, supportive families. It is hard for them to grasp why Hansen, "the extrovert," would prefer to spend holidays alone and privately. To them, that's not the norm. However, Hansen would argue it's just as vital they understand his reality as it is for him to understand theirs. He acknowledges that while some people have the desire to travel hundreds of miles to see third cousins, they need to take a moment to say that they see his viewpoint. A verbal affirmation would be all it would take.

> *"Empathy is what makes our world united. You can't have unity without having empathy."*

After college, Hansen dove into education. Being a teacher was a pivotal point in his life. Because he was thrown in the deep end, he had to learn about the human condition. He grew in leaps and bounds in terms of empathy and compassion by making himself available to listen to his student's stories. Their perspectives were just as valuable as his perspective. Learning to validate their concerns, considering their wants, and acknowledging their fears honed his listening skills. As part of his journey, he became cognitively aware that he was a Teacher of Color, despite having a White background. He became very self-conscious daily, which differed from the few jarring moments he had as a child. But the new level of awareness facilitated growth. *In* him. *For* his students. He credits his parents with planting the seed of ethnic awareness. As he matured, he became more appreciative of his Korean background. Much of Hansen's progress and growth as a human has come from being an educator. He was driven to be the best teacher he could be.

The best. Not good. The BEST.

To achieve that goal, it wasn't going to be about what *he* wanted, but John realized he had to truly listen to his students (from a plethora of backgrounds). He had to become self-reflective and positive for them. Being a teacher had "massive ramifications" on who he was as a person – and all in a good way. He has 150 students every year. All 150 have a unique storyline. The following year, he has 150 more new students, and so forth. Most people can't practice empathy at that level. Hansen is grateful he has that opportunity. Right now, he does not have children of his own (but would like to have some) and has the "luxury" of time. He has time for himself as well as time to reap the benefits of pouring himself into his job.

As a Teacher of Color, Hansen is exceptionally aware of his students' sensitivities to race. He likes to joke with his students about growing up with "White people." He understands that he will possibly be the only non-White teacher his students will have during their middle and high school years. He views that as an opportunity, not a burden, hoping it may be a cognitive switch for some students of color (meaning it is ambitious to connect with his students who have very few teachers of color, but Hansen wants to be up to taking on that challenge for them). At his core, he is very White because of how he was raised and acknowledges that is an odd juxtaposition with his need to relate to students of color.

Hansen also jokes about his ethnicity to strangers. He was once at a grocery store, and two Asians were in line in front of him at the cash register speaking their native language. When it was his turn, he looked at the clerk, rolled his eyes, and said, "Asians …" The clerk was confused and didn't know whether to laugh or condemn him. Then, to let her off the hook, he said, "I'm just playing." While he takes a light-hearted approach, he can be serious about being Asian on the surface and White on the inside. As an adult, he went to a Korean festival production that celebrated traditional song and dance. He estimated that Asians comprised 95% of the audience, and they spoke in their native tongue. And because of *that*, the feelings of being a fraud flooded within him. While he was very proud of being Asian, he felt like they perceived him as a *fake* Korean. When he got "stuck" holding the door open as many older Asians entered the theater, he just bowed and said nothing as they spoke to him, with his inward dialog repeating,

"Yes, I am Asian. Yes, I am Asian."

He now laughs about it and understands that his fraudulent feelings were self-induced. When he goes to the Korean market, he is very self-conscious about his behavior. He usually is an energetic extrovert but is uncharacteristically quiet when he is in the presence of many Asians. "It sucks." He feels like he is dishonoring that side of himself, a negative manifestation of his sense of pride.

His junior high and high school years were the periods of his life where he tried to fit in. (That's why he didn't associate with the two other Asian students.) It wasn't until college that he finally figured out who he was. There, he met his ex-wife (who is White). He laughed about the time when her father and brother discovered that she was secretly dating him. When they questioned her about "John Hansen," her father was relieved that he had the name of a "good Norwegian boy." Hansen's darkest moments in life surrounded his divorce. But overall, his life has been positive because his job demanded that of him.

At the time of our interview, the news of George Floyd and the peaceful protests and violent riots proliferated our media. Hansen said there were parallels between Floyd's story and his students' stories. He talked about the never-ending spiral of some police officers not understanding or having empathy towards community culture while – at the same time – the community did not have empathy for police officers. One begets the other. He said if he were a police officer, he would be conflicted. He thought that most likely, there were police officers who agreed with the protestors. Still, because they were tasked with keeping the peace, they were put in a position in which they were unable to say anything … and yet they had people condemning them, yelling profanities to their faces. He said if he were a police officer in that situation, he would probably cry … break down and bawl because he empathized with both sides. He extrapolated that situation to his students; if they lost control with him, it would wreck him as a person because he agrees and empathizes with their pain. We live in a society where empathy is not a priority, but he believes everyone should take a moment and validate others' feelings. As an educator, Hansen said it is his job to fight those things. To try, at least.

In his school district, 3% of teachers are of color, whereas enrollment of students of color is 24%, and 15% are economically disadvantaged. Hansen teaches his students empathy from both the White perspective and the

"Minority perspective." He uses standardized testing results to demonstrate the achievement gap between White and non-White students. In his opinion, standardized testing is aimed towards White students by the nature of language and the format used. Using that as a springboard for a learning opportunity, he has taught his students about the disparity between the percentage of Teachers of Color (3%) and Students of Color (24%). Together, they identified leadership and power roles (such as parents, teachers, clergy, friends, etc.). Through math and logic, he concluded the likelihood is that most students in his district will only have White teachers during their middle and high school years. He said, "So, if you go through your whole life where you never see a teacher of color, you develop your sense of who has power. It is impacted by only seeing White people in education."

That is Hansen's interpretation of White Privilege.

It's nothing to be ashamed of or to feel guilty about; it's just something he wants his students to be aware of – the reality is that some things in life are stacked in certain ways. He feels if his students can grasp that concept, they understand White privilege. Obviously, many circumstances lead to the socioeconomic gap, but that is just one of the factors. He feels the relationship he has with his students is not dissimilar to the relationship that police need to have with the community. Teachers and police officers go into their respective fields with the best of intentions. It is up to them to validate and value their students' and communities' feelings. Not only validate but to work *within* the system.

"Life is not stacked fairly for all humans. That is the reality."

It is the police officer's role to help stop the cycle of unfairness. And it is the teacher's role to prevent the same cycle through education. At the core of both is empathy. Both professions should be held to a higher standard. Hansen feels the community's pain and the George Floyd protestors' pain as much as he feels his students' pain. "Education is the key."

Hansen's ethnic role (brought about by adoption) contributed to his passion for teaching. He does not underestimate the potential of being an educator. It is an opportunity he is determined not to squander. To him, it is not only his responsibility, but it is his opportunity to change the world, and said, "Why would you not want to be passionate about it?" Adoption is the most significant component that makes up Hansen – a tool in his toolbox that gives him the ability to relate to his students.

~ Advice Through John's Lens ~

For adoptees: "I would summarize the whole international adoption concept to be interwoven with serious pros and cons. And each adoptee's experience to be unique. No single experience will define the group. Someone's name versus their looks can be a transitioning moment for people … enjoy those moments of levity; you can have fun with the difference of looking one way but having a different name. You can have fun and still be very proud at the core. If you are very confident and have self-esteem, you will have those moments. If you are defensive about it, it might be a sign that you are too proud or take life very seriously."

"I know I look Asian."

[Grin.]

"At some point, you have to ask yourself and be reflective about who you are. Who do you want to be identified as? *Hansen the Asian* or *Hansen the Caucasian*? Once you become so confident in that answer, it will hopefully allow you to move past the defensiveness … because you're THAT confident about who you are. Think about who you want to be. To help people who question you, encourage them to do a lot of self-reflecting. You can have fun with that. I came to the decision that I wanted to be 'Hansen the Asian,' AND I wanted to be 'Hansen the White Guy.' I am proud of both sides. However, if I am being honest, Asian is the weaker side for me because I know more about American culture than Korean culture. The soul-searching has to come from within."

My Thoughts, My Lens

When Hansen talked about the "classic slanty-eye" slur, my knee-jerk thought was "unoriginal." I'm guessing 99.9% of Asians growing up in America have heard that one. Bullies need to step up their taunting game (snark intended).

When I started writing this book, I didn't foresee that racism would be a major topic covered. However, since many of the interviewees were from transracial families, it was impossible to ignore. Someone told me she didn't believe me when I said that I didn't anticipate the topic of racism would be an integral part of so many stories. For several days, I didn't have a response. Of course, I was acutely aware adoption *and* racism both proliferated my life, but I viewed them as individual silos – disconnected and unrelated. However, I wasn't being untruthful – in my mind, I just never linked adoption and racism together, blind to the fact that the racism I've experienced over my lifetime is a *direct result* of my adoption. It was painfully obvious to others, but wasn't to me. Duh.

Transracial adoption unintentionally provides an easy target for racist individuals – a hard truth. But that doesn't mean we should discourage transracial adoptions. Instead, we should work to normalize transracial families through education and exposure. As Rachel Garlinghouse put it,

> *"It's important to note that though many White adults embrace the idea that 'race doesn't matter' and that 'racism is a thing of the past,' neither of these is true. Any experienced transracial adoptive family can testify that race does matter and that the world is not colorblind."*[16]

The concept of a non-colorblind world reminded me of an incident in college when I signed up to be a psychology study participant. The subjects were asked to listen to the cries of babies and rate how distressed each cry

---

[16] Garlinghouse, Rachel. *Come Rain or Shine, A White Parent's Guide to Adopting and Parenting Black Children.* CreateSpace, 2013, p. 166.

sounded. At the end of my session, I asked the teaching assistant about the study, and she told me they were comparing answers across cultures. I told her I was adopted and should be in the "Caucasian" pool. She disagreed and told me I would be in the Asian pool. When I tried to make my case that I had zero knowledge of Asian language or culture, she became agitated and said she would talk to the professor. She made sure she "put me in my place" by letting me know that my responses were mostly likely going to be in the Asian pool. I left frustrated and unheard, yet again reminded that *I* was out of place. I wish I had incorporated the same type of humor into my life that Hansen naturally integrated into his. The levity would have lightened my burden.

Hansen's opinion about the effect of names also resonated with me. I thought his parents did a good job at co-mingling his American and Korean names. Things became easier for me once I got married and changed my last name from Miller to Zmich (pronounced like Michigan with a Z – "zmish"). My name history is:

1. <u>Birth</u>: Lee Jung Sun

2. <u>Adoption</u>: Lee Jung Sun Miller (a.k.a. "Suni" pronounced "Sunny")

3. <u>Marriage</u>: Lee Jung-Sun Zmich (a.k.a. "Suni")

4. <u>Facebook</u>: Suni Miller Zmich (still pronounced "Sunny")

As "Lee Miller," living in the South in the 1980s ("Suni" is what everyone calls me, but it is not my legal name), it was hard for me to use my credit card or write personal checks because people thought I had stolen them from a White guy. Sometimes, the clerks or waitstaff clearly felt justified in their hostile demands that I show alternate identification. A young Asian woman had no business with the last name of Miller … little reminders that I was swimming in the wrong pond. At times, it was a nightmare. When I got married and took on the Polish name Zmich, it was so unusual that it matched my complexion in the eyes of many others (both were "foreign"). It was a perfect relief because no one ever questioned me again. Ever.

I suppose I should stay married.

I am sitting here rolling my eyes at the memory of a shocked Southerner when he learned that my last name was Polish, saying, "Whuuut? Pohhh-lish? Are yew kiddin' me? Well girl, ah thawt yower layast name was ORRREEEEENTALL!" I can now laugh at how ridiculous he was.

It is impressive that Hansen approaches his Asian-ness with witty banter. It is inspiring. I should take some life lessons from his playbook because I allowed the racially jarring moments to sink in and hurt me over my lifetime. Hansen is blessed to have good friends in his life who have been brothers to him since childhood. He is an excellent example of an adoptee who has learned to claim his rightful place in a mostly White state. By balancing humor with his outgoing personality, he successfully played the life cards he was dealt. And that is admirable.

The reality of transracial adoption is that racism exists in our world. While we need to acknowledge it, it need not dictate how we view ourselves. In my mind, Hansen is brilliant.

Lisa B. | College Student

Guatemala City, Guatemala
Year of Birth: 2001

During our initial conversation, the first thing I noticed about Lisa was her easy smile. The second thing I noticed was the mellow, circumspect way she told her story. It took a few conversations for me to understand her stance on adoption. When she was younger, she was insulated from how other adoptees felt, as evidenced by her innocent dismissiveness as we moved through her story. (She wasn't even sure how her own siblings felt about adoption.) At one point, she mentioned her adoptive brother had extreme behavioral issues, which was the opposite of her experience. It is worth mentioning that she did journey through varying emotions about her adoption as a child and teenager. However, she ultimately arrived at a peaceful venue with respect to her adoption.

Unlike many other adoptees, she did not view her adoption as a burden. Lisa grew up in peaceful American suburbia. Her parents were very open about her adoption with her and her siblings. They also freely spoke about it with their friends. At four, Lisa's earliest memory of adoption occurred when her parents brought her youngest brother home from Guatemala (after adopting him when he was 22 months old). It was at that time when Lisa's parents told her she was also adopted. She already had an adopted sister to whom she was very attached; on some level, she even felt biologically connected to her sister. But it wasn't until that conversation with her parents that Lisa was old enough to comprehend the concept of adoption fully. She has five siblings – one adopted brother, two adopted sisters, and two older brothers who are her parents' biological children. As child number three, she is the oldest adopted sibling. All four of the adoptees are from Guatemala, with ages spanning only six years.

It did not occur to Lisa to have any negative feelings when she learned about her adoption because she was excited that she was getting another sibling.

119

She did not see the arrival of her brother as *charity*. Instead, she focused on the joy of getting another brother. She bonded with him as she helped him learn English (as a toddler, he already spoke Spanish). As Lisa grew older and her parents adopted another girl, she became the self-appointed caretaker to her siblings. As a third grader, she would go with them to an in-home daycare. She was the oldest kid there but still too young to be at home by herself. However, Lisa liked going because she felt special when she helped with the younger children. It was at daycare that she and her baby sister bonded.

Over the years, Lisa's peaceful caretaker role spilled over into her other relationships. Most of her friends were younger than she was, and she often checked in with them to make sure they were doing well. She is now a college student studying to be a social worker. In her mind, her career choice was natural because she was adopted. Foster care is her passion. She wants to champion system-change and yearns for reform.

In Lisa's early elementary school years, she was affected by her adoption. She wasn't angry with her parents but was mad because she was put in a situation that necessitated her adoption. When she was in the fourth grade, her class was given an assignment (during the 2010 Vancouver Winter Olympics) to find their ancestral home country's representatives. Guatemala had no athletes that year. She said, "I hated my school for making me do that." However, her feelings changed later that year when Lisa's class was assigned projects on countries outside the U.S. She chose Guatemala and learned about its history as a nation in the developing world, which directly affected her life. Most of the population is poor and lives in villages known as "unmarked cities" because they consist of only a few dozen people.

Like many other Guatemalans, Lisa was not born in a hospital. Her mother's story is vague. The adoption agency told her family that Lisa's mother was a widow, and Lisa was undocumented because her mother was illiterate. The only documentation Lisa has is a photograph of her mother and her fingerprints. As a female, it was dangerous to live in Guatemala because many young women were victims of sex trafficking. Young boys and young men were expected to join the militia or cartels. Lisa believes that her mother wanted something better for her. I asked Lisa if she had ever wanted to save her birth mother. She answered yes but didn't want to get her hopes up. Her birth mother would have quite a few obstacles to overcome if she were still alive. When she completed the research for her project, her anger over her adoption melted away. Lisa pivoted from being angry to being grateful that her mother gave her up for adoption.

Lisa accepted it. She said,

> *"I felt like I was being selfish and knew I couldn't be angry anymore."*

Lisa does not know if her siblings are as accepting of their adoptions as she is. They've never shared their feelings about adoptions with one another. But in her view, having a large family influenced her positively. Lisa sees herself as being an integral part of her big family and therefore never felt the need to discuss adoption at length. She is also surrounded by friends who are adoptees or people connected to adoption, so her life feels normal to her.

When our conversation turned to race, Lisa was casually dismissive. Skin tone does not matter to Lisa. She does not question her physical traits because she doesn't see herself as different from her White adoptive parents. Lisa unapologetically shrugged her shoulders as she said she did not see her adoption as something that needed to be addressed as a negative circumstance.

Lisa did another project about Guatemala in high school. Her parents adopted Lisa's youngest sibling a year before Guatemala closed the borders to international adoption in 2007. During her research, she learned that the shutdown was due to many reports of children who were abducted or of parents who were tricked into signing away their parental rights. Many of the parents were illiterate and did not know what they were signing. The Guatemalan foster care and adoption systems were so corrupt that they would destroy the documentation after the adoptions were finalized. Like Lisa, many Guatemalan children were undocumented because they were not born in hospitals and therefore did not receive birth certificates. They were not even registered as citizens of Guatemala, making it easy to hide the exploitation.

Before 2007, when the adoption business was booming, American couples paid upwards of $30,000 to adopt Guatemalan babies, bringing in more than

$100 million annually.[17] The Guatemalan government took over the corrupt system in an effort to protect their children after receiving international pressure to comply with the Hague Convention (a mandate to protect children in intercountry adoption). A Guatemalan government report concluded that at least 333 children were stolen and sold for adoption to parents in the United States, Sweden, Italy, and France during the 36-year civil war. Sometimes, parents were killed so the children could be adopted abroad.[18] Sex trafficking is also a problem in Guatemala. According to Reuters, "Nearly 60 percent of the 50,000 victims of sex trafficking in Guatemala are children."[19]

At 16 years old, another pivotal life event happened for Lisa when she traveled to Chattanooga, Tennessee on a youth mission trip. She had the opportunity to learn about American Indian history and how they honored their land. She also worked with older adults and children in need. But what impacted her the most was when her youth group visited the popular tourist places; they would also see the homeless people who were hidden away from the rest of society. To witness homelessness so close in proximity to the wealthy area of tourist attractions jolted Lisa's social awareness. She journaled about her experiences and how she felt like she wasn't doing enough. The poverty reminded her of her Guatemalan roots.

During our follow-up conversation, Lisa said since our first interview, she happened to click on a TikTok video that introduced her to the term *transracial adoption*. The young woman in the video said she was not only a "minority" at school but also a "minority" in her own home. She continued to say she loved her family. "But there will always be an element of true

[17] Fieser, Ezra K. "Guatemala Confronts One of its Largest Businesses: Adoptions." *ICWA Letters,* EKF-18, Nov. 2009. www.icwa.org/wp-content/uploads/2015/10/EKF-18.pdf. Accessed 11 May 2021.
[18] Brice, Arthur. "Guatemalan army stole children for adoption, report says." *CNN,* 12 Sep. 2009, www.cnn.com/2009/WORLD/americas/09/12/guatemala.child.abduction/index.html. Accessed 29 Apr. 2020.
[19] Moloney, Anastasia. "Guatemala 'closes its eyes' to rampant child sex trafficking: U.N." *Reuters,* 8 Jun. 2016, www.reuters.com/article/us-guatemala-humantrafficking-idUSKCN0YU29V. Accessed 29 Apr. 2020.

empathy that is missing."[20] The video impacted Lisa because up until that point, she was content. She said, "I never questioned things. I'm just happy, you know, but I don't want to ignore other stories." Lisa did not share the woman's experiences in the video because she was not a "minority" in her own home, having four White and four Guatemalan family members. But the random TikTok click caused her to open her mind to the feelings of others. She applauds social media sites for creating platforms for adoptees to share their feelings without backlash.

While Lisa now understands that other adoptees (and even her own family members) have had vastly different experiences than she did, she is at peace with her adoption. She knows what her life would have been like if she had not been adopted and understands the polar differences between her idyllic American life and her humble birth country. That acceptance freed her to bond with her American family.

~ Advice Through Lisa's Lens ~

For adoptees: "You don't have to be ashamed of being adopted. It's not very common, but it's also very unique, and you should be proud of it."

For adoptive parents: "If you're adopting a child of a different race or ethnicity, be cautious of the looks you're going to get. Ignore them. It's more important to be focused on your child. You will gain a backbone and become stronger mentally. Don't take it personally. Adoptees feel like outcasts. It definitely helps adoptees figure out who they are and where they belong in the family dynamics if there is more than one adoptee in the family. Telling them they're adopted is definitely important. Be aware that adoptees will face identity crises and offer 100% support."

In a follow up call, Lisa expanded on her advice for parents. She had completed a project in college about the mental health of adoptees and adoptive parents. She said,

---

[20] www.tiktok.com/@tay_jiyoon/video/6897338125752732933. Accessed 21 Dec. 2020.

"There are moments you'll feel vulnerable at times, but when the child is a young adult, or you feel the moment is right, talk about those insecurities or fears."

When Lisa's mom finally opened up about her fears, she felt much closer to her mom. Her mom revealed how sad she became when Lisa yelled at her that she wasn't her "real" mom during a few teenage fights. The conversation was fruitful for both of them. Lisa felt like a "weight was lifted" from her shoulders when she could assure her mom that she didn't mean it. At the same time, her mom felt relief just by being able to talk about her feelings with someone other than her husband. Lisa still feels a little guilty about those arguments. However, she and her mom are now in a good place, closer than ever before.

My Thoughts, My Lens

It was easy to talk with Lisa. She is a gentle and peaceful person, motivated to rescue the world. She has the perspective of situational contrast – her dangerous birthplace juxtaposed with all that comes with orderly American suburbia – manicured lawns, plenty of sidewalks, and well-maintained parks. In her mind, she has left behind her humble beginnings and has chosen to embrace life with her adoptive family. I imagine that accepting her adoption has set her up with a high probability of success in the social services field. I love her sweet-tempered personality and her ability to shed her anger *in the fourth grade.*

Many adoptees struggle for years to find that place of self-love. (I fall into that camp.) I admire Lisa for being able to appreciate her adoptive family without any resentment. During our interview, she mentioned her adoptive brother had a very different childhood experience than she did. While Lisa's story was blanketed with peace in the end, her brother's story was tangled with extreme behavioral issues and sorrow. However, we didn't delve into the details – she felt it was not her story to tell. Author Nancy Verrier wrote about the differences in sibling adoption experiences when she interviewed people for her book over the course of ten years:

> *"When there are two adopted children in a family, in every case that I have studied, one adoptee assumes the acting-out role and the other is compliant, regardless of their birth order, sex, or personalities."*[21]

As an only child, I fulfilled both roles. My mom recently told me she had no idea that the source of my childhood angst was about adoption. (Apparently, I didn't either.) Growing up, I played the role of a model student. It wasn't until I was in that weird in-between stage of transforming from a dumb teenager to a stupid young adult that I allowed my rancor to bubble up to

---

[21] Verrier, Nancy Newton. *The Primal Wound: Understanding the Adopted Child.* Gateway Press, Inc., 1993, p. 63.

the surface in college. In my opinion, people wake up to life when approaching adulthood. I know I woke up to barbed wire rage wrapped around my heart. Breaking from playing the model student role for my first few years as an undergraduate, I lost my mind, determined to numb myself with destructive behaviors.

Unlike my story, Lisa's journey provides superb context of how an adoptee can embrace happiness early in life after letting go of the anger. I feel it is important to show prospective adoptive parents that not every adoptee's story has a lingering shadow of trauma. Some adoptees are able to work through their heartache, allowing them to move forward with a fruitful life. I feel blessed to have Lisa's story in this book.

Liv O. | Graduate Student

Ansan, South Korea
Year of Birth: 1997

I've known Liv since she was a baby. She is a lion trapped in the petite frame of a beautiful Korean American young woman. When she decides to accomplish something, she goes all out. Valedictorian of a Chicago suburban school. Scholarships out the wazoo. The consummate overachiever as a student at the University of Illinois. During our interview, Liv demonstrated an extraordinary level of self-awareness, which wasn't apparent to me until our conversation. In speaking with her, it was evident she had transitioned into adulthood. When I later asked about her self-awareness, she said that years of therapy helped her have an emotionally-centered conversation.

Additionally, her supportive core family helped her "practice" these conversations. Tragically, both of her adoptive parents were killed in a car accident in December 2018. Before their deaths, Liv's world of awareness had a much smaller radius. She spoke without a trace of reservation ... to the point that I felt obligated to precisely capture her trauma. And because her adoptive mother and I were close friends, I felt inexplicably compelled to respect the legacy of Liv's parents and prove that I was worthy of the gift of her story.

Liv was brought to social services in Seoul within two weeks of her birth and placed with her foster family three days later. Years later, when Liv met her foster mother, she was surprised and appreciative that her foster mother remembered specific things about her — like the three freckles she has on the right side of the nape of her neck. With her flashy cute old lady blouses, big jewelry, and assortments of lipsticks, her foster mother was still the same person that Liv's parents had accurately described over the years. Her parents had met with her three or four times when they were in South Korea to bring Liv home. It was protocol for Liv's adoption agency to not relinquish their babies to foreign adoptive parents until the end of the visit.

127

Liv's parents could only take her directly to the airport upon departure. Korean culture dictated sensitivity to the optics of having White families with Korean babies in public. Her parents brought Liv's brother, Cory (their six-year-old biological son), along on that trip. While it was not an inexpensive endeavor, they appreciated the journey as they explored the process of adoption.

Liv cherishes the stories of their time in South Korea. Her father, Tom, could have been a successful Hollywood entertainer; he was a successful salesman. He drew people in with his affable personality. Everyone who met him liked him *immediately*. He could tell a boring story with the skill of a seasoned comedian, easily convincing every listener it was the funniest thing they had ever heard. Misadventure seemed to surround their travels in South Korea. One of Liv's favorite stories was of the time when her dad had to carry their giant suitcase because it had a broken wheel. He shoved it into the train and tried to board behind it. However, he couldn't fit in the packed car, and his leg was stuck in the closing doors, unable to pull it out. Liv's mom, Molly, had already boarded the train and was scared because an older Korean lady was freaking out. WAS HE GOING TO GET DRAGGED BY THE TRAIN???

He was not.

They ended up getting separated as the train departed but then were reunited at another stop. Another story that Liv's family liked to tell was about their 4-hour bus ride to the country's mountainous eastern part. The travel agency arranged for them to stay at a very nice hotel with a bowling alley in the basement. There was some confusion at the bus stop, and they were told to board the wrong bus, ending up instead on a high school summer vacation bus, not on a nice tour bus with air conditioning! During the ride, Liv's mom Molly started to cry; all of the teenagers were staring at her. The weirdest part of the ride was that the kids were eating dried squid snacks.

Squid. Dried. Snack?

On the plane ride back to America (after spending a week in South Korea), Liv's parents had to take turns standing with her in the rear of the plane while she sobbed the entire trip. On the leg from South Korea to Japan, she cried. On the leg from Japan to Seattle, she sobbed even louder. There were fewer Asian faces on the transcontinental flight. Molly thought the tears were because Liv knew she was being taken away, and the concentration of "foreigners" on the plane upset her.

Molly only used Liv's Korean name, "Cha Jin-Hee" in Korea. Out of respect for the Korean culture, she refrained from referring to her as "Liv" or "Olivia" until they reached American soil, thereby acknowledging that infant Liv was being taken away from a homogeneous culture. When they arrived in Chicago, Liv's extended family was at the airport to greet her with celebratory balloons in hand. Over the years, Liv's parents included her extended family in their celebrations. The Korean first birthday party is a big deal ("Dol" in Korean). Molly and Tom went all out buying Korean groceries to make japchae (a savory pork noodle dish) and homemade mandu (deep-fried dumplings stuffed with garlic and chicken – like a crispy pot sticker). They dressed Liv up in a hanbok, the traditional Korean dress with rainbow sleeves and a hat.

As Liv grew up in White suburbia, she became acutely aware of her ethnicity. In fourth grade, Liv was introduced to the concept of racism. She had to ride the bus with a neighbor boy who was a year ahead of her in school. On one particular day, she took longer to find her seat because her friends were not on the bus. He punched her in the back and yelled at her, "Sit down, Chink!" Liv was at a loss of what to do and told no one until she got home and could tell Molly. Sadly, that was the day Liv learned racism exists. And race *does* matter.

Since Molly and I were friends, she called to tell me about the boy right after she learned about the incident. She was normally a very calm and uber-organized person … the kind of mother I aspired (but often failed) to be. She had the perfect balance of protective instincts and softheartedness. Her home was immaculate and beautifully decorated. She always tastefully dressed in a classic style. Her meals were well thought out and prepared with love, and her kids were well behaved and articulate. Naturally, Molly was a Room Mom and Girl Scout leader – to which she brought her ultimate kids' party planning skills. She would read every book that her kids were assigned to read so she could be ready to discuss it with them, if necessary. The classy, modern-day version of June Cleaver = Molly (June Cleaver was the iconic perfect housewife in the late 1950s sitcom *Leave It to Beaver*).[22] The best part was that Molly was one of the kindest souls on this planet.

However …

When she talked about *that* boy, the one that hurt *her* little girl on the bus, she said she wanted to punch him in the face.

June Cleaver wanted to punch someone in the face.

The Momma bear that came out of Molly was shockingly impressive and a testament to the extent she would go to protect Liv. The altercation's impact changed Liv's life because it was the first time that she had to acknowledge race meant something in a larger context.

In middle school, Liv fit the smart Asian stereotype. She was picked on for being both "Asian" as well as being a "Smart Asian." The kids would tell her racist jokes. Rolling her eyes, she thought they were the stupidest people in the gifted and talented school program. Throughout her school years, Liv would confide in her mom about her schoolmates. Molly taught her not to engage them because they were looking for attention. She said her mom was somewhat right, and the bullies became interested in other targets. In middle school, Liv started to have serious symptoms of depression. She said, "I don't 100% know why." When she told her mother that she had thoughts of suicide, Molly brought her to a therapist who worked at the adoption agency that facilitated Liv's adoption. That therapist referred them to another excellent therapist who had direct adoption experience (she had adopted children from South Korea). When they met with her for the first time, Molly could barely speak when she choked out that Liv had thoughts of suicide.

[Tears.]

> *"That was the first time I realized that these thoughts and feelings were not bad and immoral. They just have meaning."*

---

[22] Kiddle. "June Cleaver facts for kids." kids.kiddle.co/June_Cleaver. Accessed 7 Apr. 2021.

It was her mom's reaction that made Liv realize that her feelings could be harmful … they were real, and being young didn't preclude her from being impacted by negative things such as racism.

Liv has vivid memories of high school. Even though her school was predominantly White, she initially had a racially diverse friend group. When she met her boyfriend's Laotian grandmother, she realized that Asian families differed significantly from White families. One of her Vietnamese friends had many nice Asian pieces of china in her home, including a big cylindrical utensil container filled with different kinds of chopsticks. The big ceramic Chinese ones stand out in Liv's memory, and she remembers thinking that it was inconceivable to her … her family would never have a container of chopsticks in their home. It wasn't a bad thing, just inconceivable.

By high school, she noticed other differences between her family and other families. For example, she knew her family was upper-middle class, and then it dawned on her that her friends were in a financially lower bracket. She ended up leaving her diverse friend group during her sophomore year because she became focused on other activities, such as band and speech. But at the same time, distinctly specific thoughts of depression escalated, and her stress was feeding it. Even though she didn't know *how* people committed suicide, she fantasized about dying … "What if I got in a car accident?" She pictured it very graphically and went down the path of emotional self-harm. She would purposely think about her death and the reactions of her parents. She said she clearly understood it would be life-ruining.

> *"I would have guilt over the fact that I would feel relief, but my parents would be devastated. I know I thought those things to hurt myself and exacerbate the agony."*

Liv attempted suicide on May 5th of her junior year in high school.

It was an unplanned impulse that she desperately hoped would work because she just wanted to disappear. The week leading to her attempt was filled with extreme turmoil. She had broken a beaker in the chemistry lab and cried in the band room for the rest of the day. Surprisingly, on the day of her attempt, she had the best day of the week. She felt okay during the school day, but the tsunami of despair came later at home. When the emotions returned, she felt it was out of her control. However, the one thing she could control was to take a bottle of meds and hope it would work. She was sobbing so loudly that her parents came up to her room, and she told them she took the pills. She felt so guilty but knew she wanted to go to the hospital while hoping she would disappear at the same time.

Not wanting an ambulance or an entourage of police cars at the house, her parents drove her to the hospital. Luckily, it was only four miles away. She vaguely remembers the events. *Triage … Pump her stomach? Charcoal? Poison control. Watch vitals. It will pass through her system.* Liv was sedated for 30 hours. Her parents took turns sleeping on the hospital floor with a security guard outside the door. She was exhausted and felt genuine fear that her parents couldn't handle her. When she came to, she thought she would be in solitary confinement and that her life would change in a bad way forever.

But it didn't.

She was brought to youth rehabilitation services at the university hospital for ten days. Daily visits were discouraged, so her parents visited only four times (for psychiatrist sessions). During her stay, Liv felt like her problems did not compare to the other kids in her group counseling sessions. She saw scars on their arms or ankles and heard about their abusive family situations. The patients could not have phones, shoes, or shoelaces. Everything struck her as "weird." She realized that many kids were objectively in worse situations than hers. At times, it did not make sense to her why she was even there because, after all, in her mind, she only had thoughts and feelings … but when she looked deeper, she agreed that she needed to be there.

Her mother fiercely (and successfully) protected Liv's privacy. Friends and their extended family did not know of her depression or suicide attempt. Liv shared these events with her extended family after her parents' deaths, and they were genuinely shocked.

By the time Liv left the rehabilitation facility, she was on an antidepressant medication. It did not go well. That summer, she had psychotic thoughts. She told her mom that she no longer needed an eye. She wanted to donate her eye. Molly bawled. In retrospect, Liv said that it was definitely a psychotic thought because, *in that moment*, she didn't think there was anything wrong with what she was saying. The manic symptoms presented in a variety of ways. She wanted to sell all of her possessions. She sold a ton of books and was going to use that money to save all of the homeless people by making hats and mittens for them. Because Liv's personality changed so dramatically, Molly spoke with the psychiatrist, and they changed her medication. The psychotic thoughts subsided, but the depression did not. Her personality morphed weirdly, and she became outwardly promiscuous with friends. She became hyper and got in trouble in school for the first time. During our interview, Liv cringed at the memories of her first college semester. She would yell in the cafeteria, goof around, shoot banana guns. In hindsight, she saw she was acting like a third-grader.

With the strange behavior came an intense desire to search out her Korean-ness. It had moved from the back of her mind to the front of her consciousness. Broiling. She dated a Korean adoptee who was older than she was. He had a car, his own apartment, and was very exciting. However, that relationship deteriorated in the winter when she started having emotional meltdowns, complete with violent crying, throwing objects, and the need to throw herself against a wall. She told Molly. They decided that she should do partial hospitalization instead of full-blown inpatient treatment. She moved back home, dropped out of classes, and went to a clinic for six or seven hours a day, mainly doing group therapy. They worked on grounding exercises and spiritual meditation. Liv said it was a helpful program. When the psychiatrist heard her story and learned about her diagnosis of depression, she immediately directed Liv to stop her meds; she was not depressed but had bipolar disorder. Liv had to try out a few meds before finding the right one for her new diagnosis. She started out-patient dialectical behavior group therapy with a mix of adults and college kids, which was helpful because it focused on the triad between emotions, thoughts, and the body. Classic therapy excluded attention to the body. Molly stressed to Liv that she needed to stay away from substances. Liv developed a fear of alcohol because she was exposed to people with comorbid disorders (presence of more than one disorder) at her therapy sessions. Alcohol misuse and medical or psychiatric comorbidities can often worsen each other's symptoms. Although helpful, the therapy was taxing on Liv, and she would nap four hours a day.

After Liv equilibrated, helped by therapy and medication, she returned to college. She threw herself into her studies and being Asian, or more specifically, Korean American. Her Korean language class excited her, and she developed a respect for her professor. He took an interest in her because she had a unique identity in his classroom. He would bring in Korean students to speak in his classes. Liv was infatuated with them all (not necessarily in the romantic sense). In her words, "They embodied something I wanted to know more about." She got involved with the Asian American university community and even signed up to have a language exchange partner. When she tried to build an Asian social circle, she didn't fit in well with the second-generation Asian American students. They could joke and cry about their similar experiences … the classics (e.g., "Kids made fun of my smelly Asian lunch."). Liv could not relate to those types of stories because she grew up in a White household. At first, it didn't deter her because she so badly wanted to fit in. She joined a Korean percussion group, and that was her social mainstay in college. It was a hodgepodge group of Korean Americans from Korean families, adoptees, and international students. She did not have to be a "Korean-Korean" (culturally Korean) student to be in the percussion group. She immersed herself in training. The sensory experience embodied in music helped her to feel grounded. Although she grew up playing the clarinet, it was performance-based. Whereas, with the percussion, she took the time to enjoy and feel the rhythms and sounds that were unique to Korea. A sense of normalcy developed as she practiced percussion.

The Korean percussion group maintained a certain degree of Korean decorum – i.e., hierarchies and how they organized the group. They had MT (Membership Training) and OT (Orientation Training) in the form of an overnight retreat that involved emotionally heavy bonding activities (and heavy drinking). They would lock in their group goals, get serious, and become initiated after a bit of hazing. Although she thought it was cool, she felt like she was getting an inauthentic Korean experience. Until that point, she had not been to Korea or a Korean culture-camp like many of her counterparts. Therefore, she ended up trusting the fellow students much more quickly than she ever had with any other friends. She admitted she was jealous of their Korean-ness. They had many things in common: they were all male, older than her, and had more experience with Korea than she had. Some were "Korean-Korean," and some were adopted.

In retrospect, Liv truly believes that some of the men used racial, gender, and age tactics to influence her during her quest to become Korean. She resents that the older men thought they could tell her how to have a relationship with Korea while admitting that part of it was her fault for believing in them and becoming romantically involved with a few. However, she still feels she was emotionally manipulated. She felt like a weak young woman who exposed her vulnerabilities to them. In her opinion, they had huge egos and low emotional intelligence, playing on her fears that she was getting a weak watered-down experience of Korea. They told her that she better damned well try to do as much as she could to fix her troubled relationship with Korea. They told her it *had* to be a hard experience; otherwise, she wasn't doing it right. She trusted them.

[Tears.]

Through networking, Liv went on her first trip to South Korea with a group of evangelical Christians. She was still searching for her spirituality and did not believe as they did. Liv learned from that trip:

> *"As a Korean adoptee, I am predestined to go through experiences of the hardship of feeling disconnected and abandoned that I won't fully understand myself. Those feelings were exacerbated by strong Christian evangelical beliefs that went against [my] past spiritual teaching and my own intellectualization of what it means to be an individual. My past traumas cannot be summed up to a relationship within the Bible. The people I went on the trip with thought there was a moral aspect to searching."*

During that trip, Liv went to the agency that had facilitated her adoption. The scariest emotion she ever felt happened there. An overwhelming sense of rage and frustration overtook her as she was sitting in front of the social worker's desk. The woman had a binder at least 2 inches thick all about Liv. She handed Liv a paper file that was not even 20 pages, saying that was all the information they had on her. Liv remembers thinking, "Why do I only have 5% of what you have???" When Liv looked through her folder, she realized she did not have the paper with her original Korean identification number on it (similar to an American social security number). The number was technically revoked because she was no longer a citizen, but she wanted to have it as a matter of personal pride. The social worker agreed to let her take a photograph of the original document.

As Liv took the picture, the social worker sat up perfectly straight and covered a portion of the paper with her hands so it would not be in the picture. *Covered a portion of the paper. With her hands. Sitting up perfectly straight. Covered. Covered.* Hiding what Liv KNEW was her birth mother's name and address. Liv was never closer to physically assaulting someone – knowing the woman represented that larger system full of injustice, thinking,

> *"It was ridiculous that this lady's small hands were the only thing holding me back from direct contact with my biological mother. What right did she have to do that?"*

Reflecting on that, Liv said – for a brief period of time – she toyed with the idea of wanting to work in adoption or social work. However, she decided against it when she knew she would have to be in a position where she had to do what that social worker did legally. And would get fired. There was no way she could do the same thing that the social worker did to her.

[Tears.]

Liv felt entitled to that information because she was an adult, and it was essential to get answers to her past. She felt so helpless, and that helplessness led to anger. To compound her jumble of emotions, she also felt a profound sense of melancholy. They toured every level of the adoption facility. On the second-to-the-top floor were rooms filled with cribs, filled with babies. With no parents. She was allowed to hold one, and Liv just cried the whole time. She was still struggling with her spirituality, but at that moment, she prayed.

Genuinely.

She prayed those babies would not be subject to the difficulties she had gone through or the difficulties she learned that other adoptees had gone through. Being on that floor, she had a flashback to her own infancy. The only other time she had a flashback was once in elementary school in the springtime. She walked by some beautiful trees, and for a second, she felt like the trees were not American trees, but they were the cherry blossom trees in Korea. For one instant, she felt like she was looking at a different sky and was teleported there within herself. Those were the only two times she ever felt that lucid about infant Liv.

Currently, Liv is exhausted from her birth mother search. She has written letters, sent photographs, completed a DNA test, and searched the internet and social media. When she was at the agency, they informed her they had sent two telegrams in 2017 to her birth mother's address. They use that method so that someone has to sign for the telegram. It was a vague statement, something like *Cha Jin-Hee is searching for people she is related to. She is in good health. She is searching for extended family.* Both times, her birth mother's husband (not Liv's biological father) received the mail. That's all the information the agency had. Liv has rolled that information around in her mind. Liv's thoughts ranged from neutral to horrible things. *Did he throw it out? How did he interpret it? Did he read between the lines? Did he know exactly what it meant? Is my biological mother now in trouble?* The agency's policy was that they could not try again for two years if they did not receive a response.

Liv has not had the energy to try again. She has the names of her birth parents and has extensively searched Facebook. She found a man whose facial profile looks remarkably like hers; he has the same eyes. A friend from her Korean percussion group helped her translate an inquiry. However, the man she thought might be her biological father shut it down. It bothered Liv because he was the only person that she found with his name who had her facial features. She concluded that either she was not related to him or he rejected her.

[Tears.]

Liv is no longer hopeful.

Liv has tried to push her sorrow aside by concentrating on the positive. The healthier Korean relationships that stand out to her have involved cooking. She has vivid memories of making meals with a Korean international student whom she came to love as a close friend. He was "very, very, very" patient with her and genuine. He encouraged her to practice her Korean and taught her to make kimchi jjigae – a Korean spicy broth soup with beef, pork, or tofu, and green onion. It is the Korean version of American chicken soup, as it is considered comfort food. She associates comfort with him. Their connection was very private but endearing because when he taught her how to make it, she felt like he was sharing his mom's recipe who learned it from her mom, who learned it from her mom, and so on. She felt she was getting a taste for having an experience she would have had with a Korean family. She also had another strong food experience with a friend she met over a language exchange app. She became friends with a Korean woman who took English courses and was a nanny in California. She would impart sisterly advice – even visited Liv in Chicago. During her stay, she taught Liv how to make tteok mandu guk, a salty white bone-based soup with rice cakes and boiled mandu dumplings (similar to won ton soup). These brotherly and sisterly relationships were helpful to Liv; they provided familial comfort.

Eating food in Korea was the ultimate food experience. According to Liv, dishes prepared by nice old Korean ladies tasted different than Korean food made in America. The nutrients in the water and soil are different and impart different flavors. While there certainly are nice old Korean ladies who live in America, some nuances cannot entirely be achieved. Liv talked about the "knowing" referenced in the *Primal Wound* by Nancy Verrier. In trying to describe her sensory experience, Liv said,

> *"The intuitive 'knowing' that even infants can experience, I think, is something that I achieve or encapsulate when I am able to have the sensory experiences. Things that don't require words … salt, savory, or sweet. You can just know internally that it's delicious. In the book, babies know things, because just as humans, we are able to know those things."*

In 2018, Liv and her parents were able to return to South Korea on vacation, and she cherishes that trip because that was the last summer before their deaths. On both of her trips to South Korea, she captured pictures and videos of everyday life – the food culture, people on the subway, children walking out of the school gates, and students studying in the cafes.

Liv felt like she was gathering pieces of herself through photography.

During their second trip, Liv's parents were patient with her. They took in as much culture they could. She was delighted they were with her. It was very clear they wanted to see everything that Liv was willing to share with them. They were respectful and observed her interactions with the host families she had come to love on a previous trip. She loved being able to guide them through the country. They were happy to let her do as much of the ordering and navigation as she wanted and were not caught up in being fully proficient themselves. Liv thought it was impressive that her parents would travel to a place where they were the linguistic minority and the racial minority. Her dad would get up before Molly and Liv, go to a coffee shop, and then show up with pastries for them when they woke up.

In Liv's opinion, it is unfortunate that her extended family is only willing to travel to Europe. She thinks it is because it is not a priority to challenge their sense of belonging. They are happy with living in White suburban Illinois. I asked her if she fits in with her extended family.

"No."

Liv doesn't think she is viewed as a foreigner in her family; she truly believes they see her as "family." But she said that no one ever talks to her for more than five minutes at a time at family gatherings. Her aunts and uncles might ask a few superficial questions and then move on. In contrast, the conversations they have with the other White cousins her age are much more in-depth. When Molly was alive, Liv would confide in her about their disparity of interest. Liv thinks that is why Molly was so protective and kept her depression a secret. One of Liv's friends once told her, "Your family is very White." Very true. Some of her family overheard that comment, but no one ever said anything to her about it. *"They're just very Midwestern suburban. I don't want to say it's a stereotype … but it is something that impacts me."* Liv doesn't bring up politics or diversity issues with them because they have polar opposite views. However, after Molly and Tom died, the extended family did put in more effort to connect with her, much to their credit. Liv admits that she could try harder, too. Her parents were the only ones in her family who adopted a child, so it may be hard for her aunts and uncle to relate. Liv believes there are problems with transracial adoptions. It is really easy for White upper-middle class suburban parents to blindly continue living as if their internationally adopted child belongs. In Liv's mind, "It is an atypical definition of racism." She believes that racially different adoptees need friends and people of color to help them with experiences they don't understand.

Liv is doing well now, living on her own as a graduate student. She has worked through her Korean American childhood experiences and manages her mental health expertly. She is blossoming into a grounded, well-balanced young woman. The lessons she learned from her transitioning experiences have helped her move forward. I 100% believe she will continue to draw strength from them and will succeed in life.

~ Advice Through Liv's Lens ~

<u>For adoptees:</u> "Prioritize YOUR gut feelings, intuition, and experiences … not the experiences of others." Liv thinks that if adoptees want to search for their birth parents, they should really understand their own motives because they might be hurt by what could happen.

<u>For adoptive parents:</u> "Listen to other peoples' stories about the family in general. Include mixed families. Become exposed to diversity. Be introspective about how other peoples' family systems make you feel. It's not like comparing pros and cons but really internalize … people are different. The way people create systems of support is very, very different. Know that adoptive families are part of larger family units. Expose your kids to people that match their individual demographics."

Liv continued to talk about adoptions in which no information was known about the birth parents. She advises adoptive parents, "Don't tell your child 'you are so lucky for being adopted.' Don't say, 'your biological parents loved you and wanted the best for you' *if* you don't know that. There's nothing that says that in my file – not a single word from my birth mother in any of those files. No one has the right to say she cared about me. I'm hoping it's true, but don't say things you don't know and put words in other people's mouths."

My Thoughts, My Lens

When Liv said Korean food tastes different in Korea than it does in America, I had a flashback. The best French fries in the world are in Germany and are called *pommes frites*. As an Army Brat, I lived in Germany twice. ALL of my memories surrounding German food are blissfully positive. There is something special about Germany's soil that produces potatoes with a distinctly incredible mineral-like depth of flavor that lingers on your tongue. In my opinion, even a German greasy food truck serving *pommes frites* born of German-grown potatoes could earn a Michelin star.

It's like crack. In a good way.

Right now, in this moment, I want to catch the next flight to Germany, Uber to the nearest Gasthaus, order two portions of *pommes frites*, eat them with my eyes closed, wash it down with bier (a.k.a. beer), snap a selfie, and then fly back home before the sun comes up.

Liv's authentic Korean food experience makes complete sense to me. According to the popular Korean cookbook author, Maangchi, Koreans are obsessed with food. She wrote:

> *"Koreans who were adopted as children and had never experienced their native country's food tell me they have used my recipes to get in touch with their heritage and the essence of who they are. When they tasted the food they made, they say they felt whole for the first time in their lives."*[23]

Liv associates her identity with food born of Korean soil. Her family had very little experience with other cultures. Although they did not provide her with many opportunities to experience diversity, she pursued them on her own. As Rachel Garlinghouse put it,

---

[23] Maangchi with Martha Rose Shulman, *Maangchi's Big Book of Korean Cooking*. Houghton Mifflin Harcourt Publishing Company, 2019, p. 10.

"Transracial adoptive parents should recognize that parenting Brown-skinned children involves not only parenting them and raising the children to become successful, independent, responsible, and kind adults, but also instilling in the children racial pride and an understanding and acceptance of the child's racially cultural norms, racial reality, and history."[24]

Liv once told me I was her parents' only non-White friend who visited them in their home (that she knew of). That revelation shocked me because they were very welcoming. Maybe I *was* their attempt to give Liv the culture she craved. Molly and I had many shopping outings and even took a women's weekend trip together. She and I had a few enlightening philosophical conversations about race and how it related to adoption. Still, it never occurred to me that I was her *only* "data point." (I commandeered that phrase from Alex B.) Clearly, Liv's lack of exposure to diversity shaped her because it propelled her to voraciously pursue a relationship with Korea. In my mind, this supports Liv's point that interracial adoptees should be given the opportunity to immerse themselves in their heritage. Knowing what I know now about Liv, if I had a do-over, I would have encouraged Molly and Tom to expand their data points.

Nonetheless, they were fabulous humans and instrumental in helping Liv successfully navigate her mental and emotional challenges. They lovingly provided Liv with the framework and the doorways to personal growth. I have no doubt that Liv will take the world by storm. My family loves her dearly, and I hope she has found a little piece of Korea with us.

---

[24] Garlinghouse. *Come Rain or Shine*, p. 73.

Yan Z. | College Student

Shaanxi, China
Year of Birth: 2000

My first in-person interview was with Yan, a Chinese adoptee. As a blossoming young college student awakening into adulthood, her sense of self was impressively acute, and she appeared to be at peace. She gifted me with her carefree smile as she breezed into my kitchen. She even showed me her original passport; clearly, her parents must have instantaneously fallen in love with that same smile. I could tell she *wanted* to tell her story. As she spoke, the words just poured out of her as we enjoyed our garlic chicken pasta primavera (deglazed with leftover Pinot Grigio). Yan impressed me with her willingness to reveal her tender thoughts about adoption. As she was telling me her story, it seemed as though she was validating her own existence by giving oxygen to her words as they tumbled so quickly out of her mouth. Her parents' story is also in this book (Harold and Helen Z. – see the table of contents). Even though I was charmed by Yan's easy-going demeanor, I was simultaneously puzzled as she lightheartedly talked about sailing through her adoption angst during her teenage years – and her ability to reach that often-elusive place of adoptive self-acceptance. However, about a year later during a follow up meeting, she was stunned as her sails were momentarily deflated by the wind change, forcing her to change direction into the storm of adoption reality. She described the different periods of her life as alternating between calm and tempestuous somewhere between China and America. The recent storm starkly differed from what she presented during our first meeting. Her yearning for cultural identity was now at the helm, brought about by topics covered in one of her college classes. She was no longer carefree and seemed a little jaded as she expressed how the craving to understand her past overtook her.

Yan learned she was adopted when she was about four years old. She calmly drifted through her early childhood, lacking any apprehension about her adoption. She didn't remember the exact conversation but recalled her parents' version of the story – they lovingly told her and her brother about their adoptions during bath time. Around that time, she wanted to know more about her adoption when she witnessed that her young friends were able to link their physical traits to their parents. When she couldn't do the same, she wanted to know why. (Her parents are White.) The lack of physical similarities didn't bother her, as she innocently thought being adopted was "cool" throughout elementary school.

When Yan reached middle school, she awakened to her reality of not knowing anything about her biological family. And the blustery wind of her adoption crushed her internally – she became depressed but hid it from almost everyone, pretending to be happy on the outside. After completing a family history school project about her *adoptive* family, the reality of not knowing her own biological history stung.

> *"It affects me because I have no idea what I am or who I look like. I will never find the answer to that question. I try not to think about it, but it's always there in the corner of my mind. It honestly haunts me even now – that I will never know who I fully am."*

Yan's mother was very helpful during her depression, encouraging Yan to express her feelings. Even though not knowing her history haunted Yan, she accepted the *reality* of it. (She assumed it would be very difficult to find her Chinese birth parents due to her rural start in life, unlike American born adoptees who seem to have a higher success rate with DNA tests.)

During Yan's high school years, she questioned her existence, feeling trapped in an American world in which she felt she didn't belong – and yet at the same time, she couldn't visualize being in a Chinese environment. Unlike many other adoptees, Yan was never teased or bullied about being adopted. Her angst stemmed from within, borne out of her mere existence. But Yan knew she didn't want to be locked up by her depression. She wanted to be able to appreciate her life.

During her "angsty" teenage years, Yan would argue with her parents about many things. The arguments ranged in intensity. A few arguments were about how she felt she didn't measure up to her brother, which culminated in her heatedly telling her parents she wished they never had adopted her. Mostly, the arguments led Yan to wonder, "What's the point of being adopted if I am always going to be compared to my brother and his accomplishments?" In looking back, Yan realized that their altercations happened in the "heat of the moment" but maintained, "It felt good to get it off my chest." Ultimately, the incidents strengthened her relationship with her parents as it provided the opportunity for them to deeply explore the subject of adoption. Her mother often concluded their discussions with lovingly saying, "We will always accept who you think you are." Her mother's words brought her comfort. As a young adult, Yan is glad her parents adopted her and regrets hurting their feelings as a teenager.

At this point in the interview, a fearful wistfulness overtook Yan's face. She said when she was younger, she often wondered if her biological parents ever loved her or if they were dead. Yan was cognizant of how the turmoil of her biological past spilled over into her present. She had overwhelming fears that her adoptive parents were always in danger of imminent death. (She never told them about her worries.) She was afraid that they would die *every* time they stepped outside of the house, even if they were just doing yard work. To this day, she refuses to discuss death with her parents. When they approach her about planning for the inevitability (e.g., burial wishes), she will immediately shut down the conversation.

Luckily, Yan's turmoil over her adoption did not affect the closeness she has with her brother, who is also a Chinese adoptee. Having him as a sibling has helped her navigate her struggles, and she cherishes their relationship. He and Yan have had deep discussions surrounding their dark fears, such as death. Yan doubts she would feel as safe sharing her views with him if he were her parents' biological son. She is grateful that they "live in each other's reality." She smiled, and with a contented matter-of-factness said, "He is my best friend."

In addition to her brother, Yan became very good friends with another Chinese adoptee in high school, which bolstered her search for self-acceptance. Although they never had deep conversations like Yan had with her brother, they had a profound connection because of their common circumstance. She was drawn to her friend inexplicably, believing she felt intuitively comfortable simply because they were adopted from the same country.

Yan knows her extended family *accepts* her – she is proud to be part of their family. However, she feels they do not *understand* her. Growing up, she felt like an outsider at family reunions. She said it was because, "I wasn't part of their blood." She and her brother are the only adoptees on both sides of their family. It's important to note that Yan's feelings of being an "outsider" were *not* based on her perception of race. Her family is multicultural through marriage – she has cousins who are both Black and White. But rather, it was harder for *her* to accept her extended family because of genetics – or the lack thereof.

Over the years, celebrating her "adoption day" and the Chinese New Year helped soothe some of Yan's adoption sorrow. Her family made a big deal of her adoption day every year (particularly her mom, who was always "gushy gushy"). When Yan lived close to her extended family, they helped her celebrate over wonderful meals and lots of cake. Yan loved the attention. (In contrast, her brother refused to celebrate his adoption day.) When Yan was young, her family also celebrated Chinese New Year, which included authentic Chinese food (Yan's favorite part). In recent years, her family stopped participating in Chinese cultural events, and she misses that effort. (However, they plan on picking up their former celebrations again in the near future.)

When Yan was a freshman in college, she managed to navigate past her tempestuous teenage years and reached a temporary state of self-acceptance – the calm before the proverbial storm at sea. Between our first and second interviews, Yan started her sophomore year and her position changed from easy-breezy to discordantly windward. She had taken an *Advanced Casting and Directing* course at her university. A discussion about the conflicting casting agendas for the movie *Crazy Rich Asians* brought up deep feelings that she previously didn't know existed. The directors disagreed with each other about the "look" of the actors. Their conflict reminded Yan that she doesn't look like a "typical" Chinese person. Oftentimes, she is mistaken for Hispanic; strangers have even spoken Spanish to her. (Even Asian people have told her that she doesn't look Chinese, which cut her deeply.) As a result, she felt disconnected from her birth country and questioned her self-identity. She "labels" herself Chinese American but feels like a fraud because she doesn't have any "American blood." The dissonance has propelled her to spin – unable to decide if she should consider herself "full Asian" or "American."

"I can't call myself 'American' because I'm not 'American.' I feel like I was born out of nothing. I'm literally nothing. I never noticed

that [before]. It's like a 'shadow battle' that I've been fighting my whole life – I never realized it. The majority of my friends who are not adopted, they know their place – they know their heritage. Where do I belong in this world if I don't know my history? It's something I've been trying to fully accept – trying not to get into that dark place again of being in that 'dark hole.'"

After taking the eye-opening college course, "something clicked" for Yan. Her awareness shifted – she realized she had hungered to explore her identity for her entire life. Now she thirsts for concrete Chinese cultural connections with an undiscovered past she cannot rewrite.

Yan is determined to succeed, motivated by the fear that if she doesn't, she will slip back into a "dark hole." Her fierce determination to uncover her true self will surely propel her towards a calm harbor embraced by peace.

~ Advice Through Yan's Lens ~

<u>For adoptees:</u> "The number one thing is never to forget that you have a loving family that cares about you – even if you feel like you don't belong. Find other people that are like you … the only thing that will help you come out of depression is for you to accept yourself. Adoptees are a product of both the adoptive family as well as the birth family. Try not to hold on to the past and look at the present and future. Study your culture. Don't let fear consume you. Open yourself up like a book. There's always a new chapter. Love yourself."

<u>For adoptive parents:</u> "There will come a time that your adopted child(ren) will ask about [their adoption] and honestly, you will have to be really careful about your words. Some parents have a hard time accepting an adopted child."

<u>For prospective adoptive parents:</u> "Before you adopt, think about whether you can love and care for an adopted child as if he/she is your very own. Honor it. Show your love and devotion. Make them feel safe by showing that you love the child no matter who they are. If you have one biological child and one adopted child, understand there might be tension between the two children. Love them equally and differently. If you choose international

adoption, treat your child as both an American and as a child from their birth country."

My Thoughts, My Lens

I related to Yan's childhood obsession with her parents' death because I shared that same fear. I would worry that they were dead when they were late. My angst about death was perpetuated unintentionally by my mom because she was always late. Subconsciously. On purpose. It has always stressed her out to be early for any event, so she habitually arrived 5-10 minutes late. In those 5-10 minutes, my mind would often churn with scenarios of her death. Looking back, it makes me laugh (uncomfortably) now. It took me many years to be able to talk about death without fear. My mom recently reminded me that on several occasions, she and my dad attempted to have a simple "5-minute conversation" with me about the location of their will and lockbox – their attempts occurred over the course of *three years*. (Sorry, Mom and Dad ... I appreciate your endless supply of patience.)

Currently Yan's story is *unfinished*.

She is determined to explore who she is as an adoptee, let go of her fears, and find her identity in the process. I anticipate she will arrive at a harbor surrounded by a balanced combination of Chinese and American culture. As she studies filmmaking in college and hones her craft, someday soon, she will surely create prophetic inquisitive movies inspired by her journey of self-discovery.

I can't wait to see what happens next.

Anita A. | Special Education Teacher

Sikkim, India
Year of Birth: 1982

Anita's cheerful countenance popped up on my computer screen along with her broad smile when we met on a Zoom call for the first time. As we delved into her story, her personality's warmth was reminiscent of an aromatic bowl of creamy Nepalese soup called Dahl – with hearty lentils, lemon, and autumn spices. (When I told her about my take on her personality, she laughed and said she loved the soup analogy.) I imagine Anita brings spice to any room she enters, awakening the senses of everyone there. She had an infectious energy about her, and I'm guessing she plays the instrument of life with the force of an orchestra. Her Indian name means bliss and happiness in Hindi. Fitting. As her story unfolded, it also became clear that her biological roots therapeutically fulfilled her as she discovered her birth country's history, the source of her love of music.

A very kind lady named Zubi and her husband ran an orphanage in Patna, India when Anita's story began in the 1980s. Zubi had traveled a few hundred miles to visit her own family in the town of Sikkim, India. During the visit, she learned of an infant (Anita) who was all alone in the village. Abandoned.

Zubi found her the next day and secured the appropriate governmental permission to bring Anita back to her orphanage (a law designed to prevent babies from being stolen). Anita was one of the first babies in the orphanage, as all of the other children were older. When Zubi found Anita, they had to guess her birth date, hospitalizing her because she was born premature and sickly. After Anita recovered, the women at the orphanage (who were similar to Catholic nuns – loving and compassionate) gave her the best care possible. When her parents adopted her at ten months old, it was very hard for Zubi to let her go.

151

When Anita first came to live with her adoptive family, she had severe separation anxiety. Anita thinks that it was because the orphanage care was so excellent; she may have been traumatized during the transition to her parents' home in America. Over the years, Zubi would visit Anita on her trips to the United States, where her own children lived as adults. For a while, Anita wondered if Zubi was her biological mother. Anita said she has "not sadness … but curiosity" about her adoption. She does wonder what happened in her transition as an infant and how it affects her now. Her parents have told her that she had strong emotional swings when she was a child and would become disproportionately angry. Anita was diagnosed with depression at a young age.

Our conversation turned to how Anita's emotions supported Nancy Verrier's *Primal Wound* theory, based on research that concludes babies subconsciously remember their births. "If babies remember birth, then they also remember what happened right after birth, which is that their mother, the person to whom they were connected and to whom they expected to welcome them into the world, was suddenly missing."[25]

Anita also told me about a study of puppies in utero and how they develop emotionally. Puppies form their personalities in the womb because it is survival:

> *"Most relevant to a fearful puppy, a mother suffering from extreme anxiety puts her offspring at high risk of being anxious and fearful, even as an adult. Apparently, high levels of the stress hormone cortisol produced by the mother result in fewer cortisol receptor cells in the pup (or child or monkey, etc.). This low number of receptor cells means that the pup's brain is unable to perceive and respond to high levels of cortisol in his own body until the system is overloaded with it. Then the brain goes on red alert, sending the emotions into full panic mode, even in situations that would be only mildly stressful for an average individual."[26]*

---

[25] Verrier. *The Primal Wound*, p. 5.
[26] McConnell, Patricia B., PhD "Fear in Dogs: Where does it begin?" *The Bark Magazine,* Issue No: 56, Sep.-Oct. 2009,

Humans, like the puppies in the study, unconsciously carry memories.

Throughout Anita's life, her parents thought she was Indian – her Indian name was Hindi. However, intuitively, she became interested in Nepalese culture in high school. She always thought she was of mixed race from Central Asia and India because of her round face and curly hair. Recently, Anita took a DNA test with Ancestry.com, which confirmed that she was 80% Nepalese. She found that knowledge to be reassuring. When Google first came along, Anita queried images of Nepalese women. She was shocked when she saw a woman with a child that looked like her son. Her inner history freak prompted her to continue her research. Only certain sects of people settled in her birth town, Sikkim, located in the area between Tibet, Nepal, and Bhutan (in the foothills of the Himalayas, 50 miles from Mt. Everest). Nepal is culturally very different than India. Anita discovered through her research that various countries annexed Sikkim over the years due to its geographical location. Music saturates Sikkim's culture, and most people in the town play instruments. Sikkim musicians are very disciplined. The music connection fascinated Anita as she is a classically trained musician. She plays the piano and marimba and, growing up, was part of a drumline. Music was in her bloodline and naturally fueled her soul. By researching her biological roots, she connected with her culture. She acknowledges that non-adoptees do not have the same yearning because they *know* their ancestry. But for her, as an adoptee, knowledge of her own history is a big deal. Cultural immersion became her coping mechanism.

> *"I don't think I've ever __not__ wanted to be adopted. It is more like I'm finding myself __through__ adoption."*

The revelations she discovered about her own culture catapulted her to research other cultures; she became obsessed with American Indian culture. Learning about it soothed her. She even has a tattoo on her arm of the Kokopelli, a popular Zuni tribe image of a fertility god playing the flute. Anita drew parallels between the morals and values of the American Indians

---

www.patriciamcconnell.com/sites/default/files/Bark%202009%20Sep-Oct%20Fear%20in%20Dogs.pdf. Accessed 8 Sep. 2020.

with her Indian culture. She said, "Grandmothers and grandfathers are literally gods. You respect them. You worship them."

Anita also draws cultural parallels to the Hmong Community; she is a Special Education teacher at a Hmong charter school where she has learned about her students' values and morals. Hmong history is full of trauma and persecution. Their stories of Burmese camps and torture resonate with Anita because they paralleled her early childhood pain. In the Hmong community, family is everything. The families often live in the same apartment complex. At school, the kids get to eat pho for lunch (a deeply rich beef broth noodle soup), as the families make it fresh daily. Anita always asks for the LEAST spicy version. The pho soup reminds Anita of when she was in her 20s. She delved into the Indian food culture, ordering the LEAST spicy version of soup on her weekly visits to a mom-and-pop Indian restaurant. Although she prefers the Americanized soup, she would like to revisit India someday and have the authentic version.

Anita's adoptive extended family also played a role in her values. Her adoptive mother is an assertive city girl with Scottish and Irish roots. Anita's maternal grandfather was a Lieutenant Colonel in the Army who survived the Pearl Harbor bombing. In Anita's words, that family culture was like, "Whoo-hoo-hoo-hoo." Her maternal grandmother was a spitfire mixed with a military background. If Anita's mother or her seven siblings had their hands on the table at dinner, Anita's grandfather would try to stab their hands with a fork. *Follow the rules! Do not mess around!* They were not aggressive, just very assertive.

In contrast, Anita's dad grew up in a very subtle and laid-back Polish and Swedish family on a Wisconsin dairy farm. Anita was very drawn to her grandmother's warm demeanor and had fond memories of visiting her grandparents. She believes she was drawn to her grandmother's nurturing temperament because Anita was born into a similar culture.

Anita's parents balanced each other even though they were exact opposites. She attributes her personality to traits from each side. She learned to be a justice-seeker from her mother's family, whereas she learned nurturing, calmness, and warmth from her dad's family. Anita yearns for complete balance because extreme emotions can throw her off. Anita's parents taught her the "culture of helping." Her father is a child psychologist, and her mother is a speech pathologist. As a child, she visited special education classes with her parents. As a result, Anita is comfortable with her chosen profession as a Special Education teacher.

Anita's parents also raised her to be a traditional Catholic. The church fed Anita's penchant for volunteerism, but unfortunately, the "Catholic guilt" traumatically affected her when she divorced her first husband. He was unsupportive, abusive, and struggled with alcohol. In counseling, Anita discovered that she viewed her divorce through the lens of the separation anxiety she had as an adopted infant.

That realization really hit home.

Anita's progress towards finalizing the divorce was delayed as the sadness of her childhood adoption trauma resurfaced. However, despite the lows of her divorce, through the encouragement of her mother, she picked herself up, went back to school, and got her master's degree.

One week after she signed her divorce papers, a friend set her up on a blind date by organizing a group of people for a winery tour – without telling Anita's date the underlying agenda. At this point in the interview, Anita laughed, *"Surprise!"* Her friend did fess up in the parking lot right before they walked in. Luckily, the large group of people she had invited showed up, too. Going into the date, Anita thought she would never remarry again. She was wrong. She and her current husband knew right off away that they were 100% right for each other. They were engaged within nine months and got married at the same vineyard where it all began.

Anita's husband is a clinical psychologist and comes from a mellow family that coalesces with her biological emotional needs. They are very happy; he is very nurturing, and it was his warmth that attracted her to him. Anita has a son from her first marriage and her current husband treats him well. The support he provides feels like her comfortable childhood.

Anita and her husband have talked about having more children but decided against it. He loves his stepson, and they are content. Anita is very pleased with her life because she knows that her son will be provided with whatever he needs as an only child. She innately understands what it feels like to yearn for comfort. She wants to provide her son with the best. Knowing that he will get anything and everything he needs brings *her* comfort.

~ Advice Through Anita's Lens ~

For adoptive parents: "It is okay if you aren't experts on your children's cultures, backgrounds, or experiences. It doesn't matter what you do not know as long as you have the heart to take in a baby. Just do it. Follow your instincts, but be careful not to go overboard board in birth country cultural activities, either. It's about balance."

For adoptees: "Do not feel bad about what you do not know, but at the same time, educate yourself. Look at the history of where you came from. Just like American Indians who have lost their language and culture, you need to keep that going. You need to know where you're from and who you are because if not, you will lose a part of yourself. You will be unfulfilled. Work through your feelings of denial and harshness. I knew of another adoptee that came from the same orphanage I did. Her younger sister (also adopted) set herself on fire and killed herself at 10 years old. Not everyone needs therapy but some do and should seek help. Be okay with who you are. Being able to talk about it is healthy. Exploration is healthy and therapeutic. I know it helped me. When I was younger, I had frustration, but my perspective changed throughout my life."

My Thoughts, My Lens

Food, history, and music were all ingredients that comforted Anita as she researched her birth country in her journey to self-discovery. Historical studies brought her closer to her roots through music. Anita's obsession with music clearly fuels her. Her eyes twinkled as she expressed her enthusiasm for the piano. When she talked about how music was woven into Nepalese culture, it was obviously woven into her DNA.

I get it.

Because I am tone deaf, I do not connect spiritually to music like Anita does. But her passion for music parallels my obsession with food. I found a direct connection to Korea through food. According to popular Korean cookbook author and YouTuber Maangchi, "Recipes fit together to make up our cuisine, which for us food-obsessed Koreans is the foundation of our culture."[27]

Many years ago, as I flipped through another Korean cookbook by Hilaire Walden, I was startled when I read, "Unusual for an eastern Asian country, beef is the most popular meat (pork and chicken usually reign supreme)."[28] I believe it. I LOVE BEEF. I need to eat it at least once a week because I *physically* feel better after devouring a fat juicy burger, beef summer sausage, perfectly charred medium-rare steak, beef stir fry, or a generous helping of bulgogi.

I hesitated putting the following section in this book, as I didn't want to dilute Anita's beautiful story. She intuitively knew that she came from the region in India near Nepal whose inhabitants were different than the "typical" Indian people she had encountered (she mentioned she looked very different from her adoptive Indian sister). However, I ultimately

---

[27] Maangchi. *Maangchi's Big Book of Korean Cooking*, p. 13.
[28] Walden, Hilaire, Korean Cooking. *Explore One of the Orient's Greatest Culinary Secrets.* Quintet Publishing Limited, 1995, p. 7.

decided to keep the following paragraphs because there are parallels between our stories – Anita's and my biological instincts override logic.

Just like Nepalese culture calls to Anita, South Korea's largest island, Jeju, summons me. Coincidentally, the best beef in Korea is on Jeju Island. "It was the warring, pillaging, thirteenth-century Mongol armies which decided the best place to raise cattle was on the rich pastures of [Jeju] Island."[29]

I had a similar experience to Anita's Nepalese ancestral discovery when I recently learned about Jeju Island's history through Lisa See's poignant historical fiction, *The Island of Sea Women*.[30] (Out of the blue, my uncle had emailed me, recommending her book.) The book sublimely detailed the island's Korean women divers and their families' wartime struggles in the 20th century. I was inexplicably drawn into the pages and amazed by how it compelled me to research the Island's history further. For most of my life, I deliberately ignored my personal history, not wanting to examine why I felt out of place. However, reading about the Korean island inhabitants was like reading about myself. Throughout the book, I saw my personality and idiosyncrasies in print.

I felt like I was reading about my biological family.

It was a challenging read because the tragedies told within the pages were horrifying. The main character was a "haenyeo," a Korean woman diver. Just like Anita was jolted when she saw the Nepalese women in Google images, I was also *shocked* to see I closely resembled the haenyeo shown in my Google search. Before that, I knew I didn't look like any of the Korean women that I encountered throughout my life. I am a little bit darker and beefier than the "typical" tiny light-skinned Korean ladies.

The other commonality I have with the book's characters is that natural bodies of water call to me. I can't get enough of fishing – both fresh and saltwater. (Sorry, Dad, for the endless tangled lines and the time I lodged a fishhook in your ear.) The ocean lures and hypnotizes me, while its power magnetically frightens me – the book detailed the tragic history that the

---

[29] Walden, *Korean Cooking*, p. 7.
[30] See, Lisa. *The Island of Sea Women*. Schribner, An Imprint of Simon & Schuster, Inc., 2019.

Korean island inhabitants endured over the years with the ocean as a backdrop. As I read about the heinous war tragedies, my historical spirituality bubbled up to the surface; I often feel outraged at injustice. Logically *and* logistically, my theory doesn't make sense – because my orphanage was located on the mainland along the northern border of South Korea close to the 38th parallel. Even so, I *know* my ancestors once belonged to Jeju Island.

As I melded with the book's pages, the crux of my amazement was when Lisa See wrote about a tormented author, Hyun Ki-young, and his book called *Aunt Suni*. When I read the title, I fell off the couch. Obviously, I had to order his book immediately (thanks Amazon.com). I broke inside when I read about the war atrocities he endured as a young child in the 1940s. He was tortured again as an adult in the 1970s by the Joint Investigation Headquarters when he wrote about his childhood experiences in *Aunt Suni*. His book was banned for many years. When it was finally re-released for publication, it was renamed *Sun-i Samch'on*. Just like Anita wondered if Zubi was her biological mother, I wondered if Hyun Ki-young was part of my biological family.

For Anita to have intuitively known the importance of researching her history at a young age impresses me. I took decades to look at mine. However, when I did, it knocked me over with a spiritual force I never anticipated – but surprisingly, *welcomed.*

SECTION 3

Through the Lens of Adoptive Families

In my search for book participants, overall, potential interviewees were not difficult to find, thanks to my friends, relatives, and coworkers who vouched for me. However, the adoptive mothers were harder to secure than the adoptees and birth mothers. Several said no. One said yes but then backed out at the last minute. Another said yes but then had me take out several portions of her story after reading my notes. Yet another mother told me that she used to love talking about their adoption experience, and she could "talk an ear off of anyone." But in the last few years, they have had such a struggle with their son that she has become reticent to share her story. In an online parenting advice column, an adoptive mother described her feelings of devastation when she discovered her 17-year-old daughter secretly contacted her birth mother. She said,

> *"I'm terrified that this woman might try to take over my role in her life, and become her mother figure in adulthood."*[31]

Like adoptees, many adoptive mothers yearn for validation, too.

Wayne W., an adoption counselor and adoptive father (his story is the last one in this section of the book), had an interesting perspective when I asked him why he thought many adoptive mothers were so hesitant. He said the whole process of adoption is threatening. By looking through the lens of prospective adoptive mothers as he did his job, he learned that many felt like they were not the "real thing" because the child didn't "come through them." The struggle may be that they want so badly to prove they're the child's "real" parent. Wayne believes that being a mother is a harder job than being a father – motherhood is full of insecurities, especially in the early years. If there are problems, it's easy for mothers to blame themselves, and

---

[31] Herman, Michelle. "I'm Devastated My Daughter Secretly Contacted Her Birth Mother." *Slate, Care and Feeding.* 11 Apr. 2021, slate.com/human-interest/2021/04/search-birth-parents-adoption-parenting-advice-from-care-and-feeding.html. Accessed 11 Apr. 2021.

maybe that's why they didn't want to reveal anything that would open them up to more scrutiny. Traditionally, the father's job is to have an occupation and *then* be a father. While mothers also have careers, the parental role often falls on them. Wayne acknowledges that problems do arise with biological children but believes adoption adds another tier or intricacy because it's easier for mothers to blame themselves rather than say their child had these issues lined up before joining the family.

I would even go one step further and say that not only do mothers blame themselves, but other people blame them too. And by "other people," I mean relatives, therapists, teachers, caseworkers, and even their children. As a mother myself, I can totally understand why it would be difficult for an adoptive mother to share her story.

It would be an invitation to criticism – if not condemnation.

I love to brag about my daughters when things are going well (thank you, my good friends, for your patience), but I need a compelling reason to advertise our battles. I appreciate the brave parents who stepped up to share their journeys. I hope that their efforts bring comfort to others through the common threads woven into each story.

There are eight domestic and seven international stories about adoptees in this book. I purposely did not divide up the adoptive families into those two categories because unlike adoptees, adoptive parents do *not* seem to view their children's *origin* as a notable differentiator. While international and transracial adoptions definitely add color to families, the adoptive parents that I have encountered do not view race as a factor in *how* they became a family.

Art & Emma G. | Supply Chain Planner & Care Guide

Minnesota
Year of Adoption: 1993

Art and Emma sat down on the couch with their sides touching one another like fuzzy socks in a dresser drawer. Their smiles held the warmth of a married couple tightly knitted together by happiness and grief. I knew their story involved the eventual suicide of their youngest daughter, but they were calm and friendly as our conversation started. Even before they were married, they had the same outlook about children. They were both interested in adopting as well as having biological children. After they were married, they walked the path of infertility treatments. When that did not work, they started down the path of applying for local adoption in Minnesota. After not hearing back from their local adoption agency, they pursued other avenues. They went to the neighboring state of Wisconsin to try different approaches, but three private adoptions fell through. In one instance, they were literally walking out the door to pick up their child when they got the call that the birth mother had changed her mind. After that, Emma was *done*.

But unexpectedly, they got a call from the original agency in Minnesota asking if they wanted siblings. Doubtful it would happen; Emma was hesitant to say yes. She didn't know if she could have her heart broken one more time. But Art convinced her to consider it. Once she saw the pictures of the kids, she changed her mind. The other factor that helped Emma was that they met the birth mother, Jodi. After the meeting, they felt good about moving forward.

Art and Emma learned how important stability is during the first few years in a child's life. Jodi had three children and could not handle them on her own. Because she was a single mom with no help from her family, she decided to place her younger two children up for adoption. Both children were under two years old when they went home with another couple.

163

However, after a few weeks, the couple changed their mind and gave the children back. At this point in the conversation, Art was almost breathless. He talked about how baffled he was that someone could do that. After the kids went back to Jodi, they were transferred to a foster home but ready for Art and Emma to pick them up. However, Art and Emma were not ready logistically – their home was not yet child-proofed. Regardless, they went to pick up the kids from the foster home. Art said he would never forget the first time meeting them. Rick just ran over to him, wanting to be picked up, and gave Art a big hug. Baby Elizabeth was just a little tight ball. She had an ear infection and didn't look healthy, but she was adorable. Over time, Art and Emma realized how stiff she was. Her muscles were hard as rocks, as though she had been weightlifting or working out. Both kids were absolutely aware of the chaos, but they couldn't verbalize their anxiety and stress because they were so young. It was trauma. As Art and Emma were driving home, they realized that they didn't have any supplies for a baby and a toddler, so they had to stop at the store.

Art smiled and said, "Instant Family."

They brought the children home in mid-May, the same month as Rick's birthday. To celebrate, Jodi asked Art and Emma to let her bring the kids home to her apartment. She wanted Art and Emma to pick them up later that evening. Together, Art and Emma had to passively watch Jodi pick up their children from their home to take them to her subsidized housing apartment. Later that day, when they walked into her apartment, a haze of cigarette smoke greeted them while it hung over many little, little kids. Elizabeth and Rick were covered in cake, icing, and ice cream. Everyone was screaming.

Total chaos.

Jodi just casually handed the kids over to Art and Emma. She was talking about going out and getting drunk. Rick was screaming and holding out his arms to her, but she didn't seem to care. He definitely had a bond with her. Emma said Rick knew that they were taking him away from Jodi. It was bizarre; he was inconsolable all the way home. Art said it was heartbreaking.

On the other hand, Elizabeth did not react because she had not bonded with Jodi. Art and Emma think it was because she had lived in five different homes by the time that she was six months old. While Rick was bonded to his birth mother, he had no connection to their birth father because he was not in the picture. Rick was drawn to men – every man was "Daddy" to him. Art chuckled as she described the time Rick even followed the mailman down to the neighbor's lawn calling out "Daddy" before Art could catch him. Rick was developmentally slower; at almost two years old, he only used a handful of words. Unfortunately, because Rick and Elizabeth's life had been so rocky early on, it set the stage for future struggles.

Art and Emma were united in their approach to talk openly with their kids about their adoption sorrow. Art would tell his kids he understood that their feelings were real, and he couldn't pretend to *know* what they were going through. However, their kids were with them for a reason. It was fate; they were meant to go through three adoption failures to get Elizabeth and Rick.

During their early elementary school years, the kids had two very different experiences. Elizabeth flourished, but Rick struggled with ADHD and its challenges – medication, counseling, and doctor appointments. An evaluator said that intelligence-wise, Rick was bright – he just couldn't track or focus. So much time and energy were spent on Rick, while everything came easy to Elizabeth. She was good at sports, school, and making friends. Rick had a surly side which included the typical sibling jealousy. At the same time, Elizabeth was jealous of the amount of time Art and Emma were putting into Rick.

At this point in the interview, I asked Art and Emma if they thought their kids understood the poverty they left behind. Art said he didn't think so because Jodi was able to get out of poverty. She had another child and was able to move on with her life. Elizabeth and Rick's biological grandmother (Jodi's mother) had more interest in them than Jodi did. She would send birthday cards and small gifts in the mail. The gifts would have to stay outside for a few days after they arrived because they would smell so badly of cigarette smoke. Elizabeth would say, "That's from Stinky Grandma." During the kids' elementary school years, the interactions with Jodi dwindled. Art and Emma left it up to her to contact them when she wanted to see the kids. They didn't feel like it was their responsibility to contact her.

However, they now wonder if that was a mistake.

Many years went by without any contact from Jodi. However, when Rick was in sixth grade, she connected with him online through Myspace, and they had many conversations through social media.

At this point in the interview, Art took a long deep breath and sighed, while Emma said that she still holds a lot of anger towards Jodi. When Jodi inserted herself into Rick's life, Elizabeth wanted to have a relationship with her, too.

That marked the beginning of Elizabeth's slow emotional, mental, and physical deterioration.

Emma has no doubt that Jodi's return played a large part in Elizabeth's suicide. Emma thought they had a clear understanding with Jodi – that her interactions with the kids would be coordinated between the adults. She said, "However, Jodi just took the show and ran the bus." Up until Jodi's unsolicited appearance, Elizabeth was doing exceptionally well as an 11-year-old. She was smart, funny, talented, athletic, sweet, and fun to be around. Her personality would light up the room when she walked into it. It was when Elizabeth wanted to see Jodi again that their once tightly knit family life exploded. Jodi wanted to spend more time with the kids, and they wanted to be with her *without* Art and Emma. Jodi challenged Art and Emma's parenting to the point that the three of them went to joint counseling. During that time, the middle school counselors called and asked if they knew Elizabeth was cutting herself.

They did not know.

Jodi didn't care how tormented Elizabeth was because being in contact with the kids was what *Jodi* wanted. Elizabeth jumped in headfirst. It was extremely difficult for Art and Emma to manage Jodi and Elizabeth's relationship because there were no controls. Elizabeth convinced her friends to drive her to Jodi's place for secret visits. Jodi rewarded them with pot and alcohol. This continued for years. During that time, Art and Emma didn't know what to do without making the situation worse. They felt their kids had a right to have a relationship with their birth mother. However, at the same time, they feared the consequences if they prevented that relationship. In high school, Elizabeth's mental health continued to deteriorate. Art and Emma checked her into a treatment center in Wisconsin. Jodi knew that Elizabeth was struggling but did not visit her. Even though Art and Emma invited Jodi to family visitation days, she would never show up. She claimed she wanted to be supportive but always had an excuse (her car wouldn't go that far, she couldn't ride with Art and Emma because she couldn't smoke, etc.). Jodi only wanted to be the "fun Mom," leaving the hard parenting to Art and Emma. During Elizabeth's treatment, she and Jodi schemed. In October, they convinced the staff it would be a good plan for Elizabeth to go home with Jodi after three months of inpatient treatment. The facility released Elizabeth to Jodi's "care," which consisted of a Halloween party complete with alcohol and drugs.

For a 17-year-old.

Not knowing what to do, Art and Emma remained united in their battle with Jodi. Art often looks back and wonders what would have been best. They were trying their best, taking the experts' advice. Art questioned himself. He beat himself up. Many professionals thought Jodi and Elizabeth's relationship was beneficial, but they couldn't see the damage that was happening because of Jodi's manipulation. Elizabeth put up walls between herself and Art and Emma. The whole ugly relationship with Jodi consisted of cutting, drugs, and alcohol. Elizabeth's self-destructive behavior was accelerating, and by early December, she ran away from Jodi's home only to land in the emergency room in a drug-induced stupor. Art and Emma took her to a northern Minnesota treatment facility where she received the help she needed.

In the months leading up to Elizabeth's suicide, Jodi had started seeing a new man. Elizabeth was not as important to her anymore, except as a babysitter for Jodi's fourth child (Elizabeth's half-sibling). When Elizabeth would complain about it to Art and Emma, they would encourage her to be honest with Jodi and stand up for herself.

Until this point in the conversation, Art and Emma were pragmatic in telling their story. They would brighten up as they warmly described their children and calmly talked about their challenges. However, the vibration of their presence slowly changed as we approached Elizabeth's suicide. Art moved forward on the couch and sat on the edge. His facial muscles released control, and his face slightly wilted. Emma's expression changed like she was turning a page in a book to a forced neutral as she stared at a spot on the wall. As they shifted, I watched them surrender to tragic familiarity, wondering how often they had lowered their buckets into that well of sorrow.

For some time before Elizabeth's suicide, Art and Emma helped her become more financially self-sufficient. She was not living with them but worked towards earning her high school diploma online while living with her friend, Brittany. On the snowy January Friday night of Elizabeth's suicide, she and Brittany were at Art and Emma's house. When Elizabeth saw the ER bill from her December visit, she became very distraught over not having the money to pay for it. Art tried to reassure her that he and Emma would cover it. But she remained upset, leaving with Brittany in an SUV borrowed from Art. It wasn't very long before he got a call from Brittany, who was in hysterics. Elizabeth had dropped Brittany off at her mom and dad's house and went back to their place without her. Elizabeth had called Brittany – not speaking – but Brittany could hear choking. Art thought from Brittany's description; it sounded like Elizabeth was throwing up. He told Brittany he would meet her at the duplex. He was scared. When he arrived, Brittany and her mom were already there, and the three of them started searching the apartment – a tuck-under style with a single garage.

Art walked into the garage. He saw that Elizabeth had taken an extension cord, tied it to the rafter, and wrapped it around her neck. He untied the cord and started CPR. Someone called 911. When the police officer arrived, he took over the CPR, which was a good thing because Art said he was beginning to lose his mind. When the ambulance arrived, the paramedics got a pulse and took her to the hospital. She was unconscious and still alive but not responsive. The police confiscated her suicide note. They told Art and Emma it was a "goodbye" and that she said she was sorry.

Both Art and Emma thought that Elizabeth would pull through because she was tough. She accomplished everything she had ever put her mind to, but her determination was also what brought her down. They said she would have been a terrific lawyer. Thinking about the scene, Art noted there was a child's riding push toy nearby her body, and it must have slipped out from under her. He thought she was calling Brittany to threaten suicide (because she had done so before). On many occasions, she had used her potential-lawyer-like tenacity to go down wrong roads and manipulate people (including her parents). At 2 a.m., the hospital staff told Art and Emma to go home because there was nothing they could do. It would be some time before they had an update.

The staff cooled down her body to take all of the pressure off her heart. By Saturday morning, it was a matter of warming her body up slowly to see if she could handle it. Sadly, she couldn't. The cranial pressure was too high, and she was brain dead at that point. The hospital staff would keep her alive long enough to harvest her organs. Art and Emma had to say goodbye.

As Art shook his head and wiped his eyes, Emma spoke up and said, "I have a sweet story." Elizabeth participated in dance, gymnastics, soccer, and hockey. She wanted to play football with the boys. As a talented athlete, she received a varsity letter in hockey as a *seventh* grader. She always had 4 or 44 on her jerseys. The number 4 was special to the family for that reason. Emma was at the hospital to spend the day with Elizabeth before they took her away to harvest her organs. As she watched her lie there, unresponsive, Emma was engaged in an internal battle with Jodi. In Emma's mind, she thought about how she had done the work. Emma said, "I'm MOM. I'm MOM." She thought about how often she had been in hospitals, sitting by Elizabeth's bed, hoping that Elizabeth knew how much she loved her. Emma also wondered if Elizabeth loved *her*. The nurse had been cleaning Elizabeth up to make her look nice for the family. Amid Emma's thoughts, the nurse handed her a pendant shaped into a number 4 that she had combed out of Elizabeth's hair. The pendant was from a necklace that Elizabeth wore.

Emma exploded into sobs and knew it was a sign from Elizabeth.

The funeral was set for the following Saturday. Jodi's 40th birthday was the day before. She asked Art and Emma to move the funeral time to later in the evening because she was planning on celebrating her birthday on Friday and knew she would be hung over on Saturday. Jodi's other son (Elizabeth's half-brother) could not get out of bed, too hungover to go to the funeral because he celebrated with his mom the night before.

That winter, Emma could barely pull herself out of bed. Eating was nearly impossible. She had lost so much weight that nothing fit her. Art convinced her to go shopping to find some clothes. She decided to go to the Mall of America. She and Elizabeth shared a love for lipstick. Elizabeth called herself a "lipstick lesbian." As much as she was a rough-and-tumble tomboy, she also loved lipstick. As Emma walked through Nordstrom, she saw a pink lipstick at the cosmetic counter and said she was drawn to it for some reason. She didn't even try it on because she just *had* to have it. As the makeup consultant was ringing up the purchase, she said, "Oh, you got the *Elizabeth*." The name of the lipstick was Elizabeth. Emma started crying and told the makeup consultant about Elizabeth. They both ended up crying at the counter. Elizabeth did know how much Emma loved her. She *knew*.

Not too long after Elizabeth died, Art and Emma's son Rick decided he needed a change of scenery. He moved to Phoenix to attend a well-respected auto-mechanic school. He finished the program, continued living in Phoenix, and is now doing well. Art and Emma were clearly proud of him as they talked about how his life has turned out. Early on, they had their struggles with him. However, during the turmoil with Elizabeth, Rick stabilized.

When Jodi first inserted herself into his life in sixth grade, he was not doing well in school. As a result, Art and Emma enrolled him in a school for kids with mental health issues. The school had padded rooms used to isolate the kids with severe cases until they would settle down. Rick was the type of kid who had to learn things the hard way. But he did learn after spending two years at that school. During that time, he decided to do whatever he had to do to enroll in mainstream high school. He completed his technical classes and learned to be a hard worker. Knowing how challenging he was early on (and observing the struggles that Art and Emma had with Elizabeth), he did not want to create any more family issues. In recent years, Rick has spent more time with Jodi and her boyfriend. He knows that they are unhealthy and unstable. However, he feels that he needs to spend time with them because Jodi's sons are his brothers; he feels more connected with them than with her.

Rick does not know how angry Emma is with Jodi. Emma chooses not to share her feelings with him because she knows it would hurt him. Emma said that she would forever be grateful to Jodi for the gift of her children, but at the same time knows she played a major role in Elizabeth's mental health issues – and ultimately in her death.

Emma so desperately wanted to be a parent and said, "It didn't happen the 'normal' way." She and Art talked about how they had so much love to give and how they wanted to be the best parents. But when they learned they had to battle through it, they wondered why they couldn't have done it the conventional way. The infertility process was a loss they had to grieve. However, when the opportunity came along for them to have Rick and Elizabeth, they were an instant family. "Add water." They found parenting to be overwhelming, delightful, and exciting. Just taking the kids out of a bad situation made the experience that much more meaningful. They knew they were doing the right thing and were determined to be great parents. They did their research to educate themselves to understand their kids' situations. Art acknowledged that they could never truly understand (because they were not adoptees themselves), but they tried. Art said that the "hole" that adoption leaves was especially hard on his kids through their teen years. It was hard enough getting through those years, but adding adoption on top of that was immense. Art said he was surprised there aren't even more adoptive kids that commit suicide.

Adoptees want to hear their parents believe that having adopted children is the same as having biological children. Art said that the *situation* is different, but the feelings are not. He said that when they went to pick up their kids, he thought,

> *"These kids have no idea how much they're already loved."*

Art and Emma have had conversations with other adoptive couples. They all agree that they don't think of their children as "adopted" children but rather as *their* children. At times, Emma does wonder if they had a biological child, would he or she have had mental health issues? Would they have had to work through the same types of problems? Over the years, they took Elizabeth and Rick to endless doctor appointments or counseling. They always had one kid in counseling. Life was not easy with their kids, but there was a lot of joy, too. She said,

> *"I loved them dearly, and they are our kids. I'm the mom. I'm the mom."*

Art's brother once said that he could never adopt, asking Art and Emma, "How do you know what you're going to get?" They replied to him, "How do biological parents know what they are going to get?" Emma repeated, "They are absolutely our kids."

As a couple, Elizabeth's suicide could have destroyed them, but they didn't let it. For them, it wasn't worth battling to the point of splitting up. For the most part, they have stood linked arm in arm. They said their parenting wasn't executed perfectly, but they still remain united. Emma's hope for other adoptive parents is that agencies would provide more education. She also thinks that families need help with the transition. Parents need more counseling. No one educated them on how to parent kids who had bounced around. Art agreed there needs to be more tools and support.

~ Advice Through Art and Emma's Lens ~

<u>For adoptive parents:</u> "We were very naive. We felt we had all this love to give." Like many people, Art and Emma went into their adoption journey with idyllic feelings. While they don't want anyone to go through what they did, they do not regret their adoption journey. Emma said,

> *"Even with everything that happened, we are STILL proponents of open adoption."*

She would be willing to help anyone be a part of adoption but would hope they would be given an honest education. People need to know what they're getting into. *"It's not a storybook, but whose life is?"* Emma continued to say that communication is so crucial between spouses.

> *"Even if you're not united, you need to be united in front of your children. You need to have an open and honest relationship with your kids and tell them, I don't understand what it is you're going through, but I am here to listen and help you."*

Early on, Art, Emma, and Jodi went back to their adoption agency to give presentations for open adoption. People were often flabbergasted as to how they could do that. Many people want to get their kids, pretend adoption didn't happen and never talk about it again. However, according to Art and Emma, it becomes the elephant in the room. Emma said she wanted to ask the prospective adoptive parents, "What are you so afraid of?" She thought maybe it was because of an underlying fear that the biological parents would come back and take their kids. She understood because they had the exact same fear for the first few months. Art said that not telling their children they were adopted would be deception. Besides, adoptees need to know their medical histories.

"It's important that adoptive parents pursue what they are most comfortable with. Adoptive children have a right and a need to know they are adopted. We felt our kids should know their histories as part of their larger families."

One day it dawned on Art: *you are not tied to this person genetically.* Most likely, they will not like the same things you like, or want the same things you want, or communicate the same way. They are different that way. He and his son have different interests. His son has a unique path and handles situations very differently. Art now realizes that it was no wonder they had trouble communicating when Rick was young due to their "different wiring." It doesn't mean that biological families don't go through that, but you should EXPECT that wavelengths will be misaligned in adoptive families.

Art and Emma said with open adoption, there needs to be honesty and full disclosure. They think that a solid plan with clear expectations on both sides is necessary. The adoptive parents and birth parents need to be a good fit. When they look back over their experiences, they had many red flags with Jodi, but they ignored them because they already had experienced three failed adoption attempts. They now think they should have openly set boundaries that everyone could agree upon. They also said they could have benefited from a facilitator to help with the relationship expectations. It needed to start at the very beginning. Emma said it should even include details like what the kids will call the birth mother. It would have been helpful for the Jodi to have guard rails. Art and Emma even conceded that it would have helped if they had been given guardrails, too. Looking back, they thought that they should have reached out to Jodi more. They still second-guess their decision to let Jodi initiate contact with Rick via Myspace. They also recommended that adoptive parents not be afraid to seek counseling, as it helped them and their kids.

My Thoughts, My Lens

As we were wrapping up the interview, Art and Emma were snuggled back on the couch in their original unified fuzzy sock position. I hope their story helps other families by confirming we are not alone in our adoptive challenges. In my mind, Art and Emma have 20/20 wisdom. Hearing them say they are still proponents of adoption was monumental for me. I wonder if every prospective adoptive parent needed to hear that, too. I'm certain every adoptee needs to hear that their parents would choose adoption *all over again* – that we weren't too much for them – and that we *are* worthy of their love. As we said goodbye, their kindness and grace washed over me and gently enfolded me in warmth.

Bob L. & Melissa M. | EBD Teacher and Potter

Minnesota
Year of Adoption: 2014

Bob and Melissa were sitting close together like best friends on their porch in front of a stone wall. Even through my computer screen, I could sense their holistic country surroundings. Melissa was smiley and super attractive in a Kate Hudson doppelganger kind of way. Bob had kind eyes and a long beard that couldn't hide his laid-back confidence. Together, they were welcoming, gracious, and selfless with their time.

Our conversation began with discussing why some adoptive mothers were hesitant to share their stories. Melissa said that through this process, prospective parents are extremely vulnerable. She can understand why adoptive mothers tend to be guarded. However, she and Bob believe that adoption is about the *kids*. Their daughter, Rose, speaks with her birth mother (April C. – whose story is also in this book – see the table of contents) every week. Melissa said,

> *"It's super important they don't have any questions. That's why open adoption is so important. For me, it's important for Rose to have questions about where she came from. I want her to feel free to ask and know her birth mom. It's been cool she knows her birth grandparents and birth uncles and aunts. It does take a village."*

Bob and Melissa want to facilitate Rose's relationship with April so that she has someone to answer her questions about her heritage, personality, and medical issues. Physically, Rose blends in with their family. No one would guess that she's adopted. However, she also looks just like April. Recently, Rose was in the driver's seat of her grandparents' pontoon with a sassy expression. Melissa snapped a photograph and texted it to April with the message, "Does this look like anybody?" Bob and Melissa believe that it's essential to acknowledge the biological similarities. Melissa said that people get territorial in those situations, but they want to honor "Mama A" in all the ways they can.

When I asked Melissa why she welcomed an open adoption, she said, primarily, because it felt right – humans are inquisitive by nature. She once randomly met a woman at a potter's convention who was also adopted. When the woman discovered that Rose was adopted, she gave Melissa her phone number, encouraging her to reach out if she had any questions about adoption. The woman told Melissa that even though she was raised by the best adoptive parents, she still had a void she didn't know how to fill. Melissa has been touched by the adoption community's willingness to offer support. There's a connection in the community through everyone's unique experience. She said, "It is an amazing journey. It is a process."

Adoption was something Bob and Melissa talked about when they were dating. Melissa wanted to experience both adoption and pregnancy. After they had their first daughter, Amy, they waited until they were in a good financial position before adopting Rose in their late twenties. It took them eight months to get through the extensive adoption paperwork and hoop-jumping. Upon completion, their profile was put in a book – along with all the other prospective adoptive couples – for the birth mothers to consider. Twenty-two months later, April pulled their profile and asked to meet them. They agreed to meet for brunch when April was 20 weeks pregnant. While waiting at the restaurant for April to arrive, they wondered what she would look like but simultaneously spotted her as she walked in from the parking lot. The three of them sat on the entryway bench before being seated at their table. The first thing Melissa said was, "Omigosh, are you nervous? I am so nervous."

Yes, April was nervous, too.

Their meeting ended up being effortless. They "totally hit it off." They discovered that Melissa was from the same small town as April's dad, and they even attended the same schools. (Melissa's mom knew April's family!) At one point, as Melissa returned to the table from the restroom, April was telling Bob she loved the name Rose. Melissa joked, "Really, that's what you talked about while I was in the bathroom? Without me?" Three hours later, the waitstaff told them they needed to order more food if they were going to stay. Bob and Melissa left the restaurant cautiously optimistic that April would pick them. April had told them that the time she had spent with the other prospective parents was much shorter. A few weeks later, they met with April at the zoo, and she told them she had indeed picked them.

After they graciously accepted April's decision, Bob was hesitant to tell his officemate that he and Melissa had been selected to be adoptive parents. His coworker and his wife had been trying to adopt for seven years. Bob and his coworker had many adoption discussions through the years during his long wait. Of course, his coworker was happy for them, but it was tough on him. Bob said, "I wish there was a way to capture the look in [his] eyes." Bob wanted to show other birth mothers how devoted his coworker and his wife would be as adoptive parents. He said it was painful to watch his officemate wait for so long. As a matter of policy, the adoption agency would add new couples to the bottom of the list. Prospective parents are also featured on the adoption agency's website. If a birth mother were overwhelmed, the agency would introduce the couple on the top first because they had been waiting the longest. Melissa kept checking the agency's website for a while to see if Bob's coworker and his wife were still on the list. Once she noticed that their picture was removed, she felt better.

April, Bob, and Melissa were a match because they had many similarities. When they met, all three chose to be their most genuine selves: naked, open, and vulnerable. Melissa said it was liberating for her to be her "own genuine person." At the same time, April had to reveal her vulnerabilities on an extensive form because they had agreed to an open adoption. In Melissa's opinion, some of the questions were intrusive and unnecessary. However, she knows there are many benefits to having such a vast amount of information. For example, if they had concerns about Rose's mental health, they would have access to April's information. In extreme cases, if a severe medical issue arose, Rose would have a potential donor. It was important to Bob and Melissa that not only would Rose have access to her history, but she would actually want to know it. Melissa said,

> *"Everyone wants to know where they're from regardless of where they put their roots down."*

With all of the paperwork in place, Bob and Melissa felt prepared before Rose's birth. She was born before midnight. Bob and Melissa arrived the next day and stayed in the room adjacent to April's, and were able to take the time to bond with Rose skin-to-skin. That initial bonding was important to them. They knew that Rose would suddenly hear a different heartbeat.

She went from amniotic fluid to air, and then the cadence of the heartbeat she was accustomed to changed.

Two days later, when leaving the hospital, April's mom and dad were with her. She was holding Rose. At this point in our conversation, Melissa paused to gather her emotions. Tears pooled, then spilled from her eyes, as her voice softened:

> *"Time stopped. It was a circular vortex. Everything was fuzzy and moving so slowly. And she hands Rose to me, and we just hug. It was so hard to break from that because I knew I was physically taking her baby from her."*

Melissa wiped her tears. Bob looked wistful. He said that Rose is better with April in her life, and he continued,

> *"It was surreal. You have three people whose hearts are breaking … Two people who have joy. But then to actually have somebody hand you their two-day-old baby and say, 'I entrust in you to foster and nurture this child for the rest of their life …' Physically. It's heavy. It is a heavy feeling. Unless you've been through it, I can't describe it."*

Bob and Melissa's biological daughter, Amy, was 11 years old when they brought Rose home. It took about the same amount of time to adjust with Rose as it did when Amy was an infant. After bringing each girl home, Melissa needed about seven months to recover from the newborn phase physically and emotionally: the lack of sleep, the adjustment to a new human, the lack of sleep, the bonding, the lack of sleep, learning her cries, up every two hours to feed, and forming a routine. About nine months after bringing Rose home from the hospital, Melissa thought, "Okay, we're getting through this. Things are stabilizing." In taking care of their new baby, certain tasks came right back to them, whereas other things had to be relearned. Bob and Melissa felt like they were new parents again. They had to learn Rose's personality, just like they had to learn Amy's. Melissa said,

> *"There were many unbelievable similarities … because you're thrown into wonderful automatic chaos."*

The difference for them was that they were older and more seasoned when Rose came along. And the sisters never competed for attention or had any jealousy because they had different needs due to their age difference. Amy was crazy in love with her sister from the start. Melissa said, "Families can grow in a traditional way or the adoptive way. It's the unknown – venturing into this."

At this point in the interview, Bob jumped up to retrieve Amy's school project taped to the refrigerator. He brought back a piece of paper cut out in the shape of a heart sectioned off in a grid pattern. Within each section, Amy had drawn the answers to different questions: *What is your favorite food? (Chocolate chip banana bread) What do you do well? (Read) What is most important to you? (Family)*. The most touching section was Amy's answer to the question, what was your happiest moment? Her response: *When I learned we were adopting.* She had drawn a stork complete with the package bundled in a baby blanket.

Melissa said she sometimes forgets that she wasn't the one who gave birth to Rose. She once said that she "had all this sag under here because she nursed two babies" (pointing to the area between her armpit and breast). Then she laughed and said she had to take it back and say, "No, wait, I only nursed *one* baby. Not to take anything away from Mama A." April was exceedingly selfless, pumping and freezing her breastmilk for Rose; they met every two weeks so she could give it to them.

For six months.

When April wanted to wean to get herself back to normal, she apologized to Bob and Melissa. They couldn't believe that she would pump in the first place and are eternally grateful to her. Bob said he couldn't imagine what April had to go through and encouraged her when they were together. He would tell her things like, "You're *gold*. You've been through *this*. Now you can go through anything."

At this point in the interview, I asked if having an adopted child was the same for them as having a biological child. Bob answered with no hesitation, "YES."

Being adopted is Rose's "normal." Her preschool teacher said that Rose was very cute – sharing her story at snack time to the other preschoolers at her table ... asking them if they knew what adoption meant. She understands that Mama A is her birth mother – and that Bob and Melissa are her mom and dad. They have periodic calls with April, and Rose often remembers, asking to FaceTime with Mama A.

Bob's professional experience has been instrumental in helping Rose view her adoption as "normal." He understands what's on the other side of stability. As an Emotional and Behavioral Disorder (EBD) teacher, Bob's primary function is to ensure that his students are safe both emotionally and physically. He works with parents and social workers to point them in the right direction. He likens his career to working in a MASH (mobile army surgical hospital) unit – but he can only provide Band-Aids. In his experience, adoptees face trauma when the parenting of the adoptive parents is poor. For example, some parents make flippant remarks when they are in crisis, such as "I wish I never had kids." Horrible. Bob said that, supposedly, those same adoptive parents wanted those kids more than anything in the world. They went through the long adoption process, took on parenting responsibilities, and now they're destroying their parent-child relationship with those types of statements.

In Bob's experience, all behavior manifests itself from fear: fear of failure, fear of the dark, fear of not fitting in, etc. As an EBD teacher, he is the most consistent adult figure in some of his students' lives – specifically the most consistent *male*. He has worked with some families for nearly two decades and has seen "parents grow or not grow, and children grow or not grow." When kids are involved in dangerous situations, they are forced to trust him to be the adult who can do the right thing. There have been days that Bob loathed his job, but he understands that no matter how he feels on some days, those same feelings are his students' days. All day. Everyday. When I asked Bob how he protected his heart, he replied, "You can't." Melissa said it was hard for him to shut off the trauma when he came home because he was still on high alert. Working with students who had endured trauma took a toll on his soul.

In contrast, there were positive effects from Bob's job. He was prepared to raise a child who could have mental or emotional issues. April's biological sister has a form of autism. Because of Bob's experience, he and Melissa were not afraid of Rose's genetics. Both Bob and Melissa lit up when they talked about April's sister, Cassie. Bob smiled and said, "I have a memory of her." Melissa interjected, "I have one, too. I hope it's the same one." Bob started the story with, "The coolest thing – she's very tall." She was at the

Children's Museum with them and Rose. She held her baby niece one-armed – Rose just fit in the crook of her arm. Cassie was just doing her thing, happily walking around the museum with Rose. The connection that Cassie made with Rose was very important to Bob and Melissa. In that moment, they were very pleased that she was so comfortable with her. At the end of Bob's story, Melissa smiled and said, "Yep, same memory!"

> *"Adoption just changes the antiquated definition of family – [that is] family as mom, dad, and kids. We all have people in our lives that don't fit the definition. We have friends who are called Auntie … There have never been any negative interactions with April. Ever. It comes so naturally."*

Melissa said that she and April became like sisters during the first year, growing closer with each interaction. Emotional fostering has been so important – April is an equal participant in Rose's life.

Bob and Melissa put their girls first. They recently went through a divorce but prefer to call it a *conscious uncoupling* (despite the flack that Gwyneth Paltrow and Chris Martin received for that term). The girls now have two peaceful households. When Melissa pointed out the tension that once existed had dissipated, Amy agreed. While the traditional definition of family changed for everyone with the divorce, they are still a connected family. The person that Melissa was most nervous to tell was April. However, April graciously accepted the news, saying she noticed they both seemed happier. Once Bob and Melissa separated, the fighting immediately stopped, allowing them to exit from their marriage gracefully. They still go to family events together and sit together at band concerts. They have spoken with each other every day since the divorce, keeping rituals (such as bedtime activities) the same in both households to provide stability for the girls. Melissa said her parents got divorced when she was young, and she never wanted her girls to have the same experience she had. Parting was the best choice for the girls.

As I watched Bob and Melissa both nod their heads in agreement, they still looked like best friends – just as they had at the beginning of our conversation.

At this point in the interview, Rose literally popped up on my computer screen. Her grin fell somewhere between innocence and mischievousness:

soooo flippin' cute – she looked like a mini-April (I had interviewed April a few weeks before Bob and Melissa). I wanted to reach through the screen and gently squeeze her cheeks. She said, "Dad's new house is brilliant." Then, she continued to talk: her favorite ice cream is chocolate … she was "five and three quarters" old … she wanted to know if I wanted to hear a few jokes. (I did – and then learned that dogs from the Big Apple are called New Yorkies.) Oh, and then I needed to let Mom and Dad go so they could fix lunch because she and Amy were hungry. (Amy was nodding in agreement in the background.)

~ Advice Through Bob and Melissa's Lens ~

For prospective adoptive parents: "You just have to be your genuine self. You can't hide who you are. The right thing really will happen. Don't force the fit. The fit will come naturally."

My Thoughts, My Lens

Bob didn't hesitate for a millisecond to say "YES!" when I asked if having an adoptive child was the same for them as having a biological child. I had chills. Every adoptee needs to hear that.

His quick answer reminded me of a physician's assistant I once saw for several weeks in a row. We hit it off while I was being treated. I wanted to ask her out to happy hour but didn't, assuming there was probably some doctor-patient rule against becoming cohorts. She was an off-the-chart extreme extrovert and asked about my ethnicity. When she learned that I was Korean, she lit up and told me she had a young, adopted daughter from South Korea. After having five biological boys, she and her husband decided they wanted a girl. Every time I went to see her, she entertained me with hilarious stories about the youngest love of her life, which included Band-Aid carnage and pilfered objects. All of her sons adored and protected their little sister. She deftly described how her daughter's charming high-spiritedness was intermingled with turbulence over adoption. On my last visit, she gifted me with one of her brilliant stories, saying she loved her daughter more than life *and* just as much as her sons.

Her comment stunned me.

She was the first adoptive parent I'd ever heard say that. I had always wondered if parents could love their adopted children just as much as their biological children.

However, when I had a discussion with another adoptive mother of both adopted and biological children, she told me that my questioning whether adoptive parents have significantly different feelings about their children was "presumptuous and out-of-date." I understand I touched a sensitive nerve – which was not my intention at all. She clearly articulated *she* did not feel differently about her biological and adopted children. However, that does not change the fact that many *adoptees* struggle, wondering if their parents love them as much as they would have if they had been biological offspring. I *know* many adoptees have the same fearful question. (The doubts are not insults aimed at adoptive parents – they are just a reality of an adoptee's thought process.) I think that adoptive mother missed the point:

Many adoptees do not have a window into the emotional headspace of their parents and *need reassurance*.

Most adoptive parents fiercely love their children – a fact that adoptees are not always able to recognize. The misunderstandings on both sides highlight the need for open dialog and communication between adoptees and adoptive parents. I know my parents loved me. However, as their only child, without a basis for comparison when I was young, I could not be convinced that they loved me as much as they would have loved a biological child. For that reason, I will be eternally grateful to have met the physician's assistant – her answer gently closed the door to that nagging question I had for decades.

As I stood up in the examination room, the revelation of the physician assistant's words brought tears to my eyes, compelling me to tell her I needed to hear that. A piece of me healed that day. I told her that while her daughter's struggle with adoption seemed like it was aimed towards her, it wasn't. She, in turn, said she needed to hear that. We hugged briefly, and then she told me to get out of there, turning away, but not before I saw her eyes mist over.

Heather F. | Accountant

Illinois
Year of Adoption: 2013

Meeting with Heather was as uncomplicated as putting on slippers. Her cheerful, easy-peasy personality and effortless laugh made me feel as though I had known her for years. She enthusiastically talked about her husband, Jack, and his wonderful parenting skills. With love and admiration, she spoke of her son, Kyle, and his big heart. I'm betting Kyle felt like he was *home* when he walked into Heather and Jack's house for the first time at six years old.

Heather and Jack tried to get pregnant for three years, trying everything short of IVF. She laughed, "I couldn't do it anymore because I was taking way too many hormones and making myself a psycho." It was messy, and towards the end, they were spending nearly $5k per month on medical treatments. She said, "I don't know how my husband got through it. He is not spiritual. I got to the point [where] I was asking God, 'If it's not going to happen, [then] take the *desire* for it to happen from me.'" Heather desperately wanted her husband to be a father because kids loved him and were naturally drawn to him. She figured that if they would not become parents, it was not supposed to happen. She said,

"It was emotionally harder going through it than letting go of it."

"Going through it" was – literally – being at the doctor's [office] every day. Injections, blood draws, tests, ultrasounds, pregnancy tests, having a week-and-a-half break, and then starting the cycle all over again. She needed to step out of her crazed, medicated state. In the end, Heather was sad, but she was *done*. For her, it was harder to think about her husband not being a dad than her knowing she was done.

Heather wanted to be a parent, not pregnant.

185

Once Heather and her husband decided that they were finished with trying to conceive a child, they researched adoption. After deciding to adopt – they reasoned that they wanted to help an older child in need. Since they were not looking for an infant, they went the foster care route (as opposed to an adoption agency). As they went through the grueling foster parent vetting process, they did not request a specific age, gender, or sibling count. Adopting from the foster care system required them to go through multiple training sessions, including events like a 4-hour car seat installation demonstration. (Heather said it was riveting!) They also had to attend intense workshops on heavy topics like fetal alcohol syndrome. The workshops scared Heather, but they did not deter her. The whole process was "off-putting" but necessary. Heather thinks it was intentional – perhaps the social workers were trying to weed out those who believed foster parenting would be easy. She remembers filling out a lengthy questionnaire with many scenarios to which they had to answer "Yes" or "No" or "Maybe." For example: did they want a child who would play sports? Or could they handle a child who threw feces? How about a sexually abused child? The extensive questionnaire took her and Jack several hours to complete.

> *"This whole thing, which is grueling to go through, is also really awesome because they're not going to match you to someone you can't handle."*

When Heather told her son Kyle about the interview for this book, he wanted her to list the puzzling things she and her husband had to do to become licensed. (She felt some requirements – as she recalled them – seemed illogical.)

1. Knives had to be in a drawer. Not a knife block, not locked. They just couldn't be out.
2. All medications, whether over the counter or prescription, had to be in a locked cabinet. While Heather and Jack were foster parents, the bathroom cabinets were padlocked.
3. There were zero alcohol restrictions. (Really, the foster child couldn't have access to aspirin, but alcohol was *fine*? Weird.)
4. Water heaters had to be at a specific temperature.
5. The gas fireplace had to have a screen mesh in front of it – even though it doesn't get hot enough to burn.

6. Any weapons and bullets had to be locked separately. In Heather and Jack's case, it made no sense because they had a gun safe for their hunting rifles. They had to remove the bullets and put them in a less safe place (not in a safe) just to have them locked separately.
7. A fire ladder was required in Kyle's room but not in the parent's room.
8. There had to be a smoke detector in every room. Most people have a couple in central locations. Heather and Jack have eight.

After Heather and Jack were officially licensed for foster care, they were assigned to a social worker who would look for kids in the system and then present their cases to Heather and Jack. When they agreed to a particular child, their social worker would contact that child's social worker, facilitating a meeting if all parties felt they were a good fit. And because Heather and Jack were licensed foster care parents, they were entered into the statewide system; other social workers could reach out with potential matches. There were several stages in the process for each. The first step was receiving a little info-snippet of the child with a summary of what their life had been to that point. Jack and Heather had to say yes or no. If they said yes, in the next step, they would receive additional information, again, to which they had to answer yes or no. The information kept building until they had it all. However, the entire process could be terminated at any point if the child's social worker ruled out the parents. The last step was to interview personally with the child's social worker. They made it to three interviews and were ruled out each time, sending them back to start a new search from scratch.

And each time, it was extremely emotional.

Heather said it felt like she was shopping. She said, "This pair of shoes has this high of a heel, this color, this amount of cushion. It felt wrong." In one instance, she and Jack turned down an 8-month-old who had been abused by his parents. Because the parents' legal rights had not been terminated, they would still be involved in the baby's life. Jack said he could not be in the same room with someone who had beaten their child. Heather felt immense guilt over saying no to that child. She said, "Ultimately, if they're not the best fit for you, [then] you're not the best fit for them either."

When Heather and Jack's journey finally led them to six-year-old Kyle, there were many times they thought his adoption might not ever be finalized. The social worker told them they were the parents she wanted for Kyle, and they needed to move him into their home right away. On a Saturday in

September, the social worker told them that Kyle would be moving in with them on Monday – two days! Then when Monday came around – nope. The exact sequence happened three more times: Heather was told she would be a mom, and then Kyle was yanked back. The aunt he was living with kept changing her mind. After the fourth time, Heather said, "I'm done." She could no longer handle the rejection. She enrolled in college to get an accounting degree, thinking, "If I'm not going to be a mom, I'm going to do something with my career."

Finally, in December, Heather received a call from Kyle's social worker to ask if they still wanted him. The social worker assured Heather that she still wanted her and Jack to be Kyle's parents, but the situation had changed. A judge permanently terminated custody, informing Kyle's aunt she would no longer be allowed to play games with Kyle's adoption. Of course, Heather and Jack said yes. With the court's mandate, Heather and Jack were allowed to meet the people in Kyle's life. They met his teacher, his aunt, and the school social worker. While they were at the elementary school, Kyle was standing in the hall in line for breakfast. The social worker quietly pointed him out (because he didn't yet know that he would be leaving his aunt's house). To prevent Kyle from knowing they were spying on him, Jack turned his back to the line of children because he has a long, recognizable beard. He faced Heather to make it look like they were having a conversation. Heather could see Kyle clearly, *knowing* immediately, "Yep. That's my son." However, Jack did not even get a glimpse of Kyle. Heather loves that her husband was so considerate, putting aside his desire to see his son to ensure that Kyle did not feel uncomfortable. Heather grinned and said she wouldn't have been so nice. She said,

"I feel like I loved him the minute I saw him."

When Heather and Jack finally got to meet Kyle at his aunt's house, she had to balance her feelings of elation with the awkwardness of having Kyle's aunt present. Getting a glimpse of Kyle's life and his interactions with his aunt made Heather very sad. She could tell that Kyle didn't want to be there. He wasn't proud of anything and didn't even want to show them where he slept. The house was run down, dirty, and full of cigarette smoke. Kyle was very quiet during the visit, which they discovered was not his personality at all. When they took him to McDonald's the next day, they found that he was an outgoing, happy, and smiley kid, thrilled to get the little toy in his Happy

Meal. After eating, he was still thirsty. When Heather bought him extra milk, he was overjoyed.

Clearly, Kyle was not used to adults taking care of him. Heather speculated (she does not have proof) that Kyle's aunt played games with the court because she wanted to keep him for the paycheck. During the time of Kyle's adoption, parents in the foster care program received a base check for each child. They also received additional money if the child needed trauma services for PTSD, fetal alcohol syndrome, emotional issues, or medical problems. According to Heather, when the child is adopted, the parents were no longer eligible for the base check but could still receive the additional money until the child reached 18. Since Kyle did not need trauma services, his aunt would no longer have a paycheck if she adopted him. Once Kyle moved out, he had no interest in seeing his aunt and still does not ask about her.

From the day Heather and Jack met Kyle in person, it only took a week and a half until he moved into their home. Heather said, "That was mind-blowing to me; it went super-fast." During that week, they were seeing him every other day, if not more frequently. Heather had a multitude of things to accomplish on the off days – figuring out how she would juggle work, getting his room ready, registering him for school, and preparing a homemade construction paper scrapbook with photographs of his new life. The pictures were of his school, their home, his room, their pets, and pictures of Heather and Jack. (Years later, Heather found the scrapbook; it was well-loved. Kyle had gone through it many times, highlighting and circling things and writing notes in the margins.)

When Kyle walked into his newly decorated room for the first time at Heather and Jack's house, the first thing he wanted to know was why a decorative metal tree was missing. Heather had removed it during her redecorating frenzy, thinking a six-year-old boy wouldn't want it, but she was happy to put it back in its rightful place for him.

Heather purchased 5 x 7 frames, printed big letters spelling out his name, framed each letter separately, and hung them on the wall, certifying Kyle's ownership of the room and his rightful place in their family. Kyle kept those frames up for years. Even recently, when he moved into a different room in the house, he wouldn't let Heather get rid of them; instead, he put them in his keepsake box.

When Kyle moved in, life was normal. It took no time for their family to settle into a groove. Obviously, they had to learn a new schedule. Other than that, it was natural. Heather said, "He's a very easy kid to parent. Quite easy to be around." Another piece that fell into place was the conclusion of Kyle's therapy sessions. They were required to take him to counseling to make sure he had someone to talk to (in case he didn't rust his new parents). After only a week, Heather did not care for the counselor. She felt the counselor was off-putting, insisting that Kyle had ADD, barking at him, saying things like "Eyes Right Here" while sharply pointing to her eyeballs with her middle and pointing fingers. Heather told her social worker she saw no ADD symptoms. The social worker replied that they were free to choose a new counselor. Heather appreciated having the autonomy to change therapists – and did so. When they switched, the new counselor conducted an ADD test during the first visit, confirming what Heather already knew – Kyle did not have ADD. After the second visit, he said that Kyle no longer needed to be in therapy. It was evident that he was happy, and the therapist felt if they continued with sessions, it might have a detrimental effect on Kyle; he might start assuming that something *should* be wrong. Heather appreciated that even though they were technically foster parents at that point, they were able to make decisions beneficial to Kyle's well-being.

Kyle is now a 14-year-old happy kid at 5 feet 4 inches with size 11 feet. Heather wonders if kids are anything like puppies in that they grow into their paw size. They must wait and see because they don't have Kyle's biological parents' medical history. He has always been very proud to be adopted – which Heather acknowledges is unusual for an adoptee. They have a plaque in their hallway with his birth date and his adoption date. On one occasion, when his friends were coming over, Heather asked him if he wanted her to take it down. He said it could stay along with the collage of pictures that included one of their family with the judge who finalized his adoption.

Heather believes there are a few reasons why Kyle has a positive outlook on his adoption. The first was his age of adoption; at six, he was old enough to understand his circumstances but young enough that he could still "roll with it." He understood that where he was living was not healthy for him and remembered snippets of his many foster homes. His biological sister has told him about their early childhood and how she used to babysit him when she was four years old (and he was only two).

Kyle and his sister meet up once a year around Christmas. Heather says she is a sweetheart and still has the maternal protective instincts for him she developed as a child. Kyle has other siblings but connects with her the most. For Kyle, other memories come out occasionally – little things triggered by something else that is happening. She said, "Kids know more of what's going on than we give them credit for."

The second factor that helped Kyle is that he knows other kids who are adopted. Heather and Jack approach his adoption with care, too. They agree that it is Kyle's story to share and let him take the lead on choosing to do so. Heather understands that while many people do not talk about adoption, she believes that they should not approach it as a taboo subject. She and Jack have intentionally taught Kyle not to be ashamed about his adoption. She has told him that he is her son, and it doesn't matter how she got him. Even though she didn't give birth to Kyle, she reminds him that he belongs to them. They have told him, "We wanted you. We got to choose you and bring you home. If we had our 'own,' we would be stuck … we went out and chose you."

Recently, because many people do not openly talk about adoption or infertility, Heather felt led to email her church leaders, offering to be available to anyone who might need to talk. The next day, they connected her with a lovely lady experiencing the pain of infertility. Heather remembers that when she was going through infertility herself, she just wanted to talk to someone who knew what it was like: being turned down, having so many negative pregnancy tests, going to endless doctors' visits, coping with the frustration and stress. Women often keep their feelings private while attempting to appear as though they are fine. But it is essential to talk with someone who has been there and can validate your feelings. When Heather was going through her treatments, she feared not being able to have "her own kid." However, that fear dissipated when Kyle came into her life.

With the pain of infertility in Heather's past, she now concentrates on balancing Kyle's outlook about *his* past. She sometimes found it challenging to make sure she wasn't disrespecting how his life started; it's a fine line. She said, "You can't crap on somebody's parents, even if they are no longer in the picture."

Kyle rarely mentions his biological mother. However, when he does, he calls her by her first name and not "Mom." Heather said he has no desire to contact her – "Not that we could allow that. She's not in a great place." She had a drug problem for a long time. Early on, Kyle had asked why she was the way she was and why they couldn't get her help. Heather told him his that birth mother had to want help and trying to help someone who doesn't want it just doesn't work.

Any time Kyle had questions, Heather and Jack would answer every single one. Their therapist prepped them ahead of time. Kids are prepared to hear the answers to the questions *they* ask. Additional information can be difficult for them to process. As a result, Heather took the accountant's approach she had when answering auditors – not offering extra information (she laughed as she said that, and I laughed back; as a retired accounting manager, I found her humor to be perfection). When she answered one of Kyle's questions, she would follow up with, "Do you have any more questions?" She was always honest with him. Heather and Jack also taught Kyle that he should specifically come to either of them with his questions because nobody else completely knows their situation. That steered him away from asking a teacher or other people who would not have the details of his adoption. She told him, "You totally ask anything you want, but you need to ask your dad and me."

Heather would be open to arranging a meeting with Kyle's birth mother, but only if it would be healthy for Kyle. His birth mother would have to be in a positive life situation and have Kyle's best interest as her priority. She once showed up uninvited at a park where he was meeting his siblings. That incident scared Kyle, and he no longer has an interest in seeing her. Overall, though, he doesn't seem angry about her. Heather loves Kyle's sensitive and warm heart. Like Heather, he is very spiritual. Kyle prays often and has even written prayer cards at church requesting the staff to pray for his siblings.

Kyle is still affected by his early years; for him, possessions have meaning. Many foster kids have very few possessions. They have a bag of stuff, and that's it. He was touched when Heather saved the little jacket he was wearing when they met him. He wants to keep all of his possessions, often struggling to let go. For example, he once got a little choked up when a person came to pick up the loft-bed they sold to make room for his new bed. Heather and Jack have found it is easier for Kyle to let go of his possessions when they give him a choice to donate them to other children. Heather thinks he may always struggle with not being a hoarder, but they have found that empowering him as the decision-maker is comforting to him.

~ Advice Through Heather's Lens ~

<u>For prospective adoptive parents:</u> "When you're going through the process, especially through foster care, as weird as it sounds – try to take the emotion out of it." Heather said that it is best to think it through logically. It is difficult to say no, but it has to be the right fit for everyone. The process takes much longer than you would think, but once the match has been made, it takes no time at all. They spent two years looking for a match and then less than a week and a half once that match was made.

<u>For current adoptive parents:</u> "Once you do have a child, answer what they're asking honestly." Don't offer extra information because they're not ready to hear it. Be honest and make sure they're proud that they are adopted. "Let them own their life. A lot of kids out of foster care don't have choices, and things have been thrust upon them. To give them options gives them their power back."

My Thoughts, My Lens

When I was 21 years old, working at an emergency care house, most of the kids were teenagers. (The bulk of my social services story is at the end of Andrea K.'s interview.) However, a six-year-old little girl named Allison came to stay in the house where I worked. Her seven-year-old brother, Keith, stayed in the boy's house next door. They were both skinny little sweethearts with bad haircuts. Their eyes and noses reminded me of mischievous little elves. Allison had ginger freckles that seemed to dance when she smiled. Keith had cute thin lips that only smiled on one side. Those two kiddos were much younger than the typical teenagers under my care. During their two-month stay, they captured my heart. Just like Kyle, they were old enough to understand that their mother was mentally unable to care for them but young enough to not be jaded by years of neglect. The glimmer of their innocence was not wholly extinguished at that time, but I was afraid that it wouldn't be too long until they found themselves in the same emotional space as the traumatized and angry older kids. I hope they were able to find the love and stability they always deserved.

Hearing about Kyle's sensitive and empathetic six-year-young self soothed some of the lingering ache I have for those kids I knew so long ago. I love that Kyle, Heather, and Jack have effortlessly enriched each other's lives through love and empathy. Divine.

Jennifer A. | Business Director

Utah
Year of Adoption: 2013 & 2014

At this point in Jennifer's life, her eyes are wide open. She acknowledged that she wasn't always self-aware. I found her to be humble. Her attractive smile radiated sensitivity, and her pretty blonde hair was pulled back, punctuating her kind face. At one point in the interview, her charismatic husband popped in and said hello for about 20 seconds and then left so Jennifer and I could continue with our conversation. They met in high school, and I guessed they both were very popular. (Although after I shared my initial impressions with her, she said definitely *not*.) Jennifer endeared herself to me as she talked about her hopes and regrets, even shedding a few "White girl tears" (her words) as she described their journey to adopt two beautiful Black baby girls.

Jennifer and her husband, Evan, got married after receiving their undergraduate degrees and continued to graduate school. After a few years, they decided it was time to start a family. They assumed they would have no problems because they were young and healthy. However, they both had significant fertility challenges, spending years visiting doctors, testing, and trying *in vitro*. After having one miscarriage and 11 fertilized eggs which failed to develop, they realized the road they were on was not meant for them. Jennifer was open to adoption, not having a strong pull towards pregnancy like some of her friends experienced. Evan was also open to adoption because his father was adopted. They switched roads and started their adoption journey.

The agency that conducted their home study recommended an adoption agency in Utah, even though Jennifer and Evan live in a different state. Utah state regulations favor the rights of adoptive parents and allow for agency care of expecting mothers. Jennifer and Evan had to go through a detailed vetting process. Jennifer said,

"It was wild thinking about what situations we would be open to. [Whereas], when you're pregnant, so much is out of your control."

Jennifer and Evan agreed to an open adoption. After their paperwork was in order, the agency put them in a profile book. They were quickly matched with three birth mothers. It was the third birth mother, Jackie, who selected them to be her baby's parents. Jackie is Black; it did not matter to her that Jennifer and Evan are White. Jennifer spoke with Jackie on the phone a few times before she and Evan made the 23-hour drive to Utah. Jackie was to be induced one week before her due date, and they wanted to be there when their daughter was born. They arrived in time to have dinner with Jackie the night before their daughter, Alicia, was born. Conveniently, they were able to stay in the hospital.

After Jackie's labor, Jennifer and Evan came into the room to meet Alicia. Jennifer thought it was both awkward and sad, not knowing what to say to someone who had just gone through labor. Utah birth mothers could legally relinquish their rights 24 hours after giving birth. Jackie signed the papers after the waiting period, and Jennifer and Evan moved into a hotel with Alicia for a week until they obtained an interstate adoption agreement.

Jennifer radiated joy as she talked about positive memories of their time in Utah: juggling bottles, museums, hiking, and restaurants. Alicia was a very contented baby, and she mostly slept. The 23-hour drive back was easy. When they returned home, the company Jennifer worked for closed its doors. She felt blessed to no longer have professional obligations, which allowed her to stay at home with Alicia for a while. After eight months, Jennifer was more than shocked to learn that she was pregnant!

After all the infertility treatments, she thought it would be impossible to conceive, "a one in a billion chance." Because they had an open adoption, Jennifer told Jackie her news during one of their conversations. Jackie revealed that she, too, was pregnant (and was already raising three other kids at home). When Jennifer was six months along in her pregnancy, the Utah agency called. Jackie wanted Jennifer and Evan to adopt her baby after she was born. They did not hesitate – they always knew they wanted to adopt again, thinking they wouldn't have another "bio baby." Sensitive to the fact that Alicia was a Black child being raised in a predominantly White community, they wanted her to have a sibling who looked like her. Having the opportunity to adopt her full biological birth sister thrilled them.

Jennifer gave birth to her daughter, Hope, in September. In October, Jennifer, her mother, and Hope flew out to Utah to adopt Alicia's biological sister, Natasha. Jennifer's husband stayed home with Alicia. Again, Jackie relinquished her rights after 24 hours of giving birth. The second adoption worked much like the first (but without the 23-hour drive). Jennifer and her mother flew back with two babies who were only five weeks apart in age. The girls were like twins, and Jennifer was able to nurse both of them. She recapped the sequence of events for me:

1. 2013: Jennifer and Evan adopted Alicia.

2. Fifteen months later: Jennifer gave birth to Hope.

3. One month later: Jennifer and Evan adopted Natasha.

4. Jennifer and Evan thought they were finished.

5. Four years later: Jennifer gave birth to their son, Keegan.

6. Evan got a vasectomy.

When we had our interview, the COVID-19 quarantine was still in effect. Jennifer said that all four siblings were weathering the quarantine well, as they had built-in playmates. While all four get along, Alicia and Natasha are definitely linked the tightest. Alicia is the ringleader, and Natasha willingly follows her. While Hope and Natasha are in the same grade, they do not play with each other in class, but they are certainly bonded as sisters. Hope is more like Jennifer, content to play by herself. Natasha and Alicia's personalities align, much like Hope and Keegan's interests line up; Jennifer believes the similarities are due to biology.

Although Jennifer feels blessed that their family was created in such a short time period, she carries tremendous guilt when she looks back over Alicia and Natasha's adoptions. When they worked through the adoption process, Jennifer said that she "put blinders on" to what she believes was subtle coercion. Utah agencies take outstanding care of their *birth mothers*. (The agency was wonderfully welcoming to Jackie.) They housed, clothed, and fed birth mothers, even flying them in from other states. Jackie was able to stay with her other children while the agency expertly cared for her health and essential needs. At that time, Jennifer rationalized her decision to go with the Utah agency was because of how attentively they provided for Jackie. Jennifer believes those birth mothers have a choice when they give birth and the adoptions are technically legal. However, she also believes that those birth mothers definitely experience what she refers to as "emotional coercion."

In Jennifer's opinion, Utah's adoption laws are very *adoptive parent* friendly. The 24-hour waiting period before birth mothers sign Termination of Parental Rights (TPR) paperwork is significantly shorter than in other states. And it is irrevocable upon signing. In Jennifer's home state, birth mothers have a 72-hour waiting period after giving birth before they can sign the TPR papers and an additional ten days to revoke their decision. I imagine that adoptive parents in Jennifer's state wouldn't be able to exhale for nearly two weeks – knowing that the baby in their arms, the one they are falling in love with, is not yet theirs legally. However, the 24-hour Utah law benefits the adoption agency; they can give prospective adoptive parents a statistically favorable percentage of successful adoptions. Jennifer said, in looking back,

> *"I have a significant amount of guilt about using that agency and the potential for a feeling of coercion with the birth mothers."*

Jennifer said that if she had to choose an agency *now*, she would probably make different choices. She would look for a very ethical agency that champions birth mothers' rights, giving them true freedom of choice. Jennifer understands that if she and Evan chose an in-state agency, they probably would have been much more stressed having to wait longer for a match – and waiting during the longer revocable period. She now recognizes that birth mother protections are in place for a reason. However, if given a choice to go back, she said,

> *"I wouldn't change anything because I have my girls. They're mine. I realize how very selfish that is. I'm a very privileged person."*

Jennifer was forced to take off her blinders a few years ago when Black birth mothers called her out in a transracial adoption online group chat. She initially joined a few groups because she knew she had to become educated about Black culture and Black transracial adoptees. She was forced to open her eyes to the birth mother and adoptee perspectives. The birth mothers shook her. They told her that she was selfish. After listening to them, Jennifer realized that she only had the adoptive parents' perspective without the "full picture of the adoption triad." Many of the online conversations revolved around ethical adoptions. The women told her,

> *"There are no ethical adoptions. You're raising someone else's child."*

Jennifer forced herself to look at the meaning behind their harsh words. They asked Jennifer to imagine herself in their shoes. You're told you have other kids at home, you may not have a job, the father may not be in the picture … Then, someone tells you they will fly you and your kids across the country and will take care of you, giving you respite from being in "survival mode" for nine months; you won't have to decide if you want an abortion, you have the opportunity to be in denial for nine months …

It is very enticing.

But in the end, your child will be raised by someone else. Additionally, if the birth mothers changed their minds before giving birth, they would have to leave the facility. The women told Jennifer they questioned the "ethical" agency rules – who were they *really* protecting? Probably not the birth mothers. One woman told Jennifer that her baby was taken from her because she couldn't afford to raise her. Jennifer said,

> *"That broke me. I couldn't look away from it. I had to face that guilt. I'm raising children who are still mine, but they're also someone else's. They were born. They were formed by another mother – smelled her, knew her voice, had this connection I never did. She will still be their mom. I came to terms with accepting that. It doesn't make me any less of their mom. [Jackie's] still their mom, too."*

The agency told Jennifer that the birth mothers would have loved to raise their own babies if they could have. Jennifer opened her eyes and faced the reality that she had the opportunity to parent her girls because of the financial advantage she and Evan have. Through tears, Jennifer said that it was a broken system.

> *"I got two very beautiful girls by taking advantage of a broken situation. It's hard to admit. I'm not saying they would be better*

off with their birth mother or better with us. What's done is done. There's a lot of dark places in the system."

Jennifer tries to keep in touch with Jackie but thinks it's not as often as she should. They are both very busy – Jackie has a new baby at home. Jennifer and Jackie email pictures of their families to each other a couple of times a year. Jennifer loves seeing the pictures of Alicia and Natasha's siblings. The girls have recently asked to have video conversations with Jackie. They plan on starting those meetings soon. Jennifer would love for her daughters to meet with Jackie – acknowledging that video cannot replace an in-person connection. (She is looking forward to seeing Jackie again, too.)

Jennifer has concluded that adopting children forced her to look outside of the world she and Evan created for them. Parenting has made her a better person. She laughed when admitting that she's not the parent she thought she would be. She had to adjust herself to who *they* are. When asked about her hopes and dreams for her kids, Jennifer said she hopes they eventually find something they love to do. She hopes they will find someone they can spend the rest of their life with and have the joy that comes along with it. Jennifer wants all of her kids to be happy – to build lasting, valuable, and healthy relationships.

~ Advice Through Jennifer's Lens ~

<u>For prospective adoptive parents</u>: "Do your research from the perspective of everyone in the adoption triad." Jennifer said that when choosing an adoption agency, look at it from every perspective. Ask yourself, "Is this the best for everyone involved?"

My Thoughts, My Lens

The expert care that the agency provided for Jackie and the quick turn-around time for Jennifer and Evan seems like a win-win situation. Jackie signed the irrevocable Termination of Parental Rights (TPR) paperwork after the Utah mandatory 24-hour waiting period. However, I can see why Jennifer believes that some adoption agencies have the potential to subtly coerce birth mothers without breaking any laws. Jennifer's assertions troubled me and prompted me to look into it further.

The majority of states only allow a TPR to be signed *after* birth. Additionally, most have a minimum waiting period with an average length of 3.12 days. In roughly two-thirds of those states, the TPRs are irrevocable upon signing. In three states, birth parents can sign a TPR before birth, but they all have revocable periods until after the birth ranging from 4-10 days.

The most disturbing part of my research was learning that 14 states did not have a waiting period to sign the TPR after the birth. Of those states, seven were irrevocable upon signing. I tried to imagine what it must be like for the birth mothers in those seven states – those signing the TPR on the *same day* they gave birth. After giving birth, I remember feeling like I had been hit by a freight train followed up by a Mack truck. My entire body ached, my mind was foggy, and my emotions were scrambled. Honestly, I have my doubts about whether I would have been of sound enough mind to sign a black-and-white – yet profoundly gray – legal document on the same day I experienced the most emotional event in my life. I wonder if it would be morally prudent to mandate that all birth mothers are allowed a reasonable period of time to recuperate physically *and* emotionally before signing a TPR.

Conversely, I tried to imagine what it must be like for the adoptive parents who live in states with more extended revocation periods. During that time, it must be excruciating trying to fall in love with a baby who is not technically 100% yours; *joy partially cannibalized by fear.* Undoubtedly, the infants would sense the hesitation of their parents during the waiting periods.

I am not a lawyer, and therefore not fully informed on the legality of state adoptions. However, Jennifer's moral struggle is acutely real. I'm delighted that her adoption experience went smoothly. And I am also sad for her that it is peppered with guilt about her White Privilege. In a well-written NY times article about transracial adoptions, one adoptee was quoted as saying,

> *"You need parents who can talk about White Privilege, who can say: 'You might experience some of this. I'm sorry. We are in this together."*[32]

Jennifer actively sought out the perspectives of Black birth mothers – and that is admirable. It's not easy to turn the proverbial mirror on oneself, especially when guilt outlines one's reflection. We have all had times when we had to choose between seeing reality or turning away. The fact that Jennifer chose to look at her reflection makes me respect her that much more. I believe her ability to replace her prideful blinders with empathy for birth mothers will be invaluable as she helps her daughters grow and nurture their relationship with Jackie.

---

[32] Jones, Maggie. "Why a Generation of Adoptees Is Returning to South Korea." *New York Times Magazine,* 14 Jan. 2015, www.nytimes.com/2015/01/18/magazine/why-a-generation-of-adoptees-is-returning-to-south-korea.html?fbclid=IwAR16ht9RZYKmlwh74IX2jXPL7gg9rabtfOloeMQU8ZNCBTe vYDdHhS6FwBg. Accessed 5 Sep. 2020.

Anissa M. | Business Administrator

Virginia
Year of Adoption: 2008

I had a blast with Anissa. She was an upbeat ball of fire, forging our interview into what seemed like a conversation between old friends. I admired how well informed she was due to her extensive adoption research over the years. She sprinkled in sparks of energy and humor while hypnotizing me with her enthusiastic firework display. Her emotional accessibility and sincerity also emerged as she talked about parenting two children with Fetal Alcohol Spectrum Disorder (FASD). I was surprised (and even inspired) that she spoke about the upsides of their adoption downsides. I felt energized for days after speaking with her.

Anissa and her husband, Richard, chose adoption, believing it was something they were called to do. They were already comfortable with their decision because her husband and sister-in-law are both adopted. She said, "It wasn't a second or third choice to having children biologically." When the three-year journey to start their family began, they focused on Eastern Europe. They narrowed their search region to Kazakhstan, an ethnically diverse Central Asian country near Siberia (formerly part of the Soviet Union). Anissa and her husband took a Russian class and a course on *The Internationally Adopted Child*. The first thing the doctor said in that course was, "Your child will not be normal." They learned about the intellectual side of parenting ahead of time and prepared themselves for the likelihood that their children would develop both physical and psychological issues. Three years and three failed referrals later (the last one on Mother's Day of 2008), Anissa received a phone call asking if they would take a brother and sister duo. Anissa immediately exclaimed, "Yes!" and told the caller "No!" when he asked if she needed to speak to her husband.

Off they went to spend ten weeks in the city of Pavlodar, Kazakhstan. She said, "It wasn't terrible, just boring."

"Like going to Fargo."

But everything was very modern. Their rented apartment looked like a Soviet Bloc building on the exterior, but the interior was furnished like *page 36* of an Ikea catalog. Anissa's husband returned to the United States to work for part of the ten weeks, but she remained in the country the entire time. They hired an interpreter – a young female college student, fluent in five languages. She became Anissa's buddy for the whole visit, taking Anissa on a cultural experience and showing her the country's rural parts. She not only introduced Anissa to the warm people of Kazakhstan but also fixed her up with a sheep's head on a platter!

A few days after arriving in the country, Anissa and her husband went to the orphanage to meet their kids. The cleanliness of the establishment pleasantly surprised them. However, it was woefully understaffed, and the building had way too many open electrical outlets for so many young children. Their three-year-old daughter, Ava, scared them the first time they met her. She marched into the director's office and let out a maniacal, "Hee-hee-hee" in a wicked movie villain voice. Anissa said, "That pretty much summed up the last 12 years." Her son Max, who had just turned two, "was a harder nut to crack." During their time in Kazakhstan, they went to the orphanage every day for a few hours so that all four of them could get used to each other. Anissa continued to go when her husband was not in the country.

Anissa and her husband decided to keep Ava's name but added Grace as her middle name because they needed some "Grace." Max's original name was Alan, but they changed that to his middle name because Anissa and her husband both have Uncle Alans – and they decided Max was not an "Al" but a "Maximillian." They knew both kids probably had Fetal Alcohol Spectrum Disorder (FASD) before they adopted them. Max's case was more severe than Ava's. His symptoms presented like someone with autism. Currently, he is enrolled in an autism specialty program. Both go to private schools for kids with executive functioning disorders.

Ava's symptoms lean more towards the mental health issues accompanying the FASD diagnosis, such as depression and anxiety. Anissa said, "They have therapists galore." When the kids initially came home, they had unusual issues, "weird medical stuff, like parasites." They were also contagious. Anissa was on antibiotics nine times. She and the kids had mysterious skin infections on their faces and bodies, finally diagnosed by an Infectious

Disease Specialist. The kids were staph bacteria carriers. They took 30 days of strong antibiotics, and Anissa had to put a few teaspoons of bleach in the bathtub to bathe them. Ava recovered, but Max is still a carrier. He was scrawny at two years old, not even weighing 20 pounds.

The doctors thought that Max was clinically depressed. He couldn't walk when Anissa and her husband met him, but they taught him to walk during their orphanage visits. It took him an entire month to smile at them; the first time was when Anissa blew on his tummy, which made him laugh hysterically. He was on a soft food diet due to swallowing issues and required an occupational therapist's help. Textures of foods were "wonky" for him. He only ate eggs, yogurt, and peanut butter. (When they got home, Anissa ordered nine pounds of peanut butter from Amazon.) But Max now has a very typical teenage boy's diet.

Besides occupational therapy, both kids have been through (or are currently enrolled in) behavior therapy and speech therapy. Anissa reduced her working hours to part-time, as she is "always driving them around, meeting their needs." She does wonder what kind of life Max would have had if he had not been adopted. He now has resources in the United States that were not available to him in Kazakhstan. She thinks that he probably never would have gotten out of the institution or might not even be alive. But now, she said he is, "Like woooooo! A bundle of energy" (just like Anissa).

Ava had typical physical growth development. However, she has under-receptive pain receptors. (She doesn't feel the same sensations of pain that people normally do.) Strong kid. When Anissa first met Ava, she was surprised at how many caretaking and cleaning jobs she could do. As a three-year-old.

The orphanage staff gave her extra jobs because she was a troublemaker. When she learned about her pending adoption, she would walk down the halls of the orphanage and tell every staff member,

"My mama and papa have come for me."

Anissa said, "She was a tough little spitfire of a kid and virtually uncontrollable. Ha-ha." When they went to Almaty, the largest city in Kazakhstan, to get their visas, they were desperate to find a pet store to buy a leash. At this point in the interview, that memory sparked emotions for Anissa – she opened her eyes wide, plopped her hand over her mouth, half laughed, and half coughed in disbelief. She told her interpreter she knew it sounded bad, but they had a hard time corralling her. Since then, Ava has gotten lost on several occasions – at parks, zoos, etc. She wanders and doesn't stay with the family.

When the kids were in the orphanage, they spoke two different languages; Max spoke Russian, and Ava spoke Kazakh. Because Max was blonde-haired and blue-eyed, the staff had him in the Russian group, whereas Ava was in the Kazakh group because she looked Mediterranean. The siblings couldn't understand each other, but she would try to hug him and speak to him in Kazakh. And to reward her efforts, he would punch her in the face.

Anissa and her husband had learned some Russian before going to Kazakhstan but got a crash course in Kazakh from their interpreter so they could better manage their wild three-year-old daughter. Their linguistic efforts were focused on her and not Max, who was quiet, sweet, cute, and younger. The first time Anissa spoke Russian to Max, "Give me your hand," he gave her a look, like "Oh, crap." While in Kazakhstan, anytime they spoke with the kids, they used English, Russian, and Kazakh. After returning to the United States, they phased out the Russian first, and then the Kazakh, eventually transitioning entirely to English. However, now, if their kids are in trouble, she still speaks to them in Kazakh, saying things like, "Knock that shit off." They appreciate it because it doesn't embarrass them in public. She said, "I'm still saying it but in another language."

> *"It's been wild. It's been great. I wouldn't change a thing. It's hard for the kids because they have to work so much harder to pay attention in school … to claim their bodies and brains. It's not that they're deficient. It's the way their brains function."*

When they first came back as a family to the United States, they cocooned themselves in their home so the kids could adjust. Anissa couldn't even take them to the library because they were so feral (she laughs about it now). Some of their friends bailed on them, which was upsetting for Anissa. She had assumed that when they got their kids, they could play with their friends' kids because they were similar in ages. Unfortunately (or perhaps, fortunately), she discovered who their true friends were.

Developmentally, Max has reached his milestones but at a slower pace than neurotypical children. When Anissa first held him in the orphanage, he didn't know how to grip as babies do – he would just dangle there. She also had to teach him how to cry because he didn't know how. She thought that made sense for a baby in an understaffed orphanage – he learned not to cry when he was hurting because nobody would come, the inverse of "Peter and the Wolf." He has a sensory processing disorder with regard to touch, sight, and sound. For him, gently touching him feels like someone is twisting his sunburned arm. When he was younger, he would protect himself by biting anyone who got too close. Given a choice between "fight or flight," he chose fight. Anissa's family celebrated when he got through his first dentist appointment without biting the dentist. They also celebrated when he got through a haircut without yelling. It took Max a few months to hug his parents. As a teenager, he still can't handle a full-on frontal hug – but will hug from the side.

Ava has always been very accepting and compassionate with her brother. She would stand up for him and "mothered" him. Early on, to relieve Ava of her motherly duties, Anissa would ask her, "Who's the mama?" Ava would answer, "Mama's the mama." As time passed, Ava grew to realize that her younger brother has more severe issues than she does. Unlike Max, when given a choice between "fight or flight," Ava initially chooses flight and then internally retreats. Max and Ava had to learn how to bond when they were brought into the family due to a lack of touch in the orphanage. Ava would climb all over Anissa, whereas Max didn't want any touch. Their grandparents favored Ava because she asked for the attention. Max had a hard time bonding with them but ultimately became close with Anissa's dad because, for years, he patiently waited while respecting Max's space. Anissa once caught them eating brownies at 7 in the morning. At 8 years old, when he finally hugged his grandmother for the first time, she almost cried. Anissa pointed out, "If you want the kids to meet you on *your* terms, you're going to be sorely disappointed."

The school has been fantastic about empathetically meeting the kids "on their level." In a conversation about Ava, one principal told Anissa, "You have to remember she suffered a lot of loss in her short life." The kids see Adoption-Competent Therapists.

Adoption trauma never goes away. The loss and despair are real.

*"You never know what you're going to get as a parent. You just
don't – biologically or adoptive. We did know before we adopted*

207

them. We felt we could give them the resources they needed to be successful and happy. That's what's important to me – that they feel fulfilled. They're good kids. Don't get me wrong, the kids drive me nuts sometimes. I can handle the adoption-related stuff. I can't handle typical surly teenage stuff. I have no patience for that."

Anissa has heard the classic, "You're not my real mom" argument, to which her reply was, "Oh yeah? *Actually*, I am. I love you, and you are my *real* child." (Insert hot attitude with the head moving in a side-to-side bob and weave with a pointing finger perfectly in sync.) During those times, Anissa said she has to realize it's not about her.

Then will go cry quietly in the corner.

Anissa said that their adoption story belonged to her and her husband until they actually adopted the kids – "then it wasn't about us anymore." It is the same being a biological parent. She said, "The difference is that they have so much extra baggage, so, soooo much extra shit they have to wade through." It manifests differently in both siblings. Max doesn't seem interested in his biological family, whereas Ava is very curious. The disparate interest levels parallel Anissa's husband and his sister's stories. Her husband has zero interest in meeting his biological family, but his younger sister was very curious. She found them in her late teens but was crushed when she didn't have the fairy tale she had previously imagined.

Ava and Max know that their biological parents never took them home after they were born. They also know that their birth mother chose to drink "a shit-ton" of alcohol when she was pregnant. They know their disabilities are not due to an organic or naturally occurring condition. Ava wrestles with the knowledge that she has depression because of her birth mother's choices. She wrestles with reconciling the fantasy of her birth mother and the knowledge of her FASD. Anissa tries to teach Ava to be compassionate for her birth mother: maybe she didn't have much of a choice, maybe she didn't consciously make that choice to drink, maybe she had alcohol exposure in the womb herself because of Russia's cheap vodka.

Many sources have reported that alcohol is a significant revenue source for the Russian government and is used as a tool to gain compliance from the masses. An article in *The Atlantic* reported some historians claim that "heavy consumption of alcohol was also used as a means of reducing political dissent and as a form of political suppression."[33] Anissa tells her kids they have every right to feel angry, but also asks them to consider how will they choose to deal with this.

Are they willing to mix grace and compassion into their anger, or will they choose only anger?

After getting the okay from their therapist, Anissa shared the adoption paperwork with Ava. Anissa said, "That's some hard shit to hear." It was hard for Ava to hear how her birth mother was characterized on legal documents as amoral and living an amoral life. She hasn't quite wrapped her head around it but is getting the tools and support she needs from Adoption-Competent Therapists. Anissa hopes it is enough to help Ava with her anxiety and depression.

> *"Not knowing about one's birth parents sucks. But knowing their story doesn't necessarily make it any better either."*

Ava's fantasy bubble was burst when she read her adoption documentation. Before reading those, she thought her birth mother gave her up for adoption because she couldn't take care of her. She viewed it through "rose-colored glasses." However, Ava was forced to face her reality through the clinical and dispassionate words describing how her birth mother's parental rights were taken away. Social services took three children away from her when they were between 5 months and 3 years old.

While in Kazakhstan, Anissa and her husband discovered that the "dynamic duo" also had an older half-sister, Anastasia, in another orphanage. They tried to adopt her. Unfortunately, even though they lined up the paperwork, Kazakhstan blew up its international adoption program when joining the Hague Convention in 2009. The convention is an international agreement that "provides safeguards for children and families involved in adoptions between participating countries and also works to prevent the abduction,

---

[33] Fedun, Stan. "How Alcohol Conquered Russia." *The Atlantic,* 25 Sep. 2013. www.theatlantic.com/international/archive/2013/09/how-alcohol-conquered-russia/279965/. Accessed 29 Oct. 2020.

sale, or trafficking of children."[34] The United States signed the Hague Adoption Convention in April of 2008, while other countries have signed at different times (currently, 86 countries are members). While the safeguards for orphans are absolutely needed globally, sadly, the timing of when Kazakhstan entered into the program prohibited Anissa and her husband from legally adopting Ava and Max's half-sister.

Ava and Anastasia have been processing the knowledge of their birth mother together through a phone video app. The communication with Anastasia has helped keep the kids connected to their heritage. Anissa has encouraged that relationship. Ava has been in Russian Outschool classes, and Anastasia has been studying English for several years. For Anastasia's birthday, the kids wanted to give her American candy. Anissa wanted her to have sturdy cold weather socks. $200 and 17 sugar varieties later, they sent her a package of socks and sweets. Anastasia sent them a picture of herself on her bed surrounded by her candy (but not the socks).

Anissa's family indulges in Russian food. They eat pelmeni – traditional Russian dumplings with pork, beef, onions, and dill (served with a side of sour cream). The dumplings originated in Siberia when the moms and the aunties would come together to make them. They would store the finished dumplings in the snow all winter. The kids love the pelmeni and borscht (purple beet soup with cabbage and beef) and plov (rice pilaf with lamb). During International Week at school, Anissa brought in vegetarian plov to share with the class while sitting on small, felt rugs they brought from Kazakhstan. They read books from Central Asia like *Peter and the Wolf*. Kazakhstanis are not ethnically Mongolian, but rather Russian and Azari (Azerbaijan) descendants.

While in Kazakhstan, they befriended another family who was also adopting a young girl from the same orphanage. They have kept in touch with them and recently met up with them at Kazapalooza, an event that started as a group of Kazakh adoptive families getting together. It has now turned into a charity festival of 150 families descending upon Frankenmuth, Michigan

---

[34] Child Welfare Information Gateway. "The Hague Convention on Intercountry Adoption." www.childwelfare.gov/topics/adoption/preplacement/intercountry-adoption/hague-convention/. Accessed 28 Oct. 2020.

(Michigan's little Germany). They raise money for an organization in Kazakhstan that helps single moms who had grown up in orphanages and then became single moms themselves as they aged out of the system. It provides housing, schooling, and job training for the mothers. The United States families have a weekend of fun with other people who understand the journey. They stay together at the Bavarian Inn. The kids play games, go to the pool, and make crafts. There is a silent auction with flags, ornaments, knitted and crocheted items, etc. Everyone is able to get the extended Kazakh experience. When they were in Michigan, Ava said her skin was vibrating because she was "with her people." Both she and Max have Kazakh flags in their rooms and bumper stickers on their doors. They own a Yurt (a felt round tent used by the Mongolian and Kazakh tribes). The total darkness the handmade felt provides is just as comforting as embracing other families also living their Kazakh adoption journeys.

While the common threads of their experiences bond the adoptive families, outsiders can be cruel in their ignorance. For example, when Ava was in the fourth grade, she and her best friend (who was adopted from Guatemala) were bullied by kids who told them, "Your parents are dead, they don't love you." Anissa noted, "It pissed me off – and still does - when people say 'oh, your kids are so lucky.' Pisses me off. My response – rather than jumping down their throats – is 'I think my husband and I are the lucky ones.' People say stupid shit all the time about adoption to adoptees."

> *"Adoption is messy ... It's awesome, it's awful, it's everything in between."*

To help sort out the messiness, Anissa's kids go to an adoptee camp where they are able to talk about the adoptive experience in a safe environment. Many of the social workers are adoptees themselves. They can process the "goods" and the "bads," along with the "highs" and the "lows." Participants are of many different races. To help her kids, Anissa has read a plethora of adoption books (her daughter tires of her sentences starting with, "I read this book ..."). Anissa said Sherrie Eldridge's book, *Twenty Things Adopted Kids Wish Their Adoptive Parents Knew*, blew her away. It helped her understand the loss that adoptees feel. Anissa feels she really "got it" when she had to help her own kids walk through it. Sherrie's book helped her realize that adoption is not about *her*. She also recommends Kirk Martin's *Celebrate Calm* because it taught her self-control as a parent. She attended one of his speaking engagements; she said some of the best advice was from Kirk: Never look a teenage girl in the eye.

Since receiving that advice, when engaging Ava in a disagreement, Anissa looks down and to the left – because if she sees an eye roll, it will send her over the edge. (No doubt, millions of mothers can relate!)

Anissa's mantra is: Information is power. She concluded the interview by saying, "It's been a wild ride. They're awesome kids."

~ Advice Through Anissa's Lens ~

For prospective adoptive parents: "Do your research. Do your homework. The important stuff isn't physically taking care of the kid. You have to be aware of the loss and grief that your child is going to experience. And they will experience it. You have to be aware of how it's going to come out, and you have to give them the tools to deal with it. Realize that once you have the child, it's not about you anymore. Yes, it's about the relationship. The relationship is more important than homework. The bumps in the road that you'd experience with a 'typical' child will be different. It will be centered around identity, loss, and the inevitable fantasies about what their life could be like when they're mad at you. When they stop talking out loud, they're thinking about their biological family. It's not about you. [It's about] giving them what they need."

Anissa believes that biological parents probably see their kids as extensions of themselves. Therefore, adoptive parents need to make the distinction; their kids come with different DNA embedded with their biological ancestors' experience. Trauma was the catalyst for adoption. There are things that adoptive parents will never know, and yet it's going to manifest itself somehow. Shortly after returning to the United States, Anissa read the neuropsychological evaluation about her children's FASD. When she saw the words "Fetal Alcohol Spectrum Disorder" in print, it really hit her. She and her husband knew about it before they met their kids, but the *official diagnosis* made her weep. She allowed it to floor her for 48 hours and then picked herself up off that floor. Initially, she thought her kids would not have time for fun because they would always be in therapy. She was wrong. They have been able to find ways to have fun. For example, Max is in the

Challenger division of Little League Baseball, the adaptive program for kids with physical and intellectual challenges. Anissa's family has found "their people" through that. Most of the time, he chats with his buddy who was assigned as his neurotypical match.

Many adoptive parents don't want their kids to know they're adopted. Anissa disagrees with that approach. She said that knowledge of their adoptions does not undermine their happiness; it makes them richer as people.

My Thoughts, My Lens

I agree with Anissa. Knowledge is power. The more I read, the more I interview people affected by adoption, the more I unclench. For years, I ignored my feelings about my adoption, and the dark ignorance was slowly eroding my spirit. In the words of Brené Brown:

> *"Denying our stories and disengaging from emotion – means choosing to live our entire lives in the dark. When we decide to own our stories and live our truth, we bring our light to the darkness."*[35]

Anissa harnessed knowledge to help her children live in the light. When she said, "Adoption is messy," I immediately thought, *"Yep."*

Adoption is an amalgam of grace, fear, joy, anger, and love, which pushes us to know WHY we exist.

> *"Struggle happens. We give our children a gift when we teach them that falls are inevitable and allow them to participate in a loving, supported rising strong process."*[36]

The building blocks welded together by Anissa's strength and energy will surely help her children understand and know their complex stories as they navigate the challenges that accompany adoption.

---

[35] Brown. *Rising Strong*, p. 75.
[36] Ibid., p. 154.

Mary R. | Teacher

Iowa
Year of Adoption: 1989

When I met Mary, the juxtaposition of her being both timid and fiercely protective struck me as intriguing. She was extremely loyal to her daughter. It was apparent that she worked hard to create a safe nest for her family. While I found her to be cautiously reserved, she shared a portion of her growth and awareness journey. As an elementary school teacher for 40 years, she had learned to be in tune with her students' incongruous family dynamics. It was obvious that the devotion she had for her students also permeated her personal life.

Over three decades ago, Mary went down the infertility path of many tests and even a few surgeries. She said, "We didn't have the sophisticated procedures for infertility they do now." She struggled with the guilt of being jealous of her friends and relatives who were having babies effortlessly. The only thing that helped her was a short book written by a woman who graphically described her feelings of resentment and shame. Mary found solace in knowing that someone else had harbored the same taboo, angry feelings of injustice. After prayer, she and her husband decided to adopt because they knew they would have a baby in the end. After a long 6-year process of home studies, questions, and assessments, Mary's father died. On the day they were finalizing funeral arrangements, she received a phone call from a social worker with the news they had a baby girl named Leigh. When they learned that she was born on the same day her father had died, Mary *knew* it was divine intervention.

Recently, Mary had a tussle with grace. During her infertility treatments, she was very private and chose to hide her pain from her friends and relatives. Year after year, more babies arrived, but she and her husband had to leave holiday gatherings with no children of their own. She never expressed how much she suffered, especially when they would complain about things like

"only having boys and no girls." She reserved her struggle for herself; they never knew about her grief. However, recently, one relative had to experience the pain of infertility through her daughter's eyes (Mary's niece). Over lunch, the mother told Mary that she did not realize the agony of infertility. She said, "Your heart must have been broken every time we said, 'I'm pregnant, I'm pregnant.'"

Uh, yeah.

Mary now understands that they were young and consumed with their own lives, never recognizing how hard it was for her. She decided not to dwell on how she felt wronged so many years ago. She reached out to her niece to let her know that she had not forgotten the pain of infertility and would be there if she had any questions or needed support.

Mary recalled that her anguish vanished when she and her husband adopted Leigh. Instantaneously. The painful memories. The painful days. The painful holidays. Gone. Philosopher Lao Tzu is credited with saying, "New beginnings are often disguised as painful endings." Mary characterized it as,

"It was like the pain of childbirth but worth it."

Leigh had been staying with a foster family for three weeks. During that time, Mary and her husband drove a few hundred miles to meet them and their social worker. The foster family gave them letters and a journal detailing Leigh's time with them. They also received a box of things from the birth family, including a blanket, a fancy dress, other clothing, and letters for Leigh. The birth mother, grandmother, and great-grandmother explained in the letters that Leigh was special to them and was loved. But because her birth mother was only 18 years old, she was not in a position to raise her.

When Leigh was 20 years old, Mary gave the letters to her. In hindsight, she questions whether she misjudged the timing and should have given them to her sooner. She said, "All of a sudden, she was 20 … Who knows if I made a mistake?" Mary said she *wasn't* consciously *not* giving her the letters but wonders if she held off subconsciously. Mary had deliberated over the years, trying to decide what the perfect time would be. Mary said she didn't want to say anything that would hurt Leigh or be misinterpreted.

For the first five years of Leigh's life, Mary wrote letters to the birth parents, letting them know about Leigh's development. For Leigh, she kept a touching journal that contained yearly letters "Dear Leigh, from Mom." It was like keeping a diary of life events. Mary gave me the privilege of reading the first letter. She wrote to Leigh about the initial phone call with the social worker and the preparations for her arrival. She told her that their friends and relatives were so excited about her arrival that they threw Mary a surprise baby shower. Mary even described the beautiful spring day they had when they drove to pick her up. She recounted the love that everyone shared, how blessed they were, and how they just wanted to show her off to the world. When Mary and her husband brought Leigh home, many people came to their home to welcome her.

From the time Leigh was little, she knew she was adopted. When she was four years old, she asked, "Why didn't my Mommy want me?" Mary told her it was because she was young, wasn't married, and wanted Leigh to have a better life with both a mom and a dad. The answer satisfied Leigh, and occasionally – over the years – she toyed with writing a letter to her birth mother but then would get busy with her life and never got around to it.

For a short period after the adoption was finalized, Mary experienced a twinge of fear. They had friends who were foster parents on track to adopt, but the birth mother changed her mind and took her child back. She described it as "not actual fear" but something that stayed in the back of her mind. She knew their situation was different because their adoption was locked down legally. As Leigh grew older and their mother-daughter relationship got stronger, Mary's initial worry was replaced with curiosity. When they visited Leigh's birth city, she watched random strangers and wondered, could that be her birth mom? How about her? Or what about that woman? Mary is now at the point where she would like to meet Leigh's birth mother. She is respectful and grateful for the gift of family that she and her husband received. Mary would be supportive if Leigh wanted to initiate a search for her birth mother. However, she is cautious because it could be a "wonderful meeting or it could be a heartache." She said,

"Right now, faith trumps fear."

This past year, she and her husband had a near-death experience. They had carbon monoxide poisoning and had to be flown out of state for treatment. Leigh had to sign their medical directives because they were unconscious, and the doctors told her that she might lose them both. Throughout Leigh's life, Mary was the protector but that night, in Mary's words, "Leigh stood up to the plate" and, at 30, protected her parents that night. That incident changed the bond of their relationship. It gave everyone involved a renewed perspective on the preciousness of life.

~ Advice Through Mary's Lens ~

For adoptive parents: "Have an open mind. Do the best you can." Show love and support. Provide opportunities. Expose them to their culture if it is different. Provide the most caring environment you can. Model good character and teach spiritual values.

For adoptees: "Be open with your parents ... pray they're open with you." Understand that your parents may not have the answers, but sometimes, they do.

My Thoughts, My Lens

Ever the diligent teacher, Mary was highly involved with composing this chapter from start to finish. She carefully chose her words to ensure there were no misunderstandings. I respect Mary's rationale – she said she didn't want to unintentionally hurt the feelings of her loved ones. I'm sure it was hard for her to open up to a complete stranger.

Ultimately, I knew Mary's story needed to be included in my book because of the kindness she showed to her niece. It saddens me that Mary carried her infertility grief in silence, but at the same time, I admire her for finding the courage to support her niece who was experiencing the same anguish – despite Mary not having that support herself decades ago. I do wonder how many people are capable of doing what Mary did:

How many people on this Earth compassionately choose to give purpose to their past struggles?

I'm not so sure I would have done the same. I sometimes default to being a cranky old lady. At times I think, *[insert gravelly voice]* "Well, since I struggled about such and such, you should, too. By gosh, you young Gen Z'er!" It is a good thing not everyone is like me; the world doesn't need more hardheaded fools. One of my biggest challenges in life is learning how to impart mercy. I am masterful in the art of carrying a grudge – my husband knows this well. Sometimes I wonder if my whole life (up until this point) has been about carrying a grudge about my adoption.

But seriously, how exquisite was it that Mary was able to rise up and offer her young relative the gift of grace?

Reese S. | Acupuncturist

New York
Year of Adoption: 2009

When Reese and I met via FaceTime, my tired old iPad cropped her face off at the bottom. I could only see her doe-like eyes for most of the interview. Her mellow countenance matched her docile personality I had known for nearly three decades. She and I both moved away from the city where we met, and we became busy with our own families. Although we hadn't spoken for 13 years, seeing her again was as natural as it was when we hung out together in person.

For a long time, Reese and her husband Joe wanted to have a family, but it didn't work out for them biologically. She had two extremely physically painful miscarriages. After the first one, fear overtook her, and she obsessed about having another one. Sadly, her fears came true, catalyzing a change in their journey to start a family. They decided that the route for them would be to adopt a child who wanted to be loved. Unlike many other mothers, Reese didn't feel the need to mourn the loss of biologically bringing a child into the world. She said, "In all honesty, I really felt it was not in the cards for me to be pregnant and give birth to a child." Reese and Joe believe that they were *meant* to have their son, Jaeden. They adopted him when he was ten months old. The only regret Reese has is that she wasn't able to see his birth or be with him for the first ten months of his life. As an acupuncturist, when Reese's patients or friends shared their newborn stories, it was hard for her to relate to them. But after listening to many accounts, she laughed as she said, "Actually, I'm glad I skipped the pregnancy and the birth."

For Reese, adoption was a natural decision because she has adoptees in her family. She is an only child and White; Joe is Chinese. They wanted to adopt internationally and researched different countries. They decided against China because of the five-year wait time. They had already tried to have children for many years. Reese was *ready* to be a mom much sooner. They turned to Vietnam and initiated the adoption process. However, they had to change their focus because Vietnam's borders were shutting down. The U.S. had stopped approving Vietnamese immigration documentation; they were investigating allegations of mothers selling their infants.

Not wanting to take that risk, Reese and Joe switched their sights on South Korea. They worked with an adoption agency in Connecticut. Reese has fond memories of the social worker (who had also been adopted from South Korea). The process moved quickly. Six months later, they were matched with Jaeden. He was placed with a foster family when he was five months old, staying with them until he was ten months old – when Reese and Joe adopted him. Reese said the foster family was "awesome." Jaeden was their first foster child, and they treated him like their own. Reese and Joe corresponded with the family before going to Korea. The family sent them pictures along with a lengthy description of Jaeden. After he was adopted, they sent another letter with a photo album of his time in their home.

Reese and Joe stayed in Korea for a week, enjoying the country as they prepared to take Jaeden home. The first time they saw Jaden was very brief – they were with the social worker at the foster family's apartment. Reese said it wasn't a monumental moment because they weren't allowed to take him at that time. However, it was absolutely monumental when they got to have him a few days later. Reese started crying the minute she walked into the room (Jaeden's foster mom was crying, too). She said, "It was ridiculous. It was great. He was happy." Reese was too emotional to hold him. Joe had to carry him out because she thought she might drop him. What she remembers the most was that Joe kept kissing Jaeden's cheeks.

Reese and Joe had prepared themselves for a baby that might be traumatized by their adoption. They had read the research that showed adoption is an immense process for them. Some babies are overwhelmed by the difference in language and the different smells and sounds. However, Jaeden was not traumatized. He was excited. The first night, he woke up giggling and laughing. In the 1990s, the Korean adoption agencies did not allow adoptive parents from other countries to take Korean adoptees in public (as demonstrated by Liv O.'s story in this book). They were only allowed to take the infants directly to the airport. However, in 2009, Reese and Joe were allowed to have him the day before they left the country. The plane ride was easy; the flight attendants were familiar with U.S. adoptions of Korean infants and were very helpful. Jaeden slept in a bassinet that hooked on the wall in the bulkhead aisle.

Upon returning to New York, Jaeden didn't take his bottle for a while because he had a bad case of nasal congestion. Other than that, the transition went very smoothly. Reese was ready to be a parent. She cherishes the time that she and Jaeden share. She was able to "hang out" at home with him during the weekdays while attending acupuncture school on the weekends. After two weeks of being back in the U.S., she took him to a pediatric visit. The pediatrician said something like, "Wow, you've only had him for two weeks; you don't really know him." Reese was offended and thought, "What are you talking about???" She remembers feeling like he had already belonged to her for a long time – she had stared at his photograph for months before their trip to South Korea.

She changed pediatricians.

The second pediatrician was just as insensitive, asking Reese how much they paid for him. The third pediatrician was better, but Jaeden didn't like her. In Reese's experience, New Yorkers do not hold back their curiosity. A neighbor in their building also wanted to know how much they paid for Jaeden. However, unlike other transracial adoptive families' experiences, Reese was surprised that they were never questioned about his ethnicity. Many interracial families exist in New York, whereas interracial families are less common in other parts of the country where populations lean more homogenous. New York nannies are often of a different race than the children they watch, so Reese's playground experience consisted of casual questions like, "Oh, is he with you?" or "Oh, are you his mom?"

When Jaeden was four years old, he understood the concept of adoption when they adopted their cats but didn't have a strong reaction. Similarly, when he learned about his adoption (at nine years old), he didn't react negatively. He already had an inkling because somewhere along the way, he had picked up the knowledge that he didn't "come out of Reese's belly." He started asking her questions about his birth, but she kept putting it off because she wanted to find a good time when she and Joe could sit down with Jaeden together. However, it didn't happen that way. She finally decided that she needed to tell him, and "for whatever reason, it happened naturally." It wasn't like a big "sit down – we have something to tell you." Reese wasn't even sure what Jaeden's exact question was because it wasn't a jarring event. She thinks he might have been asking about the hospital where he was born. After she told him his story, she could tell he was processing her answer. When she brought out the photo album from his foster mom, he was very touched and thought it was very special that they took care of him.

Reese and Joe wanted to make sure they were the ones to tell him about his adoption – instead of him randomly hearing it from someone else. Although she felt it was definitely Jaeden's story, she felt guilty that family and friends knew about his adoption before he did. She was uncomfortable with other people knowing – of course, family knew, a few friends knew, people in the building knew (because they had never seen her pregnant). And it was troublesome to her.

Although many children learn of their adoption at a younger age, listening to the advice of Jaeden's therapist, Reese and Joe waited longer to tell him because he is a special-needs child. Special-needs children process their emotions differently. Reese prefers to keep his clinical diagnosis private because labels are often associated with them. When Jaeden was younger, he was very aggressive due to his chemical sensitivities to artificial colors and flavors. Once they detoxed him, his behavior changed dramatically. They considered putting him on medication, but they opted to treat the root of the special needs. Many other families choose medication. In Reese's opinion, that is not always a bad thing. She believes it takes a collaborative effort with therapists and medical doctors to determine how each child can succeed.

Jaeden also has sensory sensitivity. Reese assumes he wasn't held much for the first five months of his life. When they were in South Korea, she and Joe were not allowed to see the floor where the infants were kept at the agency. Reese always wondered if that lack of stimulation during the first five months of Jaeden's life played a role in his receptiveness. He could be inflexible at times, becoming disproportionately angry at things that were seemingly innocuous to others. Developmentally, babies are very self-oriented until around age two. However, Jaeden never came out of that phase. He still sees things from his perspective. He goes to a special needs school and has a very strong need for attention. Reese wonders which factor plays a role in his perception. Adoption? Special needs? Only child? He requires external regulators, such as structure and positive behavioral support at school, because he does not have internal regulators like mainstream population kids do.

Reese talked about the YouTube influencer who adopted an Asian child but then gave him up for adoption when he was diagnosed with special needs. She was careful not to condemn the YouTuber but said, "Definitely thoughts come into your mind, but that's part of processing – you realize you're a special needs family. I would never say I had the thought of returning Jaeden. I realized he was *so* meant to be ours. We had a 5-year span of trying to have a baby. We were so ready to have a baby. He was meant to be *ours*."

She did say that when she had negative thoughts about Jaeden's special needs, she had to *consciously choose* to look at the big picture.

Jaeden loves the fact that he's from South Korea. Reese assumes it's because they already have Asian culture in their family, with Joe being Chinese. She also practices Chinese medicine along with acupuncture. They eat Asian food. Both Korean and Chinese people celebrate Lunar New Year. Joe wants Jaeden to understand his Korean culture. The two even watched a Korean movie together recently. Reese wonders what adoptee percentages are special needs vs. neurotypical. In an article from Disabled-World.com, "The number of children waiting to be adopted shows that from thirty to fifty percent experience a form of developmental disability."[37] Included in those percentages are very mild to severe cases. The article also points out, "Parents who have adopted children with disabilities feel they receive far more from the experience than they give."[38] According to the CDC in 2011, fifteen percent of all American children have a developmental disability.[39]

---

[37] "Adoption of Children with Disabilities." *Disabled World,* 13. Jan. 2011. www.disabled-world.com/editorials/disability-adoption.php#:~:text=Synopsis%20and%20Key%20Points%3A,a%20form%20of%20developmental%20disability. Accessed 2 Nov. 2020.

[38] Ibid.

[39] Shute, Nancy. "CDC: Developmental Disabilities Affect 1 In 7 U.S. Kids." *Shots, Health News from NPR,* 23 May 2011. www.npr.org/sections/health-shots/2011/05/23/136582348/cdc-developmental-disabilities-affect-1-in-7-u-s-kids#:~:text=Fifteen%20percent%20of%20American%20children,for%20Disease%20Control%20and%20Prevention. Accessed 2 Nov. 2020.

(In a later article the estimate was updated to one in six, or seventeen percent.)[40]

Reese talked about the healing theory that children come into the world with history. For example, two generations ago, someone could have gone through the holocaust. A grandchild is born, and they have residual emotional and physiological anxiety. She speculates that perhaps "Jaeden is coming with all of these ancestors we don't know about." Given Jaden's disposition, it seems his ancestors were good-natured. They must have been good friends with Reese's ancestors, given her lovely gentle countenance.

~ Advice Through Reese's Lens ~

For adoptive parents: "Just love your baby and be grateful for them. That's it. Just be grateful. It's a gift to have a child this way."

---

[40] Centers for Disease Control and Prevention, Page last reviewed: 12 Nov. 2020. www.cdc.gov/ncbddd/developmentaldisabilities/facts.html. Accessed 11 May 2021.

My Thoughts, My Lens

When I asked Reese if she would be interviewed for my book, she reminded me that we had a conversation about 25 years ago about my adoption. Apparently, when she asked me about it, I shrugged it off. I have no recollection of that conversation, but my defense strategy doesn't surprise me. For the latter part of my adult life, if someone asked me about my adoption, I deflected or changed the subject. (Although, early on, it didn't occur to me that I could simply say I didn't want to talk about it.) I didn't want to be vulnerable. The rage I felt was ugly, and I detested the thought of examining my own eclipsed insides. It took me half a century to be able to peel back the layers.

I told Reese I always felt like I was White. Everyone in my family was White. It didn't occur to me that when I looked in the mirror, an Asian face glared back at me. Reese said she understood – because when she lived in China for two years, she was the ethnic minority. She often had dinner with Joe's parents and wanted to look like them. She's convinced she was Asian in another life. That made me smile. If humans actually do have other lives, I'm sure that she and I were friends in that one, too.

Anna B. | Dental/Orthodontic Assistant

North Dakota
Years of Adoption: 1992 & 1994

When Anna and I met, she was relaxed and nestled in a comfy chair. She looked poised to open a novel and sip from a cup of tea. Recently widowed, she seemed to have that certain repose as only one who has journeyed with a long-time spouse can understand, like she had been resting for a while after stepping off a tilt-a-whirl. Anna struck me as uncomplicated and good-natured.

The first thing Anna told me was that she knew a woman who chose adoption after giving birth to a baby girl in high school. That woman moved on with her life and had a family of her own, unaware that she and her biological daughter lived in the same town. The astonishing part was that she was unknowingly carpooling with her biological daughter's family!

At the time, as an adoptive mother of two girls, that story was very threatening to Anna. Her girls were still young, and she felt vulnerable to losing them if they found their birth mothers. She worried that they would like them more than her. Since Anna was always the disciplinarian, she worried that she would end up being their scapegoat. She prepared herself for them to use their adoptions against her. Anna's husband, John, told her she was being ridiculous. But in Anna's mind, because he was the "fun" parent, of course, he wasn't worried. The other reason she thought John wasn't worried was that most adoptees prioritize finding their birth mothers, not their birth fathers. As the girls grew older and became teenagers, Anna feared that they did not view her as their legitimate mother. Her oldest daughter, Erica, did lash out once and said that she and her husband were not her "real" parents. In that moment, Anna's fears were realized. She wondered if her daughter really believed what she said. But because she had prepared herself for that type of event to happen, she was able to move beyond it. Looking back, she understands her daughter was just going through a typical "ugly teenage" phase, and it never happened again.

When their girls became adults, Anna no longer feared their birth mothers. She said,

"It's really humbling when your kids grow up."

During the year after John passed away, Anna's friends and family told her how much both of her girls appreciate their childhood and Anna and John's loving relationship. Anna talked about how her late husband parented with an "all in" philosophy. If they had a party, it had to be a *great* party. If they went on vacation, it had to be a *memorable* vacation. She laughed and said John's philosophy was, "If we weren't going to have good food and good booze, then let's not even do it." Hearing that the girls appreciated their parenting style caused her fears surrounding their adoptions to dissipate. In fact, she has become so secure that when their youngest daughter, Alex B. (whose story is also in this book – see the table of contents), recently found her birth mother, Anna was surprised by her own reaction because she was genuinely happy for her.

Anna and John adopted their two daughters in North Dakota. Erica is White. Alex is half Chinese and half White. When Anna and John applied for adoption, they specified they wanted healthy babies with birth mothers who did not abuse alcohol or drugs. They did not specifically request White babies. Within six months of adopting Erica, they were eligible to reapply for a second adoption. The agency called and said they had a "special needs" adoption. As detailed in Alex's story, in North Dakota, the adoption agency classified someone who is not fully "Caucasian" as "special needs." They chose to adopt Alex because, for them, being fully White was not a factor. Anna said that Alex has been *anything but* special needs.

Anna and John met both daughters' birth mothers on the day of their placements. Both times, each birth mother literally placed her birth daughter into Anna's arms. Erica was one month old, and Alex was two months old. Both girls had been placed with foster families until their birth mothers legally relinquished their parental rights. Anna remembers that it was sweltering when they went to pick up Erica. The agency did not have air conditioning. But when the birth mother gave Anna her baby, she and John were so overjoyed that they forgot about the heat. Everyone in the room was crying. She said that for a while, she even forgot that Erica's birth mother was in the room. Anna wondered how she was able to hand her over. During the second meeting when they adopted Alex, Anna and John were able to meet the foster parents, as well. Both times, Anna was perplexed as to how the birth mothers were able to trust her and John to take their babies. She felt empathy for the birth mothers. She said that both young women were very capable, but they knew it was not their time to raise a child.

As part of the adoption agreement, Anna wrote letters to both women to give them yearly updates on the girls. She would take the letters to the adoption agency, and the agency would forward them. Anna included pictures and would always thank them for entrusting her and John to raise the girls. As the girls became older, she kept the letters to 95% positive – she didn't want the adoptive mothers to think that parenting was 100% rainbows and butterflies. She kept copies of every letter and gave them to the girls when they were adults. Erica's birth mother reciprocated with letters over the years. Alex's birth mother did not, and not hearing from her disappointed Anna. She wasn't sure if she got the letters and hoped that she was still alive.

Anna always felt that because Alex was Asian in a White family and town, she would need her birth mother's help to find her own identity. When Alex was younger, she was very reserved at home. However, after she went to Europe on a high school trip, many of the parent chaperones surprised Anna when they told her how funny and entertaining Alex had been on the trip. Anna had no idea that Alex was gregarious and wishes she had known that side of her when she was still living at home. Anna sees that side now and understands that it took a while for Alex to find her own identity.

Over the years, Anna sensitively handled issues surrounding Alex's race. Anna and her husband were good friends with a couple from Tennessee who would travel to visit them in North Dakota. One year, they accompanied Anna's family to a school assembly during which Alex read a

Norwegian book full of "uff das."[41] The husband said that he got a kick out of hearing a "Chinese girl speak Norwegian." He thought it was the funniest thing he had ever heard. Anna said to him, "Earl, what are you?" He said, "What do you mean?" Anna said, "I'm German and Dutch." He replied, "I'm Tennessee-an." Anna repeated, "Who are your ancestors?" He replied, "They're from Tennessee." Anna let his answer hang in the air like a silent gong. He later told her that he did a DNA test and discovered his ancestry.

While Alex was an extreme rule follower, Erica was the "typical naughty teenager" and is now a lovely busy mother of little ones. Anna enjoys her grandchildren. Erica and her birth mother have been in contact through email and have exchanged pictures. However, they still have not met in person. Erica wanted to travel to meet her, but it has yet to happen. Her birth mother has young children of her own, and like Erica, she is also very busy. Anna is hurt and frustrated for Erica. She could not understand why her daughter's birth mother has not tried to meet her. She said that if she were in that same situation, she would travel "around the world" to meet her birth daughter. She said that not as a judgment but from a place of empathy – unable to imagine how hard it would be to choose adoption for a child. Overall, though, Anna said, "Our girls, both of them, as far as I know, are very content and happy. They know why they were adopted. We had a great life together. We always talked about adoption. All the way up. It was never a secret."

~ Advice Through Anna's Lens ~

For adoptive parents: "Be open. Share information when they are mature enough, and always speak of adoption in a positive way."

---

[41] Griffith, Michelle. "Where does 'uff da' come from, and why to Minnesotans say it?" *Star Tribune*, 1 May 2020. www.startribune.com/where-does-uff-da-come-from-and-why-do-minnesotans-say-it/569326271/. Accessed 5 May 2021.

My Thoughts, My Lens

The story of Anna's "Tennessee-an" friend cracked me up. It reminded me of a conversation I had with a Latina when I lived in North Carolina many years ago. She and I talked about when random strangers feel entitled to know our ethnic backgrounds, asking questions they think we are required to answer. I often heard the question, "Are you Chinese or Japanese?" Whereas she was asked, "What are you?" She said she always chose to answer but then would turn the question around on them. If they didn't know their ancestry, she would follow up with a confused expression and a calm head tilt, "What do you mean you don't know?" Quizzing those people in a noncombative voice made them pause, just like the way Anna deftly and gently talked with her friend.

Anna's easy-going attitude and approach to adoption are commendable. I love that she was truly happy when Alex found her birth mother. In my experience, her selflessness is atypical. Many adoptive mothers I have met are threatened by their children's birth mothers. I can see why they feel that way because most adoptees cannot deny the pull towards their roots.

Biology is real for adoptees. The *fear* of biology is real for adoptive mothers.

When considering the adoptee's "biological pull" (from my perspective as a mother), I *know* that it is possible to love more than one child. When my second daughter was born, I did not love my first daughter less to make room for her sister. But rather, the scope of my love expanded.

Love multiplies and is inclusive, not exclusive.

By the same logic, I believe it is possible for a child to love more than one set of parents; one does not usurp the other. I believe Anna intuitively knew that, which ultimately allowed her to relax. So wise.

233

Harold & Helen Z. | Guardian Ad Litem & Account

Executive

Pennsylvania
Years of Adoption: 1999 & 2001

Harold and Helen were sensible in their approach to the interview. They each had the perfect posture of polished news anchors as they sat at their kitchen counter. As they presented the facts of their son's and daughter's adoptions, Harold was articulate, and Helen was tenderhearted. Their daughter's story is also in this book (Yan Z. – see the table of contents). It was evident they cherish their children.

For Harold and Helen, adoption felt like the normal way to start their family.

They could not have children biologically, so they changed lanes and considered different adoption avenues: domestic, international, special needs, and cross-cultural. They had mixed feelings about having a special needs child, but it turned out that they "got one anyways," as their son had issues that they didn't know about at the time of the adoption. They later found out their son has Asperger's Syndrome. They initially wanted to get some parenting experience before they took on a special-needs child, or in Harold's words, "Subjected that child to *our* parenting." In hindsight, they realized their plan was naive. They also were mindful of race and cultural differences. Harold and Helen are both White. They were aware of the experiences some of their Black friends had with prejudice. For that reason, they decided not to adopt a Black child because they thought there would be fewer instances of discrimination with children of other races. Helen pushed for international adoption because of a disastrous well-publicized news story near their home in Pittsburgh. The birth mother had lost her parental rights due to her drug abuse. However, when she kicked her addiction *several* years later, the court granted her parental rights – even though the foster family had adopted their son as a one-year-old. He was taken from the only family he consciously remembered. Helen couldn't fathom losing a child in that way and didn't want to take that risk with domestic adoption.

After researching many countries, Harold and Helen chose China. The wait was longer than in other countries, but the process was more reliable and predictable. Chinese adoptions had a reputation for being well prepared and giving accurate information about the adoptees. Many children were having difficulty being adopted in rural orphanages due to the one-child-per-family law. Harold and Helen felt there were sensible benefits with going through each planning stage. For Harold, the process itself was exciting because it was the start of their family. They went to China to adopt their son in 1999 and their daughter in 2001. Both times, they traveled with a small group of other adoptive families. As a result, all of the couples developed a strong sense of a mini-community. When they returned, they would run into the same families at Chinese cultural events in Pittsburgh. On their first trip, Harold and Helen traveled to a small province in the southern part of China to get their son. Many Chinese people would stare as the group of ten American couples walked around with their Asian babies. But many were friendly and seemed appreciative – the broad acknowledgment made Harold and Helen feel that their child was meant to be part of their family. Neither Harold nor Helen had any doubts or anxieties about what they were doing.

Helen's motherly protectiveness kicked in very quickly after adopting her kids. Strangers would say things like, "Are those *yours*?" or "Are they adopted?" Helen even encountered a nasty man at a post office who told her that her daughter needed to go back to where she came from. People would even make comments about how horrible it must be for the children to be taken away from their families at such a young age. One lady followed Helen around a department store with questions. Strangers were so tenacious with their questions to the point that Helen felt compelled to be rude and cut the conversations short. She hoped that the comments would not negatively affect her children on a deeper level.

Harold, on the other hand, had a very different experience. He never was subjected to rude comments or events that necessitated an intervention. He always felt proud to be with his children in public. He was also proud that he and Helen actively sought out their children. But looking back, he thinks that perhaps his thoughts were presumptuous – because that perspective was more about what *he* did than the little baby he was holding in his arms.

Harold and Helen believed they had a responsibility to take on their children's emotional needs. They attempted to bring Chinese culture to their family by attending cultural events and celebrating Chinese New Year. As their children became older, their son outwardly rejected his Chinese culture, while their daughter Yan yearned for information.

As Yan became older, the topic of adoption became very important to her. She went through a challenging time, not knowing who her birth parents were. On one occasion in the car, she told Helen, "I'm looking at these stars … I'm wondering if [my birth parents] can see the same stars," and then burst into tears, letting out heart-wrenching cries. It was so painful for Helen that she could hardly drive. Yan was always comfortable in expressing her feelings. Yan wanted to find her birth parents and even asked about DNA testing. Harold and Helen wanted to support her search, but it is almost impossible to find birth parents in China. Even though they always allowed Yan to take the lead in adoption conversations, Helen said it was hard not to question herself and wonders if she could have done more. The turmoil Yan shared with them at home contrasted with how she presented herself in public. She was a model child. Her teachers and coaches always gave positive feedback, saying she seemed like a happy, well-adjusted kid.

When Yan's interest in adoption was increasing, her brother's interest was decreasing. From a very young age, he rejected numerous things that were culturally intrinsic to him. He often became distraught because he felt like he was being criticized. He adopted a mantra of his own making, an "unholy trinity" of statements: "Put me in harm's way. Call a stranger. Break a bone." With his peers, he never felt as though he fit in. Sadly, he didn't feel like he was worthy of protection or respect. Being Asian with Asperger's Syndrome was a challenging combination. Even to this day, he doesn't want to talk about his adoption.

When the kids were young, Harold and Helen were active in the Pittsburgh Chinese cultural group, which included a few hundred families. Because their son didn't want to attend them when he got older, they stopped going. Looking back, Harold and Helen regret that decision because it was important to Yan. They feel they could have done better. As time went on, they saw their family as "any other" family. Unfortunately, the importance of Chinese culture slipped out of their consciousness as they became less involved with the group. Their son's and daughter's needs were very similar, but the manifestations of those needs were very different.

> *"If you become a parent expecting your kids would never be a challenge or cause you pain, then you are naive. It's not a judgment. Human relationships will cause pain. It's easier to be friends with somebody than to be a family member."*

As a Guardian Ad Litem, Harold works with dysfunctional families. Helen holds a tender place in her heart for her children, but Harold's work helps her put their family life in perspective – she feels they don't have a right to complain. On one end of their family's teeter-totter, Harold (who embraces practicality) sits with Helen (who embraces protective instincts); on the other end, reality balances their parental partnership. Through his work, he has learned how *not* to handle family situations and appreciate the particular challenges of having an international adoptive family. Helen said,

> *"I don't think about my <u>adopted</u> family. I look at it as <u>my</u> family. Even when I look at my kids, they're Asian. I'm not … but they're my kids. My siblings have their families. We have our family. Adoption is <u>how</u> we became a family."*

While they do have a few regrets, overall, Harold and Helen wouldn't change their adoption journey. In Helen's words, "Any parent, whether their children are adopted or biological, wants to take away the pain and the hard stuff." To which, Harold added, "You can't take away someone's pain, but you can help them deal with it, even if it is just being there for them."

~ Advice Through Harold and Helen's Lens ~

<u>For adoptive parents:</u> "Always try to be mindful of their particular experience and that their emotional needs might not always be apparent and come out directly. Embrace other families that have adopted. Continue [to keep] those strong bonds as your kids grow up. Recognize, acknowledge your own limits of what you can do to support your kids. Just love them."

My Thoughts, My Lens

Helen's protectiveness of her children impressed me. As adoptees, we often believe that we are not the owners of our own destinies and do not protect ourselves. The perceived lack of control was welded into our psyches at an early age by the hands of other people. I admire Helen for shielding her kids.

A parent's sacred duty is to protect their child and teach them how to create safe boundaries.

As a college student, I resented nosey co-eds who wanted to know my adoption story. Like Helen's encounters with rude strangers, I was confronted by a particularly assertive student on the university bus. I remember feeling boxed in (literally, because I had the window seat). He was an international student and thought I was one, too. When he discovered I wasn't, he peppered me with questions about my adoption. As he kept probing, I kept answering his questions, somehow unable to shut down the conversation. *No, I don't know my birth family. No, I have no desire to find them. Yes, I think my adoptive parents are my parents.* And on and on. By the time my bus stop came, I felt like I had been violated. I couldn't get off the bus quickly enough. As I pushed past him, I resisted the urge to kick him in the teeth.

Now that I have several decades of emotional distance from that situation, my advice for other adoptees is that you don't have to answer any questions from strangers that make you feel uncomfortable. It is perfectly acceptable to say you don't want to discuss it.

It is *your* story. You are not obligated to give it away.

It is crucial to face your fears and internal conflict (with people who love you or with a trustworthy Adoption-Competent therapist). But after self-assessment, put away your fears so you can move through life unencumbered. In my case, I was very young when I endured the bus ride. It didn't occur to me that I could have taken the obvious "Helen approach" of blowing him off.

239

And now I (sort of) feel bad that I wanted to kick another human in the teeth.

After thinking about the bus incident, I had an epiphany. Not understanding I could set my own boundaries spilled over into my professional world, too. I was a workaholic, trying to fulfill every request – as well as my own futile need for perfectionism and acceptance. A competitive coworker told everyone who would listen that I was a martyr, but she got it wrong. It simply didn't occur to me that I had any power. But by writing this book and meeting many phenomenal people, I have now found my power.

I appreciate Harold and Helen's pragmatic approach as adoptive parents. As a result of protecting their children and offering them empathy for many years, their son is now finding his independence, and their daughter is opening her eyes to adulthood with determination.

Sara W. | Regional HR Director

Texas
Year of Adoption: 2014

Sara had just jumped out of the shower the first time we met on FaceTime. At first glance, she startled me because I thought she was naked. I breathed easier when I saw her pretty dark brown skin was wrapped in a fancy towel with elastic around the top. She was completely uninhibited and smiley, eager to share her story like that first spring breeze clearing away the winter crud. The second time I spoke with her, new developments had happened since the first meeting. The breeze had died, leaving a gloomy pallor. Sara has a unique perspective of being both an adoptive sibling and an adoptive mother. She is the adoptive sister of Benet T.'s birth son. (His story is also in this book – see the table of contents.) Growing up with an adopted sibling helped shape Sara's parenting.

Sara's first experience with adoption occurred when she was 5 years old. Her biological parents adopted her baby brother. They wanted her to have a sibling. He was only six weeks old when the social worker put him in Sara's arms, and she instantly bonded with him. When Sara asked her parents what his name was, they asked her what she would like it to be. She said, "Thomas."

Sadly, Thomas always struggled with his adoption. When he was 6 and Sara was 11, their mother died due to diabetic complications, which compounded his adoption trauma. After her death, Sara became extremely protective of him – as many adoptive siblings do, they take on the parental role. Both she and her father "parented" Thomas. She even made him tag along on her dates so she could keep an eye on him. But because Thomas was unable to have a relationship with either his birth mother or his adoptive mother, he grew restless and destructive. Even through his contrary behavior, Sara would defend his actions. He, in turn, would defend her. When he was nine years old, Sara had a new boyfriend that Thomas did not like. On one

241

particular day, she and her boyfriend were standing on the cement church steps. Little Thomas seized the opportunity to sucker-punch the 6-foot 4-inch interloper in the crotch. That was Thomas, a cavalier rogue, constantly fighting in the present to stop the pain of his past, protecting the family he still had.

When Thomas was in his early 20s, he reunited with his birth mother, Charlotte, and his birth father, Benet, on two separate occasions. He and Benet formed a healthy bond. However, when he tried to bond with Charlotte, she did not reciprocate. According to Sara, Charlotte despised Benet so much that she transferred her resentment to Thomas. Over the years, Thomas was married twice, and each time, she bonded inappropriately with his wives. Unfortunately, she never bonded with him. For instance, when his first wife cheated on him, Charlotte threw her support behind the wife, telling Thomas that he was "nothing." Sadly, Thomas interpreted her actions as evidence that he was worthless. No love. No attention. As Sara was telling me about her brother's low self-esteem, she shook her head, grimaced, and said, "Try living it and see the pain and struggle in his eyes - and you can't do anything about it." Charlotte rarely contacted Thomas, but when she did, she manipulated him emotionally. He would fight with her, sometimes defensively, sometimes offensively. However, because he still wanted his mother's validation, he never turned her away.

Eventually, Thomas self-destructed. His descent into drugs, alcohol, and suicidal behaviors propelled him to hit "rock bottom," landing him in a long-term substance abuse private rehab program. From the safety of the facility, he has been able to make great strides within his sobriety. Sara credits Benet for Thomas's improvement. She said, "Benet makes up 150%, showing Thomas the love that he missed. Thomas loves Benet dearly. I appreciate all the love and support he gives him. Even though Thomas was going through tough trials, Benet was calling him, being supportive." Currently, Thomas is nearly finished with the program and has plans to move out in a few months. Sara is looking forward to his release and is very proud of his progress.

Even though Sara watched Thomas slide down into despair over the years, adoption was her "normal." At 40 years old, it was natural for her to decide to become a foster mother so she could adopt. She went through the rigorous foster care training and knew that she was agreeing to take on her foster child's struggles. Linda was Sara's first and only foster daughter when she came to live with her at 11 years old. After five months, Sara made it official and adopted her.

Up until her adoption, Linda's life was a series of abandonments. When she was 8, the first abandonment occurred when her mother tried to murder her and her half-siblings. Her mother admitted in court that she had intended to kill her children by driving her car as fast as possible and purposely crashing. Consequently, she lost her parental rights and was incarcerated. As a result, Linda was separated from her half-brother and half-sister. She was sent to live with her maternal grandmother, whereas they were sent to live with their grandparents in Texas. Shortly after the separation, Linda's grandmother told her they were going on a trip and flew to Texas. Her grandmother pretended they were invited to visit Linda's half-siblings and *their* grandmother. She knocked on the door, dropped Linda off, and said she would come back to get her the next day.

Her grandmother never returned – abandonment #2.

The grandmother (of Linda's half-siblings) called Child Protective Services and said, "I can't do anything with her. Come get her." Abandonment #3.

Sara was up to the challenge of being a mother, knowing that Linda felt like no one wanted her. When they met, Linda's hair clearly had not been cared for properly; it was broken and unconditioned. She was very needy and desperate to eat. Her hunger stemmed from the time when she lived with her stepfather and half-siblings. He treated her poorly and would favor his biological children over her, giving her meager portions of food while giving them as much as they wanted – in a twisted Cinderella fashion. When Linda first came to live with Sara, she was distrustful and unsure of her new environment – but very obedient. As time passed, she did the normal sneaky teenage things during most of her high school years. But she did turn off her emotions outwardly as a coping mechanism. (Sara has never seen Linda cry.) After a while, Sara won Linda's trust. Linda even told Sara she was her best friend. But Sara insisted that she call her "Mom," not her friend. At this point in the interview, Sara laughed and said that "Dream Maker" was more appropriate. Even though Linda does not show her emotions, Sara knows she loves her. Linda walks and talks just like her! Sara said, "She has my swag."

Over the years, Linda has witnessed Thomas's sadness about his adoption. Sara recalls Linda telling her that Uncle Thomas was crying about his mom. Sara said, "I knew she was sad because she talked about it, even though she didn't shed a tear." Despite his extreme sadness, Thomas supported Linda as much as he could, calling her "Niecie." They had a good relationship, but she could never completely bond with him because there were times he had to deal with his own demons.

Conversely, Linda and her adoptive grandfather, "Paw-Paw" (Sara's father), became "two-peas-in-a-pod." She loved him dearly, and he provided the father figure she never had. Unfortunately, that was short-lived; when she was 12, she and her grandfather were T-boned in a car accident. He survived but only lived for 36 days before dying. Even though it was unintentional, that loss became abandonment #4.

Linda carried the guilt of surviving, thinking she killed him because they were not supposed to be driving. (Sara had explicitly told them to not drive without her – there were too many one-way streets.) Linda had convinced him to take her to school because she had forgotten something and needed it right away. The accident sent her to another level of despair. Although she could successfully suppress her emotions, she couldn't fight off the urge to act out. She started stealing cell phones, refused to do schoolwork, and stole Sara's clothes and shoes. Knowing Linda needed intense therapy, Sara enrolled her in a 30-day inpatient treatment program. When she was discharged, the follow-up treatment consisted of monthly sessions at their house and weekly sessions at the school for a year. The stress took a toll on Sara, too, but Linda never knew how heavy her burden was. Sara believed that she could not be weak in front of Linda. She knew that if she did break down, Linda would have followed her down that path of despair.

Remarkably, despite the turmoil that pervaded Linda's life, she had the mental strength to make the honor roll throughout high school. She was academically competitive, believing she had to do far better than her peers. She had her eyes set on becoming an Occupational Therapist. Because she had come up through the foster care system, her college tuition and books would be paid for by the state. As graduation approached, Sara even bought her a car in preparation for university life. Unfortunately, when Linda turned 18, she decided that she no longer wanted to live by Sara's rules. She moved in with her boyfriend, smoked marijuana, ditched her college plans, and hasn't spoken with Sara since she left.

In many ways, Thomas and Linda had parallel lives. Their despair began when both learned to distrust women. Linda responded by running towards men. Thomas reacted by lashing out at women. (The details of his story are also in this book within Benet T.'s chapter.) Thomas is currently climbing out of his hole through intense therapy. With the certainty that only comes from personal experience, he told Sara that Linda has to hit "rock bottom" before returning. He reassured Sara that she didn't waste her time on Linda. Sara holds on to his words. Linda has kept in touch with Thomas since she moved out and once told him, "I think my mom is done with me." But he assured her Sara has not shut that door. Sara prays that Linda will come back to her with a new perspective. She said,

> *"I am going to be still …The chapter of her story hasn't closed yet."*

Sara has witnessed Thomas turning the corner and hopes that Linda will, too. She sent Linda $20, telling her to save it for getting an Uber to come home when she was ready. She is hopeful and waiting with open arms for Linda to come back.

I asked her if she would adopt Linda if she had to do it all over again. She responded, "Absolutely. I still have a whole lot of love to give."

~ Advice Through Sara's Lens ~

For adoptive parents: "We are one. We are family. I'm Mom. She's the child. The main thing both of us need to strive for is to continue to learn about each other, grow, and continue to be a family. Always be open-minded. Don't be quick to judge. You don't know other people's struggles. They had to put on that survival mentality and had no one to take care of them." Sara continued to say that adoptive parents should be patient and let nature run its course. She has no regrets at all about being an adoptive mother.

My Thoughts, My Lens

Sara's protectiveness and endless support of her brother, Thomas, reminded me of a recent study by Jana Hunsley (a sibling of adoptees), who described *parentification* as a child acting in a parent's role, writing:

> *"I felt invisible as my parents focused all their attention on my siblings' needs. I still loved that adoption was part of my family's story, and I became like a third parent in my family to help manage the chaos."*[42]

In turn, I am hopeful that with Thomas's recovery, he and Sara can help Linda find her way out of her darkness when she is ready. Sara's story intrigued me because her "eyes wide open" approach punctuated her strength of character. As an adoptive sibling, she grew up *knowing* the pain of adoption through her brother's eyes. Through foster care training, she knew that jumping into a caretaker role would put her in the challenging and troublesome situation of mothering a wounded child.

And yet, she did it without hesitation.

In my mind, the most reassuring part is that *even* on this side of their adoption story, Sara looks forward to Linda's return. And if given a choice for a "do-over," she would still make the same choice to adopt. Now *that* is devotion.

---

[42] Hunsley, Jana. "Adoptive Siblings: The Invisible Family Members." *Adoption Advocate,* No. 147, 1 Sep. 2020.
www.adoptioncouncil.org/publications/2020/09/adoption-advocate-no-147. Accessed 8 Nov. 2020.

Sue B. | Scientist

Minnesota
Year of Adoption: 1999

Initially, Sue was businesslike, matter-of-fact, and not eager to dip into her emotions. I couldn't help but wonder if she was like a duck on a river – calm on the surface but with webbed feet swimming furiously beneath. When I requested a follow-up interview (because the first conversation felt incomplete), she agreed. During that interview, her tone did a complete 180. Our conversation began by talking about how her adopted son, Mark, is acutely aware that he is "Brown." That subject seemed to tap into Sue's previously inaccessible emotional well, and then her words flowed easily from there. It was refreshing speaking with her and learning how invested she is in her family. I'm guessing her calm logical demeanor has been a pillar in her relationship with her son.

Sue and her partner, Kathy, planned to adopt from the beginning of their relationship. In fact, before meeting Sue, Kathy had tried to get pregnant but was unsuccessful. Sue said, "When I came along, *I* didn't want to get pregnant. Adoption seemed like the better route for us." Since the beginning of their relationship in 1993, they talked about adoption. They were together for six years before adopting Mark. Although they couldn't legally be married until 2014, they were mentally and emotionally married for over two decades. Knowing they wanted to adopt was a part of their plan "from the get-go."

Two years into their relationship, an event happened that "sealed the whole thing." Friends (who had adopted a child) told them that their lawyer was looking for a couple to adopt twins from North Dakota. The unexpected opportunity just fell into their laps in a round-about way. They became connected with the lawyer and the woman who was pregnant. After much deliberation, they decided, "Yes, twins!" They started down the legal path, but a month into their journey, the woman had a placental abruption, a spontaneous abortion in which the body violently expels the fetus (in this case, fetuses). Tragically, she lost the babies. Sue and Kathy felt the loss as well, going through a mourning period for about a year. As Sue described it, they had mentally committed to adoption, and it was suddenly gone. She said, "Yeah, we were very sad. A lot of sadness."

After they healed, they decided to move forward with adoption once again, debating how to go about it. Unlike the first round, they decided to go the international adoption route. They reasoned they were not legally married at that time and didn't want to deal with someone in the United States who might change their minds. After considering different countries, they chose Guatemala; they had developed a connection with the people there when they were on a church mission project. Sue describes the Guatemalans as very gentle people who really love their children. Initially, they had dismissed that as an option because Guatemalan adoptions were out of their price range. However, they learned about a Guatemalan private lawyer who could handle the adoption and charged fifteen thousand dollars less than American adoption agencies. The first step was a home study. The second step was a leap of faith. They knew somebody who knew somebody who had used the Guatemalan lawyer. Sue and Kathy were wait-listed for several months. When they finally got the email inquiring if they wanted to adopt a boy who had just been born, of course, they said yes. They didn't even think about it. Then came the paperwork stage – forms, visas, approvals, fees, etc.

The bureaucratic process took six months. It would have been shorter, but it happened during Christmastime. In Guatemala, the country shuts down for at least a month at Christmas. During that time, their son, Mark, did not stay in an orphanage like most orphans do in Guatemala – instead, he went to live with a foster family right after he was born. At the six-month mark, Sue and Kathy flew to Guatemala. The lawyer and foster family met them at the hotel. Because Sue and Kathy were pretending to be friends and not life partners, Sue refrained from crying. However, Kathy and the foster mom cried.

The lawyer did not cry.

The whole foster family came to see Mark off. On the advice of the lawyer, Sue and Kathy brought gifts for the family. In return, the family gave the new moms information (i.e., how to feed him or details about things he liked, such as riding in a car, etc.). The foster mom, in particular, was very sad – she even called the hotel the next day to see how Mark was doing. Sue noted that when he was with the family, he was "great." They all said goodbye to each other at some point, and Mark stayed with Sue and Kathy. He was fine later in the afternoon … he was okay when they went to their hotel room … he was great when they bathed him …

However, when they put him in pajamas, it suddenly dawned on him that the foster family was not coming back to get him.

Mark just cried and wailed for over an hour; he was beet-red and unhappy. It's like he used up every ounce of his energy with those cries, finally falling asleep from exhaustion. It was apparent he was mourning the loss of his foster family. But when he woke up the following day, he was ok. He never had another crying episode like that again. Sue believes all those feelings had come out during that one intense hour. She said that was the only significant outpouring of emotion he ever expressed over the foster family.

The hotel they stayed at was next to the American Embassy. Sue called it the "Adoption Hotel." It seemed like everybody there was adopting somebody from a variety of agencies. Some people had been in that hotel for three months because they came prematurely, thinking the Embassy's paperwork would be completed soon after it had been initiated. Wrong. Sue and Kathy were lucky because their lawyer gave them good advice as to when to come. They only had to stay for four days, getting Mark's passport and resolving some other paperwork. However, because their lawyer was in the country, they sailed through the Embassy's procedural requirements. He said all the appropriate things and promptly got the correct appointments, unlike many of their fellow hotel guests. Sue attributes the ease of their adoption to using an in-country lawyer.

On the plane ride, Mark was very active. Everyone on the plane held him – he got passed around. He was very happy and liked people. He only cried a little but would perk up at new faces. In 1999, before 9/11, people were allowed to meet their loved ones at the airport gates. When they arrived, Sue and Kathy waited to deplane last because they knew a huge crowd would be waiting for them; they didn't want to impede the other travelers. A big group of friends greeted them. She said, "It was a very cool landing." Mark got passed around, again. He loved it. Sue said, "I even cried a little bit … I try not to cry very much."

Sue could tell from the look in his eyes that Mark was frightened when they brought him home. However, they had a big fish tank in their living room, which calmed him down. He adjusted pretty quickly – Sue estimates it only took a few weeks. She and Kathy took consecutive leaves of absence and were with him for as long as they could be. During Sue's leave, she brought Mark to her office, and when a co-worker spoke Spanish to him, he immediately turned and looked at her. Sue said she knew he was missing the language. Even though Sue and Kathy didn't speak Spanish to Mark, he adapted quickly.

Sue had some trepidation at first, wondering if Mark would be accepted the same way her brothers' biological kids were accepted into the family.

> *"Actually, my mother likes Mark as a person a lot more than she likes them. Ha-ha. So, that fear is totally gone … [you have] fear at the beginning when you're first introducing [your child]."*

Sue said that she had other fears, too. However, after she made it past the initial introduction to her family, she realized her fears were no different than those of a biological mother.

The next few years were pretty normal. Mark went to a daycare two houses away – very convenient. Kindergarten was fine, too. However, when he started first grade, it became clear he had ADHD. Sue admitted they probably already knew that on some level. She said, "You go to the store, and other kids are standing by their parents. My kid would be climbing on the display and jumping off. He was not like the kid that wanted to pay attention." Another example she gave was when they were at the airport; Mark would hold on to the people-moving-walkway guard rails and let it drag him along the outside … having a blast. Because he spent his first-grade year running around and not paying attention, they hired a summer school tutor after his first year to help him catch up.

In early elementary school, Mark's sadness over his adoption surfaced. Since Kathy worked with children as a teacher, she was attuned to his emotional needs. She recognized that he needed to get professional help *right away*. Like other adoptive parents, it didn't occur to Sue that adoptees need to see Adoption-Competent Therapists. Sue is grateful that Kathy knew what to do and admits that she would have "muddled around" if she didn't have Kathy as a guide.

When Mark was in second grade, they brought him to a therapist who specialized in counseling adoptive children. The adoption-focused therapy taught them that Mark actually had more feelings about adoption than what he had verbalized. During one session, they shared the adoption documentation they had with Mark and his therapist. Mark hadn't seen the papers before that because Sue and Kathy felt he was too young. When he started asking about his adoption, that was a sign he was ready. The paperwork consisted of his family history written in Spanish and a poor picture of his birth mother – a photocopy of an ID card. She was unmarried with several children already and didn't feel she could manage any more. They had her health history but few other details. The only information they had on Mark's birth father was his last name.

After a few sessions, Mark wanted to discontinue therapy. He wasn't sad anymore and felt there wasn't much more to talk about. He said that he felt like he was *expected* to be sad and didn't want to keep rehashing the same theme. He appreciated learning about his history but wanted to move on. According to Sue, the base of Mark's personality is "happy."

Years later, Mark went to therapy in Junior High, but it was not adoption-based; it was general therapy focused on his school performance. He was struggling scholastically because he preferred to run off and do other things. While he enjoyed the social aspects of school, homework was always a chore. Initially, Sue and Kathy were present at the sessions, but toward the end, he went by himself (at his request).

When I asked Sue how she felt when Mark was in therapy, she said,

> *"I didn't have any feelings for myself. I was mostly concerned about him and that he would be able to work through this ... I'm not sure I could put it into words. He was sad he didn't know who his birth mother was, but he was uncomfortable talking about it. [And] because he was uncomfortable talking, it built up in him. I didn't want to put my feelings on him. I don't want to put my feelings on anybody, not just him. It's just what I'm like. I was told from a young age that people don't care as much about you as you care about yourself. Keep it to yourself if you're unhappy."*

After pausing, Sue said that sounded harsh. She was trying to say that she doesn't easily share her feelings. After the therapy, Mark seemed to be very happy. He hasn't mentioned any sadness since then.

School and organized learning muted Mark as a teenager. He was no longer the lively baby passed around on the plane coming back from Guatemala. In Sue's opinion, the American school model is not set up for ADHD children – or males, for that matter. Many boys have trouble concentrating. Now that he's in college and can choose when he wants to work, he feels freer. He loves online learning because he can do his schoolwork at 2 or 3 a.m. and sleep until noon. As a young adult in college, he's back to being his core happy self.

Sue's relationship with Mark is better than the relationship she has with her own family. She is very pleased with the young man Mark has become. In contrast, she is not emotionally close with her mother. Sue's family was originally from Lithuania, and in keeping with that culture, they are emotionally reserved. Sue has a logical personality and is not comfortable sharing her emotions. She and her mother share history but are not close and do not share their feelings. Sue trusts Mark because he tells her things she would never tell her own mother. For her, the reward is that he *does* share. She said, "If I started to shut him down, he would stop – because I know that from my own feelings. I know enough … I am not going to react negatively and give a lecture or put up an emotional curtain."

At the time of the interview, Mark was in his early 20s and had no interest in finding his birth parents. Sue and Kathy are very open to him searching but think it's more appropriate for him to take that initiative. Sue said she didn't want to make him feel like he is *supposed* to search.

> *"I get the sense that all adoptees are different. They all have different ideas of whether they want to find their birth parents. Nobody's the same. I couldn't even begin to guess what Mark's feeling. I don't know what it would feel like. During that time, I wanted him to feel better. I don't want him to feel like I have any feelings for myself and have no desire to hold things back from him."*

Sue didn't want Mark to feel pressured on her account. While he doesn't have an interest in finding his birth parents, he would like to go to

Guatemala to see the country. They considered traveling there when he was in Junior High. However, it wasn't safe at that time, so they chose not to go. He recently asked to see his paperwork again. Finding it is on Sue's to-do list, and she is confident they should be able to understand the paperwork more thoroughly now that they have access to Google Translate.

When I told Sue that some adoptive mothers feel threatened by birth mothers, she was surprised. She does not feel threatened at all and said, "If Mark wants to have that experience, I think he should." In her mind, she thought that having a relationship with his birth mother would enhance, not detract from their relationship. It would improve his life because he would better understand where he came from and his history.

Both Sue and Kathy are White, so Mark grew up in a predominantly White environment and is "very aware that he is Brown." He has been pulled over by the police a few times. They were never able to figure out why, other than because he was a person of color in a White neighborhood. For example, when he was leaving Target, a cop pulled him over, asked for his driver's license, and then simply got back in his car and left. On another occasion when Mark was 15, he went with Sue's brother and his family to the Mall of America. It was past 3 p.m. – and per mall rules, it initiated the curfew in which anyone under 16 must be accompanied by an adult 21 years or older. A cop detained him because he thought Mark was pretending to tag along with his family to avoid curfew. Sue's brother didn't realize he had been stopped, and it took a while before it dawned on him that Mark was no longer with their group. He had to go back and explain to the cops that Mark was his nephew. Sue said, "It's always in his face that he's adopted."

Sue understands how it feels to be a non-White person in the United States; when she was a young woman, she was in the Peace Corps for a few years. She lived in an African country where she was the only White person in town and experienced racial discrimination.

"I have a sense of how it feels to be told that you think or are of a certain way because of your race. It doesn't happen to most people of my race in this country. I have had that experience. I know it made me feel angry. First of all, that's the biggest feeling you get, that someone could tell you that you think this way because you are White … or you are this kind of person because you're White. In

my case, it was a two-year thing, and I knew it was going to end,
and I would go back to my comfortable life."

For non-White people living in the United States, they do not have the option to leave the racism behind as Sue did after her Peace Corps assignment. She said, "I don't know how I would handle it if I were them. I have some understanding of the anger and where it is coming from. Otherwise, it's just sad that racism continues. I don't know … it makes me a little *angry* towards people that don't recognize it. It also makes me *sad* towards people who don't recognize it."

For Mark, being Brown is what makes him perpetually aware that he's adopted.

However, even though Sue's relatives are very racist for *other* reasons, they never discriminated against Mark. She said individuals in her family discriminated against her for being a lesbian, which differs from the type of racism Mark has encountered with other people. She says you can't hide race.

> *"People don't know I'm a lesbian when they walk in the room.*
> *With race, before you say a word, somebody has formed an opinion*
> *of you. In my case, that takes a while for them to have an opinion.*
> *I prefer for people to get to know me first. It doesn't come first.*
> *Whereas your race is the first thing somebody sees."*

Mark has been able to work through his encounters with racism, ADHD issues, and his adoption sadness. With patience and consistency, Sue and Kathy helped him through his struggles. They told him he had to go to college. He went to a community college for three years and got a 2-year business degree. (The first year he was catching up on coursework he missed in high school.) During that time, his ADHD symptoms decreased. After working as a camp counselor for several summers (and loving it), he realized he should be a teacher and work with kids. In the fall, he will be transferring to a 4-year university with a strong teaching program. Sue said, "Now, he's like an incredibly mature person in the last year and a half. It's like talking to an adult. I'm really happy with Mark … He's going to be a really great person. He has become this enjoyable, not fidgety, normal guy that is wonderful to be around."

~ Advice Through Sue's Lens ~

<u>For adoptive parents:</u> "Don't have any expectations. The way I feel it, we got this wonderful, wonderful little kid, and I'm trying not to screw it up. Obviously, *be parents*, but let them lead where they want to go and who they want to be because they're not you. That's true for all kids, but for adoptive kids, they may even have a little bit more to think about."

My Thoughts, My Lens

When I learned that Sue's mother was Lithuanian, I felt like I had an instant window into her family's dynamics because my mother's extended family was from Lithuania and Latvia. Both countries share a border and history as part of the former Soviet Union. When Sue explained how she was taught to keep her emotions to herself (but taught Mark differently), I inwardly applauded. My adoptive mom believes that emotions impede progress. (In fact, she has said on more than one occasion that "emotions are inefficient.") I love my mom dearly and know she raised me well. I've learned charity, generosity, and discipline from her. She taught me how to keep my emotions under control when a task needs to be done. My mom will always be the first love of my life, but not being able to connect with her on a deeper emotional level was always something I yearned for as a kid. When I was growing up, we knew a mother and daughter who were very close. They shared every thought and experience. A few times, I told my mom that I wished we were close like them, but she thought they had an inappropriate relationship (in some ways, she was right). However, she kind of missed my point; and undoubtedly, I'm sure I didn't articulate it very well. I just wanted the connection that some mothers and daughters seem to have because they share the same genes, somehow knowing what each other is thinking, feeling, and living. I've tried to teach many of my mother's lessons to my girls but have loosened up on the emotional front.

Through my own life experiences, I have learned that emotions are healthy when fully explored within self-regulated guardrails. The reward for being emotionally accessible with my daughters is that we are now very close. I get to have a connection with my girls that my mother and I never quite reached. My oldest daughter and I recently discussed death. She began tearing up when we talked about my inevitable passing. I told her that when I die, she should allow herself to cry and be despondent for a week. Then on the eighth day, she should get out of bed and wash her face. (When I said the same thing to my youngest, she half-rolled her eyes, laughed, and said, "Yeah, yeah. Ok Mom. Ok.")

I gave my daughters a seven-day waiting period because bottling up my emotions about adoption for seven-times-seven-years was unhealthy. Clearly, I had seepage that lasted *far* too long.

I respect Sue and Kathy. The fact that Kathy knew to send Mark to an Adoption-Competent Therapist in elementary school was prescient. She probably saved him from years of unnecessary angst. Rock on.

Wayne W. | Counselor

North Carolina
Year of Adoption: 1995

I was very fortunate to meet Wayne, a West Coast transplant settled in North Carolina and yet a Southern gentleman, too. He had adopted both a Southern accent and a son while living there. It was clear he was deeply committed to his Christian faith and open to helping others with the experience he gained as an adoption counselor and adoptive father. He facilitated over 200 international adoptions in the 1990s. As a social worker and family therapist by training with a master's degree, Wayne was invaluable to my research in that he had both personal *and* professional adoption experience. Luckily for me, he was extremely helpful. At the time of the interview, he had been a widower for about a year. I appreciated his friendly, supportive, and accommodating nature because he could have written an entire book by himself filled with well-informed advice for prospective adoptive parents.

During his time as an international adoption counselor, Wayne learned that the information parents received from orphanages was not always accurate; the orphanages often would only report what benefited their mission to place children in permanent homes. International adoption can be risky, but working with a credible agency that does the legwork is paramount. He counseled prospective parents to understand that it's hard to get perfectly healthy kids because the children from nations in the developing world are often sickly due to a lack of medical care. He said, "Simply put, they're orphans." Another risk with any international adoption is that the process could fall apart at the last minute. Wayne said, "It's a leap of faith."

Some of the issues with adoptees are not immediately apparent. Even in well-kept orphanages, there is never enough attention to go around, and children can be neglected emotionally. And due to language barriers, the orphanage staff might not translate illnesses in the same way Americans would. Wayne counseled parents that accurate medical information wasn't always available. Most kids Wayne placed were under a year old, and therefore they would always not have information about physical issues because the orphans had yet to develop fully. Emotional attachment issues would come out later. Sadly, he witnessed a few situations in which the children didn't work out behaviorally. Wayne also had to guide parents through a lot of disappointment due to bureaucracy. He had to prepare them to accept the realities of time delays or losing a child because someone else would get the child first. Some prospective parents were understandably upset. He said, "People could get really mad."

More often than not, though, things worked out. Wayne's agency not only placed children in the United States but also in Ireland. He formed fond memories of working with those families. He traveled to Ireland, met prospective parents, and has even received postcards from them after their placements were finalized.

Wayne characterized his job as a good experience because he was able to conduct parenting workshops. He taught the parents they needed to realize that they would not have as much information as they would with a biological child. He didn't want parents to have a romantic view of adoption (e.g., parents who thought having "all the Christian love to give" would solve their problems). The reality is that some adoptees have to rework their process of attachment.

At the very least, Wayne wanted those parents to be prepared for the grief that their child will have. He emphasized,

> *"It doesn't matter how good of a parent you are; the feelings of loss the child will have are inevitable."*

Adoption is birthed through loss. Somebody had to "give up" the child. Wayne acknowledged that people would often say "placed the child" because it sounds better than "giving up the child." When adopted children are young, adoption is not a "big deal." However, anywhere between seven to nine years of age, their emotional awareness catches up. They are intelligent enough to understand what it means that someone "got rid" of them – even if it was a mother who loved them and "placed" them. To the adoptee, it feels like a loss and that they were unwanted. Wayne advised prospective adoptive parents to take their children to counseling when they are between 7 and 12 years of age – even if they weren't showing negative signs. If nothing else came out of the sessions, at least the children would have an opportunity to talk about their adoptions.

Years later, when Wayne's son journeyed through adoption loss as an adoptee, they went to counseling. Wayne admitted that training other people on adoptive parenting and experiencing it for himself were entirely different. He said that he became a better professional because he went through it himself. For him, it brought home the knowledge that no adoptive parent wants to think their kid will have problems. They presume having "all the love in the world" makes them good parents. As true as that may be, adoptees will surely feel that loss – and parents need to be ready for that day.

Wayne also counseled parents who were having a hard time bonding with their adoptees. The lack of connection starts with the child not attaching in the way they are expected to and, subsequently, it hinders the way the *parents* attach. For example, some children have sensory-related issues because they were in a crib with no human contact. Hugging literally feels *physically* painful to the child. However, some parents are unaware of the sensory pain and are devastated when their children do not want to be hugged. As a result, the parents do not bond with their children. Attachment issues can be so severe that some parents return their children to the agency. I asked Wayne if the aversion to being hugged could change. He replied, "Yes." Prospective adoptive parents need to be educated on the level of care at the orphanages. They also have to understand that by choosing adoption, they are choosing to go above and beyond "regular" parenting because of the unique challenges that come with adoption.

*"In my mind, you make a commitment to the child and before God,
and then you have to deal with what you have to deal with."*

Years ago, Wayne attended professional training sessions for therapists at Texas Christian University, in which he learned about adoption trauma related issues. The same institute started a 3-week camp for adoptive children and their parents to work on their attachment skills.[43] For some

---

[43] Karyn Purvis Institute of Child Development, child.tcu.edu/professionals/camp-training/#sthash.A3vmxWRB.U8z5PU1V.dpbs. Accessed 18 Apr. 2021.

attending families, it was the last resort; if their children didn't get better at the camp, they would return their child. The parents were taught that their kids were not attaching because they never had the opportunity to bond with anyone for the first few years of their life. Their children were hurt, scared, in a crib or a corner … never being held. Their initial life experience was different from biological children who were held the moment they were born. The camp has been very successful because the staff worked with both the children AND the parents (which was the key to their methodology). They would measure the children's stress hormone at the beginning, middle, and end of the 3-week period. Often the stress levels in the children would go down. After camp, the therapy would continue. Wayne stressed that:

> *"It is very important to see a therapist who specializes in adoption work because they understand issues that a regular therapist wouldn't understand. Traditional therapists [who are] not focused on adoption might contraindicate the reality of what's going on with the child."*

Through individual training and workshops, Wayne's support included preparing parents to receive inevitable insensitive comments from other people. In Wayne's adopted Southern drawl, he gave an example of a thoughtless question many people have often asked: "Who's the real mother?" To which he responded, *"What?* And here you've been raising the child for five years …ex-cuuuse me?"

He helped parents deal with maddening situations such as those, convincing them to try to understand how their interracial families stand out. He would also prepare parents for questions their own children will ask, such as "Did she love me?" Parents would also have to consider the birth mother's situation. What if she was a sex worker? Good prep courses address some of those situations. Wayne noted that even if the adoptee looks like the parents, there will still be potential issues.

There is no substitute for "good prep" in adoption.

The birth mother of Wayne's son was an alcoholic and likely a sex worker. Wayne and his wife struggled as to when and if they should reveal those details. They ended up telling him about the alcoholism early on because they wanted him to know about his genes – so he would be careful about making choices. However, they waited to tell him about the likelihood of prostitution until he was an adult. It was an awkward conversation, but they had read books on how to handle it. They learned how to phrase things in a way to still honor her, despite her lifestyle. Mostly, they focused on her knowing she couldn't care for her son, and planned to give him to those who could provide for him. Wayne once heard a birth mother speak at a workshop. Her speech profoundly altered his view of birth mothers. He said that if adoptive parents could just hear a birth mother talk about placing her child for adoption, they would change how they presented it to their children when the time came. *"Very powerful."*

When Wayne and his wife were preparing for adopting a child, they took courses. However, they found the group meetings to be the most helpful. They met monthly with parents at all different stages in their adoption journeys. Some had adopted ten years prior, others were in the middle of the process, and some were just starting out like Wayne and his wife. He said that they trusted the adoptive couples more than the agency staff because they were *living it*. The hardest part was the paperwork; mortgage paperwork is nothing compared to adoption paperwork! They also hit a few roadblocks. Their social worker almost denied their adoption application because she thought their neighborhood was too risky. However, her supervisor overrode her non-recommendation. That incident taught Wayne they would have to persevere through difficult trials. Applicants can walk away at any time in the process.

"If you're too quick to quit, then adoption is not for you."

Wayne and his wife did not walk away. Although, they did have a better experience than many adoptive parents because they personally knew the missionary couple that headed up their son's orphanage. That orphanage was a small single entity, unlike other orphanages, which were typically part of a larger group. Many people have heard stories of visitors seeing the best rooms in the building, but behind those rooms were kids in closets. It took a couple of years for them to go through the entire process. He and his wife relied on their Sunday school classmates to help them deal with those times they didn't feel like it would happen.

When they thought they were getting close, their friends threw them a baby shower, but then the adoption was delayed. They were supposed to get their son when he was three months old. However, due to government bureaucracy and paperwork delays, they weren't able to get him until he was ten months old. Wayne said the delay felt like a miscarriage. They had already gone down the painful road of infertility, and it reminded them of how it felt to take so long to get to a place where they could even choose a child. During that interim, they were informed the birth mother drank. They took a video and photographs to their pediatrician to see if it looked like he had Fetal Alcohol Syndrome (FAS). The doctor was confident that he did not, but Wayne and his wife later learned he had ADHD, which could have resulted from her drinking. But in Wayne's words, "You can't have it perfect … even if he was our biological child, things still could have come up." He was grateful that they could lean on their church and support systems.

Finally, the phone call came that everything was a go, and it was, of course, very exciting. They booked a last-minute flight, opting to stay for a week (instead of having their son brought to the U.S.). Wayne is half Mexican and speaks Spanish fluently. He wanted to experience his son's Central American culture. When they arrived, the airport roof was open above them. The missionary's wife was on the top level, looking down at them and holding their son. They met up and held him. After a few minutes, Wayne and his wife handed him back, but the missionary said, "NO, he's yours." That shocked Wayne. He didn't know what to do. At this point in the interview, Wayne laughed, and it made me laugh, too.

The first night in the hotel was the hardest because they were so scared that he would stop breathing (even though he was ten months old). They barely got through the night. The next day, they traveled to the orphanage and stayed at the missionaries' home. Being inexperienced, the missionaries taught them how to care for a baby within their week stay. During the day, they would bring their son with them to visit the orphanage. They even borrowed the missionaries' car to make a 10-mile trip to visit a little girl they had been sponsoring through a humanitarian aid organization. Since they were already in the country, it was a double blessing to meet their sponsored child, too. Her family worked in a bakery equipped with a huge primitive stone bread oven. The family was thrilled to meet Wayne and his wife.

On the last day of their visit, Wayne was holding his son at the missionaries' house. He was preparing to give him a bottle and went into the living room to find a place to sit, deciding on the big lounge chair with a blanket on it. Before sitting, he snatched up the blanket, and a "torpedo flew out of it." In the millisecond that the bundle was in the air, he realized the blanket housed a small infant and reflexively dropped his son while catching the torpedo. His son only fell a foot and had a minor cut on his upper lip. The small infant survived unscratched. Wayne was so stunned, and at that moment, realized how parenting could be so scary. His wife later had a similar incident back in the United States when their son leaped off the edge of his changing table. She caught him by the feet with his head 2 inches from the floor. All parents know those kinds of experiences. Wayne said, "Adoption feels different … you feel so incapable – *as if* it would be easier if we had a biological child. That isn't true, I'm sure."

Wayne's wife was a quiet person, and mothering was very hard for her, but she did a good job. His son loved her very much and misses her now that she has passed away. Wayne and his son are close because he was more emotional and affectionate than his wife. He and his son also shared a love of sports. But his son had both physical and mental health issues that led to depression and suicidal attempts during adolescence. Wayne said, "It's been a rough road." Raising their son was very hard on his wife. She also had to get counseling for herself to feel more confident about being a mother. They relied on their faith to help them get through the parenting years.

When Wayne's son was 13 years old, he wanted to find his birth mother. Wayne and his wife supported him by taking a trip to find her. Unfortunately, they were unsuccessful because she was a homeless person, and there were no records they could use to trace her. Throughout the search, Wayne never doubted his son loved him. He said that a child is attached to you whether you conceived them or not. It's how you live your life in relation to that child.

Wayne *never* felt like his son wasn't *his* son.

~ Advice Through Wayne's Lens ~

<u>For adoptive parents:</u> Post-adoption training only goes on for a few years. Most adoptees experience depression, sadness, and grief after the age of seven. Adoptive parents of young children don't want to think about issues that may arise down the road when their child is seven years old. When the time comes, Wayne encourages parents to seek professional help – someone trained specifically in adoption.

There is a spiritual component that can be helpful *and* simultaneously not helpful. Wayne has a strong Christian faith but said that it is not simple; there are complexities to adoption. He said, "Just because someone may be a prayer warrior, it doesn't mean that everything [he or] she prays for will work out. We prayed for my wife when she got sick, but she still died."

> *"It's okay to have doubts. It's okay to wonder why you are going through struggles."*

It's okay.

In Wayne's opinion, the key is to have support, resources, people to pray with you, and people to pray for you. Having professional and spiritual support certainly helped Wayne and his wife. He said that spiritual beliefs intersect with adoption, but he cautions that they can both help *and* hinder. He continued, "There are misconceptions on how faith can help or not. As a Christian, some parts of society tell me that what I believe is nonsense or a crutch. That's offensive to me. They have that right, but you can take it [too far] the other way, too. Some Christians believe that because they are Christians, everything will work out. That can be just as destructive." Wayne also pointed out that the whole Bible is about being adopted. In the Old Testament, the Jews were the biological children of God, and in the New Testament, the Gentiles were adopted into the family. In the first chapter of Ephesians, Paul wrote, "Having predestinated us unto the *adoption* of children by Jesus Christ to himself, according to the good pleasure of his will. To the praise of the glory of his grace, wherein he hath made us accepted in the beloved."[44]

To conclude the interview, Wayne stated with an assured head nod, "Adoption isn't second place."

---

[44] *The Holy Bible*. Authorized King James Version. Oxford University Press, 1999, p. 1250.

My Thoughts, My Lens

I appreciated the part of Wayne's story when he talked about their second trip to South America to find his son's birth mother. He said it so casually as if the thought of not taking the trip had never entered his mind. I admire that his actions evidenced the security he had in his relationship with his son. It reminded me of the period when I tried to find my birth mother (after years of refusing even to acknowledge my adoption). Before I made the effort, I called my parents to ask if they would be offended. My dad chuckled as he let out a breath and said he would not be offended at all. My mom was in complete support, too. (Although she later reminded me that I was pretty harsh with my words when I asked them – I referred to my birth mother as "that woman.") Wow. That part I had forgotten. But I do remember appreciating that they were willing to let me freely explore without feeling like they were an anchor to my efforts.

As a military brat, I was taught to respect the chain of command, so my loyalty to my adoptive parents was and always will be solid. My dad even offered to give me his airline miles and go with me. He has always loved South Korea. He was not only stationed there as a young soldier but has made many business trips to my original country after retiring from the Army after two decades of service. Unfortunately, I could not locate my birth mother because the adoption agency said my records no longer existed (yet another "perk" of being old). The agency did not have accurate recordkeeping practices in the 1960s as they do now. Years later, my mom told me that my dad was disappointed that I could not find my birth mother because he was really looking forward to showing me the country. I had no idea that he felt that way.

Thinking about it right now makes me a little *Coffee Talk Verklempt*.[45]

---

[45] "Coffee Talk: Liz Rosenberg and Barbra Streisand – SNL." *YouTube*, uploaded by Saturday Night Live, 25 Sep. 2013. www.youtube.com/watch?v=oiJkANps0Qw. Accessed 7 Apr. 2021.

When I was growing up, my dad was always reserved, and although he was affectionate, he kept his deeper emotions out of sight. His secret generosity really touched my heart. My parents knew me when I was a raw little human. It was short-sighted of me to think that they didn't know my heart when I was an adult. Until that moment, I didn't realize my parents already knew that somewhere below my cavalier exterior, I truly wanted to know about my roots. It makes sense now. After all, they are my parents.

SECTION 4

Through the Lens of Birth Families

I had a lovely conversation with author Jill Murphy, who wrote about her experience as a birth mother in her book *Finding Motherhood, An Unexpected Journey*.[46] She became pregnant at 17. She and the birth father planned to take the adoption route, but he changed his mind and got custody. He later married, and his wife adopted his son. Years later, Jill found the love of her life, and they adopted two baby girls from South Korea. Through a series of events, she was reunited with her birth son.

Jill told me that her experience as a birth mother is her armor to help her girls. She gave me the example of when she and her seven-year-old daughter were talking about her birth son. Her daughter broke down and sobbed, wondering if her "Belly Mom" ever thought about her like Jill thought about her birth son. In that moment, Jill had the clarity to tell her daughter that she had no doubt her birth mother thought about her every single day.

The more Jill talks about her experience as a birth mother, the more she heals. She has learned that when she was young, being silent caused her pain. By saying it out loud, it became real. She acknowledged that by giving her feeling a voice, she took the chance she might discover her feelings were legitimately crazy. But it felt good. By finding her voice, she found her fight. By opening that "drawer" in her mind, she realized she should have talked to somebody many years ago.

Similarly, comedian and writer Allison Rose talked about her birth mother experience in a stand-up routine. She said,

> *"Every time anyone has called me strong, it's when I'm quiet. That's what we call strength — when you handle something alone in silence, or when you carry more than you should have to, and you don't scream about it. There's this quiet praise for silence. In a society that boasts quiet strength, sharing any part of yourself*

---

[46] Murphy, Jill M. *Finding Motherhood.* CreateSpace, 2015.

seems frightening to people. The only reason I'm okay is because I wasn't quiet.[47]

In writing this book, when I looked through the lens of the birth mothers who were not willing to be quiet, I could finally set aside my own pain.

I could see the beauty of their vulnerability.

Hearing their stories healed me because I was able to release the resentment that I held about my faceless birth mother for more than half a century.

---

[47] Rose, Allison. "She Would Never Be So New." *The Narrators,* episode 186, 10 May 2019 thenarrators.org/186-allison-rose/. Accessed 14 Feb. 2021.

April C. | Supply Chain Specialist

Minnesota
Year of Adoption: 2014

April reminded me of a young flower ready to blossom. And not in a fragile bluebell kind of way but rather in a spunky dahlia kind of way. She has already experienced a harsh winter in her short lifespan, but her spring is coming, and she is ready. Clearly, her emotional acuity has been forged by struggle, sprinkled with a dewy innocence. Her decision to use her experience to help other birth mothers ensnared in similar situations impressed me. She radiated joy when she talked about her birth daughter, Rose – and she was chipper when describing the open adoption relationship that she has with the adoptive parents, Bob L. and Melissa M. (whose story is also in this book – see the table of contents).

April was at peace with her decision when we spoke, but she admitted she wasn't always that way. She tried to kill herself in 2013 when she was a college student, moved home with her parents, and became a coffee barista. In 2014, she discovered she was pregnant. Having very little money and even less confidence, she decided that she was not mentally fit to be a mother.

Plus, she hated her baby's biological father.

April didn't tell him about her pregnancy until she was six months along. She said, "Like, we weren't a couple or anything. It was just one of those things where we were drinking. I just didn't have a lot of self-respect back then. It is what it is. I've learned from it and grew from it." April decided she didn't want to be tied to "that dude" for the rest of her life. While that was a factor, her decision to choose adoption was primarily out of concern for her future daughter. She put up a façade, showing no emotion when she told him about her pregnancy. He, of course, was very surprised. She gave him some details about her plans for adoption, told him about the adoptive couple she had chosen, and then asked him to fill out the health paperwork. He seemed relieved that she wasn't expecting anything from him and turned in the paperwork as requested. They haven't spoken since. It still upsets April that he wants nothing to do with Rose. She said, "It makes me angry and sad 'cause she's so awesome. He's never met her. Literally, since the day I told him that I was pregnant, I haven't heard from him." April has chosen to keep him as a Facebook friend in case Rose ever decides she wants to meet him. April once thought she saw him in public. Her heart dropped, and she ran around the corner to hide. Looking back, she doesn't think that was the best way to handle it.

They had many mutual friends, and April decided to cut them off, too, to avoid the risk of seeing Rose's birth father again. April now realizes that cutting off some of those friends was probably a good thing; they were not the best influence on her. Being pregnant snapped her out of her "early 20s partying zone." She found self-respect. Since then, she has two goals. One: never get pregnant again by accident. Two: work to be in a position where she will never have to place another child for adoption. Choosing adoption was the hardest thing she ever had to do.

When April first suspected she was pregnant, she said, "It was weird. I wasn't having regular periods." She went to a women's healthcare organization in search of support. Unfortunately, April's experience was not at all how they market themselves. The woman assisting her was very cold and dismissive. *"Yep, you're pregnant. Here are some pamphlets. Bye."* April needed empathy, and how she was treated made her "really, really mad." She went to her car and cried "horrible tears" because she was alone. Soon after that, she brought her parents to one of her therapy sessions. April is naturally nonconfrontational; she wanted to tell them about her pregnancy in the presence of her therapist. She was afraid that she would "chicken out" and needed her therapist to be there in case they didn't take it well. Her parents surprised her and were extremely supportive. They are pro-life, and therefore, were very happy that she didn't have an abortion. April did consider having one. However, because she grew up with "Catholic guilt," she was sensitive to abortion. She said, "I couldn't do it and feel okay about it. The more I thought about it … I heard it could be dangerous, or stuff could go wrong. I just didn't feel right doing it."

When April was 12 weeks pregnant, she started searching for adoption agencies. Working on a plan reduced her stress level. She looked at a couple of Christian adoption agencies. In her opinion, they were judgy and treated her like a "fragile flower." Because she felt insulted and uncomfortable, she went with an agency not affiliated with religion – she really liked their policy, as it listed both heterosexual and gay couples as adoption parent candidates. That distinction was important to her because she said, "I am also queer." She didn't want to work with an organization that discriminated against her. She showed up without an appointment and was immediately welcomed into their office. April said that the social worker was "amazing." The meeting was informal. When they talked about April's situation, the social worker described how the process worked, what she could expect, and her options. The agency encouraged open adoptions but would do a closed adoption if the *birth mother* chose that option. (The agency's model support varying degrees of openness, thereby giving birth mothers more control.) The legal document they put together for April is called a Cooperative Agreement, in which both the birth mother and adoptive parents agree to follow a specific plan after the birth.

The social worker visited April at her house and gave her a big binder as thick as a ream of paper, organized chronologically, placing the couples waiting for the longest at the front. The newer candidates were towards the back. April looked at it for a few hours, overwhelmed. Each couple had profiles that summed up their interests, family dynamics, pets, activities they did for fun, religious affiliations, etc. April said that the volume of the content was "insane." She didn't make it through the whole book. However, she did narrow her choices down to five couples. She emailed them and was able to set up dates with three of them.

April loved the first couple. They were a power gay couple, and both men had executive jobs. To her surprise, they had some things in common with April. She had attended a very small liberal arts college halfway across the country on the east coast. And one of them had graduated from the same school. The other man was from her father's small western Minnesota hometown. By the end of the lunch, she was 90 percent sure she was going to pick them, but because they were her first lunch date, she wanted to meet the other couples, too.

April met the second couple over pancakes. They were from a small town in rural southern Minnesota. They were "super chilled out and down to earth." She learned that Bob was a special education teacher, and Melissa was a potter. The three connected right away, discovering that they had random things in common. Melissa loved asparagus, and April was craving asparagus at the time. They all were crazy about the late 1980s alternative rock band, The Pixies. Melissa's mother was also from the same hometown as April's extended family, and went to the same school as April's father and aunt.

The third couple was not a fit. They were both scientists, and April described their meeting as, "The most horrible awkward dinner … The service was really bad, and I had to suffer through 'one point five' hours." She confirmed what her social worker had cautioned: meeting prospective birth parents was like going on a first date. You either have chemistry, or you don't. April grinned as she said that she hopes the couple found a "really awkward" birth mother. She just wasn't right for them.

After meeting with the couples, April wished she had two babies so she could give one to each of the first two couples. Ultimately, she chose Bob and Melissa for a few reasons. First, they already had a daughter. The question of whether they could conceive another baby did not come up. It wasn't important to her, and she said, "Regardless … either way, they wanted to adopt, and that was good enough for me." April also appreciated that Bob is a special education teacher and could take summers off. Because of his occupation, she also knew he could relate to her autistic sister. April loved their "hippie-dippy" attitude about life as well as their politics. They lived in a log cabin in the middle of nowhere, and Melissa could stay home with Rose. April surprised herself in that she chose a family who lived in "BFE" (Bum "eff" Egypt) because it was the exact opposite of what she thought she wanted for her daughter. The deciding factor was that they would be able to spend more time with Rose instead of hiring a nanny.

A few weeks after their pancake meal, April called them, and they agreed to meet at the zoo. After walking around for a little while, she told them she had chosen them, and they almost started to cry. They told her that they thought/hoped she might have picked them but didn't want to assume. At this point in the interview, April's face radiated. She giggled and said, "This is great, we're going to be a family forever!"

[Fist pump.]

When they were at the zoo's touch pool, a manta ray jumped out at them. Bob got a manta ray tattoo on his leg to commemorate that day – also a permanent marking on April's heart.

Then April said, "Pregnancy [Effing] sucked. Pardon my French." She had gestational hypertension, symphysis pubis dysfunction (a condition when the hip bones spread – painful), headaches, high blood pressure, and vomiting. She got a doctor's note, which enabled her to reduce her time at the coffee shop to four hours per shift and allowed her to sit while at the cash register. A week before her due date, she was induced with a Pitocin drip. After getting an epidural, she watched *Best in Show* and took a nap. When she woke up, Rose was born. April's mother supported her during the entire delivery. Surprisingly, the worst part about pregnancy and delivery for April was the hospital experience itself. The staff didn't know how to act towards her because she did not have a "normal" birth.

> *"I was excited to get her out of me and meet her. At the same time, it was very sad. It's a huge sense of loss with a lot of grief. It was 'pre-grief' because I knew I would have to hand Rose over in a couple of days. But it was very apparent that I was not ready to be a mom."*

Rose came into the world at 11 p.m. Seven hours later, a hospital staff member came into April's room to take her vitals and asked her what kind of birth control she wanted. The question infuriated April. She yelled at him, "I'm placing her for adoption; I don't think I'm going to have sex for a very long-time, sir. Get out of my vag. What the [Eff]??? Are you serious???" His response was, "Oh, we just want to make sure you don't find yourself in this position again."

Things went better later that day. April's best friend visited her before Bob and Melissa showed up. When the nurse left them alone in the room with Rose, they looked at each other like deer in headlights. "Shit, what do we do right now?"

Bob and Melissa came in soon after that. April said it was like magic. She cocked her head sideways at the memory. Her eyes sparkled as she said,

> *"It was, like, perfect. I felt like I was violating them by being there. It was such a beautiful moment. It was sad at the same time."*

277

April's family came to meet Rose, too. Originally her father was going to be out of town, but April told him, "You are canceling that trip. Your granddaughter is coming. You are going to call your boss." April's 19-year-old brother also didn't want to be there either but has since come around – and adores Rose. He made a wooden sign with her name that he woodworked for her bedroom door. Rose is loved by many relatives – both biological and adoptive. Her adoptive big sister, Amy, can't get enough of her. When Rose first came home from the hospital, Amy wanted to hold her as much as she could.

When they left the hospital, April's parents were both there to take her home. Bob and Melissa were also there. At the entrance, before they separated, a woman came over to fuss over the new baby. April remembers saying something mean to her to get her to leave but can't remember her exact words. Bob and Melissa went to their car with Rose. April went to hers with her parents. She said, "I was bawling my eyes out because that was the separation point." She cried the whole way home and for the next few days. She really wanted to see Rose – but couldn't. When Bob and Melissa didn't call right away, April's mom thought they were going to back out of their Cooperative Agreement. The paranoia that originated with her mom seeped into April's mind, and she also became afraid. Her thoughts spiraled out of control unnecessarily as her mother's fears of never seeing her granddaughter again (and maybe never having another one) made April freak out. It didn't occur to her that Bob and Melissa might not keep their word until her mother suggested it. April was exhausted, traumatized, and drained both physically and emotionally. She was also pumping breast milk for Rose. Because of her fatigue, she had a hard time processing her anxiety of the unknown. The lawyers had told her that there's nothing legally binding about the Cooperative Agreement; it's mainly about the *intent*.

However, Bob and Melissa kept their word; they spoke with April after the first few days. Two weeks later, they met halfway between their homes, and April gave them the breastmilk. She continued to pump for several months. In her mind, she thought, "I know I don't have to do this. I wish I could have parented. I can't give you much, Kid, but I can give you this."

When Rose was younger, she and April FaceTimed once a week (with Melissa on the call). Their calls occur about once a month now. Rose is five years old. According to April, it's the perfect age ... "Blah, blah, blah, it's the Rose show. I want to hold the camera … Want to hear a knock-knock joke?" Melissa sent April a video of the exact moment Rose realized her first tooth fell out. (April showed it to me. So cute!) Rose calls her both "Mama A" and "April." April respects Bob and Melissa's parenting style; they are "mellow" and deal with their girls logically and rationally.

In the past year, April has been working on her mental health by going through an intensive Dialectical Behavior Therapy (DBT) program. DBT is used to treat self-destructive and suicidal behaviors. She is focusing on herself and diligently does the homework assignments. Next month, she will graduate from the program after attending for a year. Additionally, she has recently started trauma treatment. After seeing how the program helped her, April wants to become a therapist to use her skills and direct experience to support other birth moms.

April gushed over the experiences she had while attending birth mother retreats. Powerful bonds instantly bloomed among the women. In April's words, "It was magic." She learned the one thing birth mothers have in common is that they are all too hard on themselves. They all struggle with shame, sadness, loss, and guilt. She wants other women to learn how to prevent those feelings from overtaking them. In her opinion, being a birth mother is an amazing thing. She said,

> *"It's really hard, and you have a weird relationship with your own motherhood."*

Mother's Day can be "weird" because she is a mom but isn't parenting her child. April feels very motherly even though she isn't directly parenting Rose.

Another thing April has done to help herself heal is to present her story to prospective adoptive parents at the adoption agency that helped her. She tells them she can't imagine Rose's adoption not being open. It was a little "uncomfortable" at first but maintains that it's just more people to love your kid. She said,

> *"It just takes a bit of navigating, like any new relationship."*

She found that the more people who become involved just makes it *that* more comfortable. They are one big family. She said,

"It's all love, all the time. I can't imagine not having the chance to know [Rose]. That would destroy me, I think. As hard as it was at first ... as difficult as it is, it would be that more exponentially tragic not to be a part of her life. She's never going to question, did my mom abandon me? She's never going to question why did she place me for adoption? I am a part of her life because I am obsessed with her. It is about her."

Rose clearly has April's looks, but she also shares some of her interests and personality traits. For example, they both loved mermaids at the same age. They even pose for pictures in the same way. When Rose once saw a picture of a four-year-old April, it confused her because she thought it was a picture of herself and couldn't remember posing for that photograph. Adoption is a point of pride and not pain for Rose. She once overheard a conversation about adoption when she and Melissa were at a grocery store. She stood up in her cart and announced that she was adopted. April hopes it's never something she feels bad about – it's just another thing about her – as natural as having brown hair.

April talked about how some adoptive mothers are afraid of their children's birth mothers. Her social worker confirmed they feel threatened. However, Melissa is not threatened by April. They have a personal relationship and can level with each other. They are completely open with "no bullshit." Melissa is always present when April and Rose talk. She has often thanked April for giving them the time, recognizing the importance for Rose to know April, and helping to facilitate their relationship. Rose has met April's partner and her friends, celebrating birthdays and life. Having an open relationship with Rose's adoptive family has opened April's eyes to the prevalence of adoption. She sees it everywhere now, whereas before, she wasn't necessarily tuned in to how many people have been touched by adoption.

"[Open adoption] has been cool because I think it used to be a more secretive and painful experience. Obviously, it's still painful, but it's getting destigmatized. It's great because all of the people who are linked together by adoption can lean on each other for support."

April said that her attitude has changed in positive ways. Being a birth mother has made her less cynical. The sense of responsibility that accompanies motherhood contributed to April's newfound self-worth. Her sense of purpose also made it easier for her to figure out who she wanted to keep in her life and who she wanted to boot. And that has been very good for her: she extended the mama bear vibe to herself. By protecting herself, she can protect her daughter.

~ Advice Through April's Lens ~

For adoptees: "I would almost always say, I think in almost every circumstance, a birth mother's decision to adopt comes from a place of love. [I know someone] who is adopted, and she and I talk about it. She wonders, 'Did my parents love me?' I always think that Rose is going to question that at some point in her life. That breaks my heart that she would even have that thought. I think that there's no way to make sure people understand that. This is a decision of love. Your mom did not abandon you."

For adoptive parents: "Trust the birth mother. It takes a huge amount of trust. Be open with each other as humanly possible. The more people to love on the adoptees, the better."

For birth mothers: "That's a hard one because I'm still on my journey. Don't be too hard on yourself. I would encourage people to celebrate the birth mother journey. Lean into it and accept it. Make it a part of who you are because it *is* a part of who you are."

My Thoughts, My Lens

It's a balance. Some adoptees benefit from knowing their birth parents, as demonstrated by April and Rose's story. Other adoptees struggle with the weight of unhealthy ties to their birth parents (as demonstrated in Art & Emma G's story), manifesting with mental health issues, addiction, and despondency. And yet, other adoptees wrestle with the hole left by their faceless and nameless birth parents.

But still …

What is nearly impossible for me to grasp is why adoptive parents lie to their children about their history – when the adoptees never learn that they are adopted *in the first place*. I understand lies are borne from a place of fear. However, I have a hard time understanding adoptive parents who hide the truth of their children's adoption. Perhaps I'm being too harsh?

I remember the anxiety I felt in elementary school when a friend told me that her cousin didn't know he was adopted. I was over-the-top offended that *I knew* he was adopted, but *he* didn't know. He was a cute little kindergartener with skinny legs, stringy blonde hair, pasty white skin, and a penchant for naughtiness. It was difficult for me to see him at school, knowing he was living in a home decorated with an ambient lie. In my underdeveloped child's brain, I was tempted to tell him the truth (I didn't). Over the years, I have thought about him from time to time … Wondering if he ever found out … And if he did, was it simultaneously devastating and enlightening? Wondering if the revelation filled in the gaps? Or, wondering if he never found out – always feeling like he was slightly out of place as the intangible whisper of ill-fitting genes filled his mind?

In my opinion, for adoptees, knowing the truth about their adoption – whether positive or negative – is better than *never* knowing. Surely, some people will disagree with me. But I do believe April, Bob, and Melissa have tapped into something magnificent with their openness as the three embrace Rose with love and truth.

Benet T. | Software Engineer

Texas
Year of Adoption: 1976

I thoroughly enjoyed meeting Benet, a straight shooter from Texas with a hearty laugh whom I'm sure could charm anyone with a pulse. He was very direct, philosophical, and obviously well-read. His confident deep voice commanded respect, resonating like James Earl Jones. I appreciated his refreshing honesty about his feelings about being a birth father. His birth son's adoptive sister, Sara W., is also in this book (see the table of contents).

At 16, Benet found himself caught between two teenagers, Charlotte and Susan. Both were pregnant with his babies.

At the same time.

There were messy timelines between those relationships. Because Benet was a minor, he had no influence on what would happen with either girl or their babies. Susan's parents decided that she should get an abortion. Charlotte's parents decided that she should place her baby for adoption, sending her to a well-established center that supports birth mothers. Benet did not deny that he got Susan pregnant. However, he refused to accept responsibility for Charlotte's pregnancy because she was a virgin; although they tried, they didn't have intercourse. He said, "I know now that all you have to do is get close ... and magic can happen. In my 16-year-old pea brain, because I didn't fully penetrate her, I didn't think I had gotten her pregnant. I didn't know it could work that way. We didn't have Google back then. All we knew was what the coaches told us in health class."

After Charlotte went through with the adoption, she returned and wanted to rekindle a relationship with Benet. However, he had moved on with Susan because he thought it was over with Charlotte. Susan ended up getting pregnant again when Benet was in college. To support her, he dropped out to join the Air Force.

283

A few life-filled decades later, comprised of two more sons, two marriages, and two step kids, Benet was thinking about trying to contact his first son. He was upfront with his second wife when they started dating, telling her he had a son somewhere who might come knocking on the door someday. For decades, before meeting his son Thomas, Benet definitely had a "hole" in his psyche that was formed when Charlotte gave him up for adoption. Benet moved his hand in a circular motion in the space behind his head and said, "Somewhere back here is a person I didn't know." He finally decided to try to find his son. With a phone book open to the adoption agency page, Benet intended to call them to give them his contact number in case his son was looking for him. He was literally writing the agency's phone number down when the phone rang. It was Charlotte. She said she was thinking about finding "the boy." He said, "It is interesting you should say that, so am I." A few weeks later, Charlotte called Benet to let him know she had found Thomas, arranging to meet him separately from Benet around Thanksgiving. When they met, she had a stack of birthday cards she gave him for every year she had missed. She also told him that Benet had denied getting her pregnant, which was a part of why she decided to give him up.

The following month, right before Christmas, Benet met with him. He said, "I was nervous and had butterflies … I was excited to meet him [and] see what he looked like and what had become of his life. I hoped he had done well." Thomas had bounced around from job to job, doing the best he could. When they met, Thomas had tough questions for Benet. Primarily, he wanted to know why Benet gave him up. Benet told him that he was a teenager and had no input into what was happening with the decisions of Thomas's birth mother and her parents. He candidly told him, "Even if I did have input, you were probably much better off with people who could support you." Benet wasn't sure how Thomas took everything else, but he did seem to accept that Benet did not have any input. He also explained the dual girlfriend situation with Susan's abortion and Charlotte's relinquishment of Thomas for adoption. Somewhere amidst all of the explanations, he told Thomas,

> *"I'm just glad you're here. I'm not going to force you to do anything, whatever you want to do. We can take the relationship further — as far as you want to take it. I'm not trying to push because I realize I haven't been here. You have a life now, and the choices are yours."*

Thomas chose to pursue the relationship. Benet said that Thomas was doing okay at that time. He was responsible and the type of guy who could have some fun and be cavalier about life. When Thomas's daughter was born, he was very particular and made sure he took care of her. He was very protective and engaged in her life. Benet was wistfully philosophical when he talked about how Thomas was with his baby girl.

> "There's a lot of bonding that happens when your kids are in diapers – drinking baby slobber. There's a lot of stuff you miss about that. I don't have any pictures of him as a baby or as a little kid other than the two that Sara [Thomas's adoptive sister] sent to me. I don't know what he looked like as a baby. Although, I have this picture of him and my other two boys together. It was when I saw that picture (I always thought my other two boys looked like their mother), these guys have the same mouth! That's my mouth! Other little features … Ahhhhh. All of my boys do look like me. None of them have my nose. We all have pea heads. Yeah, these are my boys."

As Benet and Thomas's relationship grew, they would meet regularly for dinner. In Benet's mind, birth fathers are wired differently than birth mothers. Benet loves Thomas the same way he loves his other two sons. Benet said he is trying to do the best he can to be present in Thomas's life. He said, "I'm sure there is some loneliness. I'm not sure what to do or say about that." When they first met, he made a conscious effort to build a relationship with Thomas, saying, "As we were talking or approaching something, I would go after it the same as I would with the other two." And after a few months of concentrated effort, his relationship with Thomas felt natural to him.

Eventually, Thomas and his two half-brothers moved in with Benet and his second wife … he said, "Which was kinda cool." Then the Tech Bubble burst, and many people were out of jobs, including the boys. Benet felt all three of them were spending too much time playing video games, and he wound up kicking them all out. He remembers Thomas being so hurt … walking backward into the dark night saying, "Okay, if that's the way you want it. Okay. Okay." He was obviously upset. A few years later, when they were talking again, Thomas told Benet he understood why he kicked all three brothers out. Benet said that he treated Thomas the same as his other two sons. He said, "Even if he thought I made a mistake, I made the same mistake with all of them. I didn't single him out. I treated him just like my other boys."

Thomas joined the Army and was sent to a combat zone in Afghanistan. He and a lieutenant were having a conversation in a personnel carrier when a large round came through their vehicle. One second the lieutenant was there, and the next, he evaporated. Thomas carried survivor's guilt. It took a few years before his PTSD overtook him. He carried (and still does) both psychological and physical pain. His wrists and feet have been rebuilt. The screws in his feet caused him so much pain that medications were of no help. As a result, he started drinking and became reckless. The downward spiral began with a DUI. After that, he started combining psychotropic medication with alcohol. His antidepressants did not mix well with alcohol. As Benet explained it, he can have one beer, but if he has even "this much more," [he held up his fingers about an inch tall], then he falls off a cliff. Benet had to bail Thomas out of jail. During the same timeframe, Thomas started mistreating women and often hurled misogynistic insults at his wife. In Benet's opinion, those behaviors were misdirected feelings he actually had for Charlotte. Both Thomas and Charlotte abused each other emotionally. She took the resentment she harbored for Benet out on Thomas, and openly treated him differently from her daughters. Also, because she comes from an extremely religious family, she was highly judgmental of Thomas's choices. Benet quoted Oliver Wendell Holmes, Sr., "Some people are so heavenly minded they are no earthly good." In Benet's opinion, being overly religious can get in the way of reality. Thomas would confide in Benet he was having difficulty communicating with Charlotte; she wouldn't answer his questions about his adoption adequately. Over time, their relationship completely broke when she refused to answer any more of his questions. Charlotte once called Benet and told him, "Your son is a liar, and he's the worst thing that ever happened to me."

As Thomas became more reckless, his young teenage daughter became uncomfortable being around him. As a result, Charlotte swept in and wielded her professional experience as a substance abuse counselor as a weapon. According to Benet, even though Thomas brought it on himself, the way she went about flipping his life upside down "got him a little bit tilted." She turned him in to CPS; they placed parental restrictions on him, making it difficult for him to see his daughter. Benet said, "I'm not blaming

CPS. In general, they are good people working hard under extraordinary circumstances. They have to make snap decisions. The decision they made, in this case, was the right one. It's just how it all came about. It's very difficult to get Thomas to listen and deal with the propriety of the situation because Charlotte got in and said some things that he's holding her responsible for" (i.e., not being able to see his daughter). "I'm assuming she knows what she's doing … [but] there can be some really awful conversations between mom and child … between counselor and abuser." Charlotte and Thomas had heated discussions that further damaged their relationship. Currently, he lives in a private substance abuse rehab program and seems to be doing okay (even though he is still angry with her). They are not allowed to have cell phones, but Thomas will call Benet when he has facility phone time. Sometimes their conversations are serious; sometimes, they just kid around. Benet only talks about Charlotte if Thomas brings her up. She will no longer take Thomas's calls, but she continues to have a relationship with his daughter. Charlotte is the only link Thomas has to his daughter because he has to get her permission contact her. She doesn't have legal custody of his daughter but greatly influences his daughter's mother. The women have become very close as they have seemingly locked arms to keep him away.

> *"I'm quite sure if Charlotte had raised him or I had raised him, his life would be very different. If she had never gotten pregnant, her life would be very different … I definitely can see the negative it brought on Thomas and Charlotte's lives for sure. Those two are not good together."*

Charlotte's actions were not the only destructive influence on Thomas. His adoptive mother also had her own set of issues. According to Benet, she was a "money-grubber" and had extramarital affairs. The family doesn't talk about her much. There were a lot of fractures. Thomas's misogyny was borne of the unhealthy relationships he had with his birth mother and his adoptive mother, a treacherous cocktail that pushed him into rehab. And, even though his birth mother has established a pattern of rejecting him, he cannot stop himself from going back for more.

While Thomas and Charlotte's lives have always been entangled, his life was also intertwined with Benet before either of them knew it. Thomas was born in Texas, moved to Michigan, and then moved back to Texas during his high school years. While in Michigan, he unknowingly lived near Benet's second wife's workplace. When he graduated from high school in Texas, Benet's mother (Thomas's biological grandmother) actually handed him his diploma on stage. As a school administrator, she knew of Thomas because he was often in trouble but did not know that he was her biological grandson. When Benet told her who he was, she had a look of recognition in her eyes. He said, "Our paths kinda came close to crossing no matter what. It was tilted that way."

Luckily, Thomas had an honorable adoptive father. Thomas calls his adoptive father "Dad" and Benet "Pops." Unfortunately, his adoptive father died after being T-boned in a car accident a few years ago. He had an undiagnosed subdural hematoma. He didn't go to the hospital right away, collapsed in the shower many days later, and passed away. According to Benet, "He did the job I didn't do. He was a good man. He did a pretty good job of raising everybody. He gave Thomas some morals." Thomas will be released from the rehab treatment facility soon. Benet hopes that the support and coping skills Thomas learned in that program will be useful as he puts his life back together. But no matter what happens, Benet will be there for him.

~ Advice Through Benet's Lens ~

<u>For birth parents:</u> "Listen and don't try to force people into various modes of thinking. Be as honest as you can with the questions that are being asked because people have a right to be here."

My Thoughts, My Lens

As children, we are shaped by the decisions of other people, and that fact is compounded for adoptees. But as adults, we have the choice to either take back the steering wheel of our lives or remain complacent in the back seat.

As children, both Benet and Thomas were molded by the decisions of the adults in their lives – with both positive and damaging effects. And while Thomas's circumstances affected him more destructively, it is encouraging that he still reaches out to Benet regularly. I find it honorable that Benet consciously put in the work to have a relationship with Thomas – and now loves him equally as much as he loves his two younger sons.

Benet's story touched me on a primal level. Before speaking with him, I didn't know that birth fathers could have a "hole" just like an adoptee. I found it inspiring that his story, while complicated, demonstrates it is possible for adults to pivot.

Kate D. | Administrative Assistant

Pennsylvania
Year of Adoption: 1976

When we met for the first time, Kate's infectious laugh rolled out of her while her presence filled my room as we introduced ourselves from 800 miles away through our computer screens. But as her story unfolded, she allowed me to look at the roiling emotions beneath her surface. It became clear that she was used to taking punches in life. And is still learning how to duck. She had a flair about her that drew me in as she talked about her hardships over the years.

Kate was 16 when she "got hooked up with the wrong guy." She started dating *the* charismatic Benny. He was 19 and drove a Firebird, which in her mind was equally as impressive as he was. Initially, he was dating Kate's friend Lex. Kate couldn't believe how lucky she was when he dropped Lex for her. Lex had everything important to a teenage girl: a huge bedroom and a closet full of jeans that made Kate envious. But Kate's nice legs ultimately got her into trouble. She admits that she was naive and didn't realize what was slowly happening – until one day, she didn't have any clothes on. She thought, "Oh, I'm naked. I'm gonna have sex." Simply put, "Benny wanted what Benny wanted." Kate was embarrassed because she didn't know how to handle the situation, not knowing how to say, *"Don't."* She continued to have sex with Benny, even though she really didn't want to. They went to a few wild parties in his Firebird. The drinking made her uncomfortable, but she continued to date him because he was *fun*.

When Kate discovered she was pregnant, she decided she couldn't have an abortion. Benny wanted to marry her. She told her older sister about her pregnancy and then knew she had to tell her parents. She said, "It was very, very scary." They were sitting in their bedroom. She walked in and said she had something to tell them. She vaguely remembers the scene now, but what stands out the most in her memory was her mother's sigh along with a guttural utterance that sounded like "uhhh-ohhh," like she was suffocating while trying to find a coherent word. With no further discussion, Kate walked back to her bedroom feeling numb.

Kate's parents contacted an agency in Pennsylvania that facilitated adoptions and housed pregnant single women and girls. When Kate was four months pregnant, they took her to stay there for the rest of her pregnancy. The saddest part was that she had to leave her six-year-old little sister – Kate was like a second mom to her. As she walked to the car, her sister hung on to her leg, begging her not to go. Kate lied and said that she was going to an art school.

Her parents had a hard time leaving her at the facility. At this point in the interview, Kate started to cry as she described the blurry scene. She remembers that her mother was crying, and in that moment, feelings of abandonment bubbled into Kate's consciousness. But in hindsight, she said there was no way her mother could have dealt with her pregnancy on a daily basis – having to watch her stomach grow and consumed with worry about what their neighbors and friends might think. Years later, her mother said that she discovered who her true friends were when they learned of the pregnancy.

The facility was homey. Kate had a wonderful roommate, which was comforting. She also liked the other young pregnant women. However, the person she came to love the most was a very kind nun who worked there. Kate said that she couldn't have survived without her. She helped Kate to sort through her churning emotions. Together they came up with the "plan," which was that Kate would give her baby up.

Unfortunately, Kate vomited for most of her stay. At eight months pregnant, she was only 117 pounds and unable to make it downstairs to eat dinner with the rest of the residents. She carried a plastic bag everywhere she went and eventually had to be hospitalized to receive fluids intravenously. When her parents visited her in the hospital, the nurse informed them that the baby was fine but said nothing about Kate, which upset her mother. She demanded to know, "What about *my* daughter???" The tone of her mother's voice made Kate realize, "Oh, oh. My mom *does* love me." Kate said, "I knew she did but not during that time."

After that, her vomiting stopped.

Kate remembers thinking, "Wow, maybe I needed that." Years later, she was not sick in the same way during subsequent pregnancies. She has concluded that her extreme vomiting was psychological – roiling emotions spewing through her battered surface.

When it came time to have her baby, Kate was given an epidural. She did not know she had a choice; the hospital staff just gave it to her because she was young. The nurses would not allow Kate to hold her daughter when she was born. After naming her baby Annemarie, she remembers seeing a little part of her hand poking up from the hospital bassinet. She said, "I sobbed and sobbed and sobbed … for the whole three days in the hospital." Kate cried so much that she disturbed the other mothers in the maternity ward. Kate got to see Annemarie on the last day of her hospital stay. Her mother brought a baby blanket and a new white outfit. They laid Annemarie on the bed and her mother dressed her while Kate stood by.

> *"I didn't hold her because I think I knew if I did, I wasn't going to let her go. It was already painful enough."*

When they were leaving the hospital, Kate remembers crying in the elevator. Her mother wanted to know why she was crying, more concerned about what the people around them would think. When they got home, Kate stayed in bed for days and cried more. Her little sister Sally would come in and jump on her, which felt good. Sally had residual emotional issues from Kate's sudden disappearance. She slept in the bed with her. Kate still feels guilty that her pregnancy affected her sister, too.

After four weeks, Kate wanted Annemarie back – she called the adoption agency to let them know. Benny drove Kate to pick up Annemarie and they moved into his house. Kate's parents were very unhappy about her decision. During the time she and Annemarie lived with Benny, Kate became disoriented and had many blackouts. She was alone with Annemarie much of the time while Benny continued to party. She remembers putting together Annemarie's crib by herself. At one point, he came home drunk and attempted to take Annemarie to see his parents in his Firebird without a car seat. As they argued, Kate protected Annemarie with her body. She knew that she couldn't leave Annemarie alone with him. He was volatile and reckless when he drove. Kate shook her head and said, "Benny was crazy." But she was conflicted because he also had a responsible side. Even though he partied hard, he also worked hard. He always had money for Kate and

Annemarie – and at least provided for them. Kate slowly concluded that her life would not work with him in it. They had scheduled an appointment with the Justice of the Peace to get married. But when the day came, she didn't show up.

Kate ultimately decided that she and Annemarie needed to move out of Benny's house. Sadly, Kate's parents would not allow her and Annemarie to live with them, fearing what Benny might do. Instead, Kate moved in with a family friend. After taking care of Annemarie for two months, Kate said, "Deep in my heart, I knew what I had to do. Again. Rocking her, I prayed. Rocking her, oh, God … God answered my prayer."

At this point in the interview, Kate lifted both of her pointing fingers together. Then she said, "In my mind, I went here, and Annemarie went here." When Kate said, "I went here," she moved one hand off to the side, and as she said, "And Annemarie went here," she moved the other hand off to the other side.

Kate took Annemarie back to the agency. When they arrived, Annemarie was sleeping. She said, "Thank God she was sleeping. In my mind, I told her I loved her. I'm sorry. I asked God to please protect my baby. That was it. It was hard. I would never advise a girl to give her baby up. It was very painful. It was 44 years ago, and I can still cry."

[Tears.]

Kate let Annemarie go physically but not emotionally. In an attempt to heal, she followed a friend to Minnesota. They roomed together while they worked for a TV evangelist. At times, Kate was okay, but other times, she was deeply depressed. Her suffering became so severe that she couldn't get out of bed and was unable to go to work. However, her friend intervened with their boss, letting her know what had happened. Kate said, "She was a Christian, and I was able to keep my job." Ironically, what finally saved Kate from her depression was that her friend was a bit of a slob. One day, when Kate was lying in bed, she looked down the hall and saw their messy apartment. And a vacuum cleaner.

> *"It was like climbing out of it … that was like soft dirt … to grab that handle and vacuum. I slowly started to make myself vacuum, make myself clean. That's how I got out of it."*

A few years after pulling herself up, Kate moved back to Pennsylvania and worked as a bank teller. Unknown to Kate, Annemarie's adoptive godmother was good friends with Kate's supervisor. One day, the godmother came into the bank with a stroller. Kate felt an invisible force drawing her to that stroller. She felt it "in her blood" and desperately wanted to run over to see the toddler with the cute pigtails. But because she was working at the teller window, she could not be on the main floor. Kate said, "I wasn't looking for it. There were all kinds of cute kids that came in the bank. It was crazy. I *knew* without knowing." Many years later, when Annemarie's godmother and Kate met, she confirmed that she was the woman at the bank. And the cute pig-tailed little girl was, indeed, Annemarie.

Kate continued to move on with her life, eventually married, and had two more daughters. Once a year, Kate called the agency to find out if they had any information on Annemarie. Eventually, the agency sent a letter that excluded any identifying information. It sounded like three-year-old Annemarie had a perfect life, complete with an older brother who was also adopted.

Annemarie's life turned out to be perfect – but only on paper.

When Annemarie was 24 years old, she found Kate. Her adoptive parents had changed her name to Marie. When they met in person, Marie hung onto Kate, sobbed, and yelped, "Mom!" Marie so desperately needed her. For the first few months following their reunion, they had a great relationship. Marie met her two younger sisters, and Kate met her biological grandsons. As they became reacquainted, Kate learned that Marie had experienced anything but an idyllic life. As a teenager, she was troubled. She partied (like Benny), and her parents were abusive. When she came home late, they would lock her out of the house, and leave a sleeping bag on the porch along with a bottle so she could pee in it.

When Kate met Marie's adoptive parents during a lunch, she was shocked by the heartlessness that emanated from Laura, Marie's adoptive mother. Kate said, "It was like her heart was encased in chains of ice, and her eyes were sewn shut." At one point during the lunch, Laura callously demonstrated how she could wrap a belt around her fist and tuck in the buckle, so it didn't leave bruises on her kids when she whipped them. Kate said, "If I had known this woman was beating my child, I would have swiped her right out of that house. I would have protected my little girl." Laura not only beat Marie but also pressured her to be elegantly perfect in public and punished her for failing.

> *"I never knew an adopted person could get parents that weren't good and nurturing ... If someone had told me that just like with [biological] parents, there is a good chance that the [adoptive parents] won't be good parents, I wouldn't have given her up. There's no way I would have taken that chance. Her mother didn't love her unconditionally."*

Kate remembers thinking, "How did my baby – that I sacrificed myself for – get *this* mother?"

Marie's DNA collided with Laura's image of a perfect dainty girl. Her genes prevented her from accepting her adoptive mother's destructive racist views. There were times when driving that Laura would joke, "How much do you think I would get for hitting that one?" And by "that one," she meant a Black person walking down the street. Kate said, "This was a woman who went to church every Sunday." Because of Laura's cruelty, Marie defied Catholicism and leaned into the Black community. She adopted the verbal slang, had Black friends, and her children were fathered by a Black man.

Sadly, after a honeymoon period between birth mother and birth daughter, Marie redirected her rage towards Kate. She verbally harassed her for choosing adoption. Kate thinks it was because she saw the mother that she could've had instead of the one she did have.

On many occasions, Marie was abusive, cursed Kate out, and lied to her. Kate said, "I don't think she realizes that I don't give it right back because I'm a mother. Our kids can hit us over the head, and we still forgive them." Unfortunately, Marie's toxic presence hurt her sisters, too. During one of their fights, Kate's middle daughter screamed that she couldn't take it anymore, holding her hands over her ears. Kate felt like she couldn't defend herself or her younger daughters, begging Marie to get help from a therapist. Marie refused and told Kate she was the one who needed to go – which is what Kate did. Kate said, "I ended up going because Marie was destroying my life."

Kate started yelling at her girls and began an antidepressant regimen (neither of which had she done before Marie's arrival). Their relationship was a rollercoaster that fluctuated between pleasant and chaotic events. Marie could be both nasty and generously kind. She once gave Kate a birthday card that said, "The best part of me came from you." Kate said that Marie's goodness was layered "between all of the ugly." Despite their turmoil, Kate loves Marie just as much as her other two daughters. However, her feelings for Marie are often entangled with guilt due to her belief that her past shouldn't have affected her younger daughters' lives – echoing the guilt she had when her pregnancy affected her little sister's life.

Marie and Kate have been unable to see each other's point of view. Kate tried to get Marie to understand why she chose adoption, but she felt unheard and judged. In Kate's opinion, most birth mothers make their choice as a sacrifice; very few choose adoption for selfish reasons.

"It's natural to instinctively protect your child."

Marie disagrees. When she became a single mother at 20 years old, she told Kate, "I'm more of a woman than you will ever be because I kept my child." Kate's response was, "I'm more of a mother than you'll ever be because I sacrificed myself for my child … why don't you just thank me that you have a life?" Despite their argument, Kate did concede that, of course, Marie wouldn't consider adoption – given the abuse she endured from her adoptive parents. Kate sometimes questioned whether she should have let Marie back into her life but ultimately couldn't turn her back on her.

Benny is still in Marie's life peripherally. He and Marie have somewhat of a relationship, but mostly, they have little to do with each other. She once stole money from him, and according to Kate, "You don't do that to Benny." He still cares for Kate. (He once bought her a stove when she didn't have the money.) She loves him because they share a child.

Kate has suffered numerous losses since she was a teenager. Her loved ones, her health, her marriage, her mother, her daughter's fiancé, her grandson, and of course, Marie.

When Kate's biological daughter was in high school, her boyfriend, Bo, did not have a place to live. Kate took him in, and he became her son. He later became her daughter's fiancé, and they were together for ten years. Bo called her "Mom," and it felt natural to her. As a White woman, Kate was particularly protective of him because he was Black, understanding that he did not receive the same opportunities in life that she did. He died of natural causes a few years ago and she has yet to recover.

With tears in her eyes, Kate talked about Bo's death, saying her grief over losing him was equally as painful as the grief she had over giving up Marie.

> *"All losses are different, but grief and pain are all the same. It took me awhile to learn that."*

Not long after Bo died, Marie's son (Kate's grandson) was murdered. At the funeral, Marie motioned for her to come down to the front row and sit with her. Kate felt a little peace when Marie sought her comfort.

Sometime after the funeral, Marie picked a fight with Kate – screaming at her that the grief she felt over losing her son was much more than Kate's grief over losing Bo. Marie's comment offended Kate because, in her mind, Bo *was* her son.

Even so, Kate attempted to communicate to Marie that while the grief they shared over losing their sons was immense, the despair she had over giving Marie up for adoption was just as painful.

> *"The pain with Marie was my pain about losing her because she was alive. I thought she would have a great life. That's not how it was. It felt as though my limbs were ripped from my body and my heart sucked out of my chest. With Bo, it was about him losing his life – his future. Both pains are pretty much the same scale; only it tips a little for Marie."*

Kate said, to her, the pain of giving up a child who still has life can be just as painful as losing a child to death. Unfortunately, Marie is not ready to accept that concept and her rage against Kate continues.

~ Advice Through Kate's Lens ~

For birth mothers: "Follow your heart and do what you know is best. At this point in my life, I would not advise anyone to give their baby away."

For adoptive parents: "If you can't unconditionally love a child that was not your DNA, you better not adopt them."

My Thoughts, My Lens

The complexity of Kate and Marie's relationship highlights the primal nature of our genes. Although Kate and Marie struggle and fight with one another, they cannot resist the magnetic draw of the mother and daughter biological bond.

Kate doesn't want to be judged by Marie.

Marie wants to blame Kate for her adoption trauma.

I believe that when we are flailing in the depths of our pain, it is hard to see we are casting our misery onto the very people we want so desperately to save us.

Kate and Marie's journey is unfinished. I have to believe Kate and Marie's bond will prevail – I hope their genetic pull is stronger than the ammunition of their anguish. I have faith that they will be able to work through their trauma together, and the charming Kate who showed up at the beginning of our interview will still be there for Marie when the time is right.

Jill D. | Deputy Clerk

South Dakota
Year of Adoption: 1975

I found Jill to be endearing, earnest, and genuine. As she eagerly told her story, her words were like a welcomed salve. They exuded from her as though they had been contained too long within her once scarred shell. Throughout our conversation, Jill repeatedly smiled and said she was "so blessed" and "so grateful."

Jill's parents' tumultuous relationship and unstable homelife propelled her to move out when she was 16. (She moved in with her brother.) When she was growing up, her family looked like a typical Midwestern farm family to outsiders. However, her mother had mental health issues. Her parents had intense fights, separated often, and then would get back together. Jill remembers a few times when her mother threw her father's clothes out on the front lawn. At the early age of 17, Jill graduated from high school. She and her high school sweetheart had broken up, but his dad passed away, and he wanted to see her. According to Jill, she gave him "a little more comfort" than she should have and became pregnant. The plan was to get married. But after thinking about it, Jill decided not to go through with the marriage, knowing it was not the best solution for her baby. She was concerned about the birth father's heavy drinking, her family situation, and not having any emotional support. At that point her ex-boyfriend disengaged.

When Jill's mother found out about her pregnancy, she was angry and screamed at her. In the 1970s, teenage pregnancy was not well received. Pregnant teens who did not get abortions either kept their babies or were sent away to a home to give birth. The girls who were sent away would disappear for a year and then come back, pretending nothing had happened. Her two brothers were married and their wives were both pregnant. Jill thinks her mom reasoned that if she were to get married, they could have a clean slate. But Jill's decision not to marry made her mother "flip out." In her heart, Jill knew that keeping her baby as a single mother wasn't right because she didn't have a healthy family support system. She also wanted her baby to have emotionally stable parents.

Both her dad and sister thought she should have an abortion. Her sister even made an appointment for her in Minneapolis. Jill had already decided against having an abortion. But when her mother found out about the appointment, *she lost it* (she assumed Jill was planning to see it through), screaming at Jill that she was a whore and slut. Consequently, Jill and her sister went to Minneapolis anyways – just to get away. (Her sister had already secured a baby sitter.) They just hung out for a few days. Taking Jill on that trip was her sister's way of showing her support.

A few years later, Jill and her mother mended fences – but they never directly discussed her decision, which deeply hurt. Things became worse for Jill when her parents were in the midst of getting a divorce. The proceedings were at the center of her mother's attention. Jill believes her mom thought she was doing the best she could, not realizing she was displacing her anger on Jill. She said, "My mom couldn't make my dad feel bad, but she could make me feel bad."

Jill ended up moving in with her sister for a while and then moved to South Dakota to be near her brother and his wife. She wanted to be able to call a nearby family member during the remainder of her pregnancy. Shortly after arriving, she walked into the state social services office and said, "My name is Jill. I'm 17. I'm six months pregnant. I need help."

They helped. Social services helped Jill secure a studio apartment and a job at the local college, working as an assistant. Jill said the professors she worked for were awesome. They called her their "gopher." An experienced non-judgmental counselor at the social service agency helped her reach her final decision by asking her to consider the pros and cons of adoption. His questions were designed to help her think long-term. The counselor emphasized she really needed to make sure she wasn't going to change her mind several months after her baby went to live with the adoptive family. While she did have time to change her mind legally, he implored her to think about that decision's ramifications. He emphasized she was not the only person her decision would affect. If she changed her mind, she would be hurting the people who adopted the child. He had seen first-hand what could happen when a birth mother changed her mind after the adoptive parents have bonded with the baby. His counseling helped Jill to make a firm decision. She became resolute in her choice because she did not want her unborn daughter to come into her life of chaos.

At this point in the interview, Jill let out a melancholy sigh, exhaling as though she was momentarily transported back. When Jill went into labor, a coworker rode with her to the hospital (Jill drove!). Her daughter was born at 4:18 p.m. on a Saturday. She named her Allison, with the understanding that her adoptive parents would most likely change her name. She promised herself that she would find Allison when she became an adult. Jill told the hospital staff she could only hold her for a minute because if they let her hold her again, she would never be able to give her up. Jill wrote Allison a letter:

> *"I am so sorry. I want you to know I will always love you, and if you can find it in your heart, I hope you seek me out."*

Somewhere along the way, the letter was lost and never made it to Allison. Jill's parents visited her in the hospital. Her mother said that if she could get to the baby, she would steal her. Jill knew her mother wasn't joking. Her mother's mental health issues scared her, so she had the nurses put Allison in the back part of the nursery. Jill sighed,

> *"I don't know. I don't know. It was the hardest thing I ever had to do."*

When Jill went home a few days later, she called her ex-boyfriend to let him know Allison had been born. When he found out she was a girl, he was disappointed. During times of extreme sadness after Allison's birth, Jill sought refuge at a Catholic chapel. She would sit in one of the pews, allowing the sanctuary to bring her comfort. During one of those visits, a lovely nun named Sister Mary came up behind her and said very quietly, "The eyes of God are shining down on you." In that moment, Jill knew God was telling her it was okay.

Over the years, people were insensitive and cruel to Jill when they learned that she was a birth mother. For example, one woman told her that she thought Jill gave her daughter up for adoption because she just wanted an "out." Another accused her of wanting to party. Others have told her that they would never do what she did. When Jill moved to a new town, she went to a Tupperware party, hoping to make some potential friends. Some of the women were bad-mouthing a young girl who chose adoption for her baby. Their lack of understanding triggered Jill's pain, to the point that she couldn't help herself and snapped at them to not judge her.

Jill did NOT make friends at that party.

On other occasions, when random people gave Jill their unsolicited opinions, she attempted not to get defensive. However, as she relayed the litany of stories, I could see the lingering remnants from her venerable wounds. She said that until you walk in someone else's shoes, you don't know what you would do if you're put in the same situation ... *even* if that situation was of your own doing. If it hasn't happened to you, you don't *know* the anguish. She said,

> *"The easiest choice would have been for me to walk out of the hospital with my baby."*

She had friends who kept their babies, and sometimes it didn't end well. Jill turned 18 right before she gave birth. As a legal adult, she and the birth father went to court to give up their parental rights. The judge asked her to stop before she walked out because he wanted to talk to her. He kindly told her he wanted to commend her for handling her situation like an adult. He also told her not to let anyone make her feel less than herself. Jill was grateful that the judge took it upon himself to comfort her. She held on to his words over the years as many people condemned her.

Jill's life continued, but she thought of Allison every day. She brought up her birth daughter in every one of her subsequent dating relationships. She talked about how she would like to meet her if she had the opportunity. For a while, Jill found happiness with the wonderful man she married. He promised her, "Don't worry, we'll find her." They had twin girls (one blonde and one brunette) and a son together. Tragically, her husband died in a car accident when the girls were five years old, and her son was only three months old.

I asked Jill if choosing adoption was equally as stressful as the death of her husband. She said it was similar because they were both grieving processes, and yet they were so different because of what she could and could not control. She had no control over the car accident. About adoption loss, she said,

"When I made that choice, it was a whole different kind of grief because I brought that grief into my life."

As Jill was reliving her pain during our interview, she automatically started rubbing her tummy, briefly teleported back into her teenage body. She snapped out of it and then laughed when she realized what she was doing. She said,

"I felt her kick for nine months and knew I already loved her ... then had to make that 'god-awful' choice."

On Allison's birthdays, Jill almost always went to church to pray or took a drive to sit by a lake – much like people do when they are grieving a loved one's death. She felt like that was "Allison's day." Periodically, she tried to find Allison by calling the state social services to get updates. However, because it was a closed adoption, they could not give her any information. She begged them to tell just her if Allison was fine or ok. No luck.

"Back then, it was frowned upon. It is better now. It was so difficult to give her up, but I gave birth to a baby that gets to have a life. I think women who choose abortion have a bigger struggle. I gave birth to a baby and heard her cry. I hoped she was alive and safe. I have a friend that had an abortion, and I don't know that she'll ever forget that she feels guilty and maybe ashamed. They carry a big load. It's sad."

As she raised her kids, she often thought of Allison. When the twin girls were 14 years old, she took them out to eat and told them, "I am going to tell you a story. Hopefully, you will understand." They did understand and somehow already knew that their mother had a secret.

Six years later, on a Thursday, Jill received the letter from the state social services she hoped would come for two decades. They let her know that Andrea had reached out and wanted to meet her. Jill ran downstairs to tell one of the twins (who was getting ready to go somewhere – curling iron in hand). She said, "We were jumping up and down and freaking out!" Everyone was very excited. Jill knew Allison wouldn't get her letter for a day or two because she lived farther away, so she waited until Saturday to give her a call. When no one picked up, she panicked and hung up the phone. After a moment, she decided not to be rude and tried again, and started to leave a message on the answering machine.

As Jill started to tell me about her message, her lip started to quiver, her voice cracked, and her eyes became misty as she said,

> *"Hi, my name is Jill. I've been waiting for this moment for 20 years."*

Her daughter picked up the phone.

They ended up having a two-and-a-half-hour phone call. She learned that her birth daughter's name was actually Andrea K. (whose story is also in this book – see the table of contents). Jill drove to St. Paul to meet her the next day. She had many questions. What did she look like? Was she happy? Was she doing ok? When they met, Jill thought Andrea looked like her dark-haired daughter.

Jill remembers that Andrea had 10,000 questions.

Why do I have big toes? *"Birth dad's fault."* Do you have health problems? Do I have living grandparents? What is this funky thing on my arm? Why do I walk the way I do? Who do I look like? Does your family have dark eyebrows? Did you ever think of me, Jill? *"Every Day. Every Day."* How old are the twins? How old is your son? What have you told them? Why did you give me up? What about my birth dad? Did you care about each other? Did you think I'd look like this? Andrea said, "At least you don't have horns." *[Grin.]* Jill replied, "What if I had been an idiot and I didn't like you at all?"

Andrea did say she was relieved that Jill was normal. Andrea was surprised to discover that she was Swedish, German, and Dutch because her paperwork said she was Norwegian. In fact, her adoptive parents almost gave her the Norwegian name Gia. Jill asked Andrea if she wanted to meet her birth dad. She said yes – but not at that time. She wanted to absorb meeting Jill and get to know her before she met him.

Through subsequent conversations, Jill was genuinely relieved to learn that Andrea had a good life growing up in South Dakota. As their conversations progressed, they figured out that she went to the same school as Jill's niece (Andrea's biological cousin) and was a waitress at Jill's sister's country club (and unknowingly waited on her biological aunt and uncle). Andrea had a solid midwestern life, went to college, and became a social worker. She saw the dismal side of adoption and foster care as a social worker. She had to make life-altering choices about babies with fetal alcohol syndrome (e.g., whether they should be removed from their homes). She visited the penitentiary, where she met with birth mothers, some of whom were unsure of who the birth fathers might be. She also met mothers who passed along their addictions to their babies. Some babies were products of rape. With that perspective, Andrea felt fortunate that Jill had zero doubts about who her birth father was.

As their relationship grew, Jill and Andrea would sometimes struggle with introductions, but they introduced each other as *birth daughter* and *birth mother* most of the time. They once went to an improv show in Chicago. The guy waiting on them joked with Andrea, saying, "After all your mom did for you, this is the best you can do???" They laughed and played along. Good stuff. Their get-togethers have been easy and comfortable.

Andrea told Jill that when she was growing up, her parents were very respectful of Jill. They told her that she was loved by her birth mother and chose adoption because she wanted her to have a better life. But after Jill and Andrea connected, Andrea's parents backed away from their deferential stance. Jill sent Andrea's mom a Mother's Day card to thank her for giving Andrea a wonderful life. Unfortunately, it wasn't received well. Jill has tried to stay out of her way. When she was invited to Andrea's wedding, she respectfully sat at the back of the ceremony.

Jill's relationship with Andrea is not a motherly relationship; it's more like that of a sister or an aunt. Andrea calls her Jill. She loves Andrea and knows she loves her back, but she also knows Andrea's adoptive parents are *her* parents.

"I can be part of her life, but it was their job to raise her."

When Andrea flies in from out of state to visit her adoptive family, Jill makes an effort not to put inappropriate expectations or burdens on Andrea. She works around Andrea's schedule, cherishing their visits which always conclude with an "*I love you.*"

Jill's family has embraced Andrea since meeting her. All of the siblings get along well. The half-siblings have great admiration for each other. They have been to each other's weddings, met on vacation, and regularly text and phone each other.

Jill knows that she is blessed to have the opportunity to know Andrea as well as she does. With glistening eyes, Jill said, "I am really lucky … I got to get that second chance that I hoped and prayed for 20 years."

~ Advice Through Jill's Lens ~

For birth mothers: "After I gave her up for adoption, I wish there would have been 'after counseling' like I had *when* I was pregnant. You have the baby, then you are done. I didn't have the financial means to go to a therapist. It would have been helpful."

For adoptive parents: "Counseling would be helpful as your child transitions to an older age and begins asking questions. Always seek ways to help your child."

Jill believes that birth parent and birth child reunions should be private. She was horrified when she watched reunions on a public stage during a Maury Povich show.

Jill wishes she could reach out to young people to let them know that while adoption may be very hard, there is nothing like the joy of knowing you brought a human into the world … and that *you* gave someone else a chance to love them. She also wishes that young people would look at choosing adoption as being unselfish. Adoption is not "getting rid of a baby." She believes that it is emotionally harder later in life for young women who chose abortion instead of adoption. Then she said, "Ah, maybe I'm overthinking it. It is both overwhelming and wonderful. Not everyone can understand or care. That's my heart."

[Sigh. Tears.]

My Thoughts, My Lens

When an adoptive mother recommended Jill D. for an interview with me, I thought I would be speaking with another adoptive mother. It wasn't until we met that I learned she was, in fact, a birth mother. After hearing her story, I realized I had been shortsighted for my *entire life* … carelessly blind as humans can be when we feel betrayed. I realized I was so focused on my own adoption trauma that I forgot that the person I viewed as my betrayer also felt pain. Through Jill's eyes, I learned that birth mothers undoubtedly mourn the loss of their birth children but are often vilified without any support. Honestly, it was healing for me to listen to her story.

I learned that her pain came *first.*

To be clear, it wasn't that I was glad to hear she suffered. Instead, it was comforting to know that I was not alone in my pain. I realized that even if birth mothers are no longer physically "in the picture," they are undoubtedly spiritually present.

Jill's encounters with many people who condemned her reminded me of a conversation I had with a friend decades ago. We were having one of those naive hypothetical debates that culminated with my friend becoming infuriated with me. In our early 20s, we were not much older than teenagers ourselves, discussing having future children and the "what if" scenarios that could come with having teenage daughters – the "what if our imaginary daughters became pregnant" question came up. I said I would likely choose adoption for her. My friend became outraged and flipped out … not just outraged – but frighteningly hostile. I seriously thought she was going to stab me in the face. She couldn't believe that I would let my imaginary teenage daughter "give away" my imaginary grandchild. She said that she would make her daughter live at home, get a college education, and take care of her child. The entire argument was so bizarre. I'm guessing my friend's outburst was similar in intensity to what Jill had experienced from others throughout her adult life. I was confused-angry-sad about why my friend was so combative and vitriolic, especially since she knew I was adopted. We never spoke of it again.

But I chewed on that altercation for years. In hindsight, I can definitely see her point – *if* both the teenage daughter and her parents have the mental and emotional bandwidth, as well as adequate financial resources needed to raise a child. Perhaps her opinion was borne from her vantage point of growing up in a wealthy family? She and her siblings all had extremely successful careers which stemmed from privilege and fully-funded college educations. The impoverished classes were not within her reality.

Or perhaps, it was because she learned that humans could be thrown away and replaced when she watched her mother move out of her childhood home so her father could replace his wife with the "other" woman? Perhaps the thought of "getting rid" of a family member hit a visceral nerve?

Or maybe it was because she couldn't imagine giving away a piece of her own heart? Now, that scenario makes the most sense to me. As a mother, I can neither imagine life without my daughters nor having to give them up by my own choice. However, I think that actually supports Jill's position that she selflessly chose adoption for her baby. It brings up the question:

Why would someone *voluntarily* wound themselves?

In my opinion, the answer is this: birth mothers intentionally slice off a piece of their souls, leaving their own hearts incomplete to create the opportunity for their children to have a better shot at obtaining a life of "wholeness."

In my view, Jill's choice was the ultimate act of love.

Natasha P. | Teacher

Colorado
Year of Adoption: 2003

Natasha embodied toughness and sensitivity, an unusual combination that was also interlaced with practicality. I imagine she is that friend whose loyalty perseveres as the years blow by, steady as the rockface of a mountainside.

When Natasha was 21, she met Garth and couldn't resist the draw of his southern drawl. She was a full-time ski instructor and was living a Colorado ski bum's life – partying and hanging out at bars. By the time she discovered that she was pregnant with Garth's baby, they were no longer dating. She had already moved on and was back in contact with her high school ex-boyfriend, Mike, whom she dated from the time she was 16 years old (and continued to see off and on for four years). As teenagers, they were serious enough that at one point, he had asked Natasha's parents for their blessing to marry her, but they said no because they were too young.

Before telling anyone about her pregnancy, Natasha went to a women's healthcare clinic looking for someone to assist her with her options. When she told them that she was pretty sure she didn't want to have an abortion, they dismissively pointed to some pamphlets on a table. She walked out the door because she felt like they weren't interested in helping her since she wasn't considering abortion. She said, "Not to be political. I have a very different outlook when it comes to pro-choice. I am pro-choice but not *that* pro-choice. Abortions are hard. If your mom chose abortion, you wouldn't be here."

Natasha extensively researched how that organization handled abortions. At this point in the interview, as she talked further and I continued to type, I had a hard time keeping up with her because she became quite passionate. She said,

"They don't give enough information for abortions. They don't tell you what the procedure is for abortions. They do not help you afterward. When you have an abortion, you're ripping your hormones into pieces and need help with stability ... It is sad. When you [choose] adoption, you're required to go to counseling and take these steps as a birth mom. I had to go through a process: 'Is this right for you? How about this? Is this right for you? Are you sure you can give your baby to someone else?' I find it odd that they don't do that for killing your child. If they [presented] full information on all four options, then abortion rates would go down. I am pro-choice the <u>right way</u>."

By "four options," Natasha meant closed adoption, open adoption, abortion, and keeping the baby. Natasha said that it breaks her heart thinking about the scared pregnant women going in to get help and wishes they were told, *"I'm sorry you're struggling. Here are your options with what you have going on. Let's take a look at each one deeply."*

After her disappointing experience with the healthcare agency, Natasha felt very alone and decided to tell her boss. Her response was, "Just get an abortion." Natasha wouldn't think about getting one. Next, she told Garth, who was in the process of finalizing his divorce. His response was, "Well, I don't know what I can do right now. You're gonna have to give me a couple of months." A couple of months? The baby was coming whether he wanted it or not. So, Natasha continued down the adoption road by herself. When Garth received the papers to relinquish his parental rights, he did not fight her on the decision. He signed them immediately because he was an adoptee himself with a positive adoption experience.

When Natasha's ex-boyfriend and would-be fiancé, Mike, learned she was pregnant with Garth's baby, it pushed him over the edge. He murdered a woman who closely resembled Natasha in many specific ways. She was shocked – she didn't think he was capable of murder because he was a ladies' man – all the girls *loved* him. The police picked Natasha up and interrogated her about Mike. Ultimately, Mike plead guilty, was convicted, and sent to prison for life.

While the investigation and trial were underway, Natasha had to finalize her pregnancy plans. She realized she wasn't ready to be a mom with the turbulence whirling around her. She said, "I wasn't going to be with Mike. I wasn't going to be with Garth. I was going to be on my own. I didn't want my parents to raise my kid – I wanted them to be grandparents. There was no reason to keep my child because I was going to be *alone*." With the lens and toughness of hindsight, she said,

> "*[My baby] saved my life during that time. My life would be different ... because I would probably be with Mike, or I could be dead, or who knows ... just because of the backstory of that whole murder and what it was.*"

The chaos resulting from Mike's actions ultimately made her decide to move back to her mother's home (Katherine J. – her story is in the following chapter). Even though Natasha was making her own decisions, her mother helped guide her. Together they found an agency that championed open adoptions. Natasha had heard of stories in which closed adoption adoptees were lost and confused because they didn't have answers about their background. Her loyalty to her unborn baby was her first priority. She wanted to make sure her baby had all of the answers he or she needed throughout life. The agency was exceedingly thorough, discussing at length the differences between open and closed adoptions. Natasha became unwavering in her decision as she learned about closed adoption adoptees who "still had that hole and that anger," even though they looked like their adoptive parents – *externally*. However, *internally* they were lost because they saw themselves as different. Natasha wanted her baby's questions to be answered up-front in the hopes that the hole would be significantly smaller.

Natasha had what she called her "team of professionals." She had adoption agency counselors, pregnancy doctors, and additional professional therapists who helped her navigate her emotions surrounding Mike and all that came with the murder. During her pregnancy, Natasha experienced many profound moments during the music portion of church. Having a small church community to give her advice was helpful; fellow congregants offered her a fresh point of view that differed from professional or parental guidance.

As her life continued to turbulently roll forward, she received an inch-thick packet from the agency – she was required to answer a multitude of situational questions like, "What would you do if your birth child showed up at your front door after having a fight with his or her parents?" Natasha responded that she would let him/her in, ask what's going on, and then say,

"Now it's time to contact your mom or dad" (and, meanwhile, she would have secretly contacted them to let them know that their child was safe). After thinking about her response, she said,

> *"And that particular answer just spoke huge words to me. This is what I want to do. It was automatic. I'm not the parent. They are."*

After getting through three or four pages of similar questions, Natasha decided not to finish the packet and requested her case be expedited because she knew exactly what she wanted. She was older than most of the teenage girls that the agency was helping. Natasha's situation was different in that many of them had become pregnant with their high school boyfriends. Because she was resolute, the agency agreed to push her through their system quicker than usual.

> *"I wasn't wishy-washy. I was like, nope, this is what I want to do."*

The agency gave her a notebook with one-page profiles of the prospective parents. She picked Peter and May, a couple from Colorado that spoke to her from the pages. When she announced her choice, her counselor informed her that she needed to pick two more. Unable to connect with any of the other couples, it took her double the time to choose. She already knew she really wanted Peter and May. While Natasha is not a deeply religious person, she knows God led her to Peter and May because they were the *only* parents she wanted. *"This is the one. Pick these guys. I really struggled with choosing other parents. Struggled hard. Can I pick just one couple? Nope ... Why? Ugghhhh. These are the ones I want."* She half-heartedly made two more choices. The agency gave her detailed information on each couple; she brought all three portfolios home to discuss with her mom.

In Natasha's mind, Peter and May were the way she saw herself, well-rounded – religious but not hardcore religious – sporty but also techie. The second couple was extremely sporty, and the third was extremely religious. She decided against those couples because she didn't want parents who would force her child into sports or religion. She said, "I wanted someone that would allow my child to be who he [or she] is ... especially because he [or she] was not coming from their 'loins.'" Peter and May are both Czech. (May immigrated to the United States when she was 18.) Natasha's first meeting with them was at the agency with a counselor present. Natasha said, "We met and kicked it off right away. We got along very well. May is very outgoing and lively, and emotional, just like me. I really loved that there were two languages in the home. Really neat and cool that my kid would get to learn two languages."

The second meeting took place at Peter and May's house. Natasha was able to see the picturesque small town (of less than 500 people) by a mountainside lake where her child would grow up. The town was worthy of Ansel Adams' camera lens. They took pictures of pregnant Natasha by the lake. By spending time in the town, she was able to easily picture her child's future. Natasha and May continued to talk on the phone off and on throughout her pregnancy. When she announced she chose not to know the baby's sex (because she didn't want to get attached), May responded, "Fine, you don't get to know the name until it's born." Natasha smiled at that memory.

When it came time to deliver, the baby was breech with the cord wrapped around the neck. To further complicate matters, Natasha's amniotic fluid was low. The doctors gave her a choice to attempt to have a vaginal delivery, but she opted for the C-section. She said, "Because it wasn't going to be my kid, I needed to make sure [the baby] came out as safe as possible." Her best friend and her mom were in the delivery room taking pictures when her son was born. Peter and May were able to hold him first. After Natasha came out of sedation, they held him so she could see him. They named him Xander. After the staff took him to the nursery to clean him up and give him shots, they brought him to Natasha so she could hold him.

The agency counselor came in for the "Entrustment Ceremony." It was a service symbolizing the openness of their adoption. I was blown away when Natasha described it to me. They even videoed it. The counselor read an adoption poem, a blessing for the baby, a prayer for the birth mother, and a blessing for the adoptive parents. During the part that symbolized giving the baby, *"From Loving Arms to Loving Arms,"* Natasha placed Xander into Peter and May's arms. Everyone present was overcome with emotions as their tears and feelings spilled out.

When Natasha handed him over, although sorrowful, she knew it was right. She said,

"It was very nice. Hard but really good – happy but sad all at the same time … overwhelming with the kind of emotions that were going through me … really hard to explain, but I really felt that it was the right decision. It was meant to be. I had a lot of nurses tell me that they could not believe what we did for an adoption. They had never seen something so open – never seen adoptive parents in the same room with the birth parent."

[Tears.]

When I asked her if she thought Xander knew on some level what was going on she replied,

"I don't know. I know now how we interact. There's still that connection. There's that unconscious, unknown explanation of that connection. As far as he's concerned, May's his mom, and Peter's his dad."

Natasha showed me pages from her scrapbook with Peter and May embracing her – both before and after Xander's birth. Natasha's mother and stepfather were also included in the photographs. As I studied each picture, they looked secure and confident – like a happy family.

Natasha, Peter, May, and Xander moved on with their lives. Natasha had another child years later (named Matthew) whom she kept. The two families visited from time to time. Peter and May made sure Xander grew up knowing about his adoption and birth mother from a very young age. Natasha said when he was young, May explained to him that "her belly couldn't carry a baby and mine could."

Eight years passed, and by then Natasha was teaching kids how to disc golf. On one of their visits, Xander joined her disc golf outing while May stayed back and visited with Katherine. In the middle of the game, he decided it was the appropriate time to ask about his adoption, wanting to know why Natasha gave him up. Luckily, Natasha had been preparing herself for that inevitable moment. She had to quickly mentally pivot from the game. She said, "I had to flip my brain." She gave him the same answer that May had already told him – she wasn't ready to raise a child. When he asked why she kept Matthew and not him, she explained that by the time she had Matthew, she was ready to take care of a kid. She told him,

"Your mom really wanted a kid, and I thought the best thing was to give you to someone who really wanted you in that moment, AND I could still be in your life."

Her answer seemed to satisfy him – he had no other questions or concerns. Xander and Matthew now have a strong brotherly relationship. Natasha hopes that as adults, they'll continue to connect and join each other for the holidays. She would like them to have a closer relationship than she has with her half-sister; they are not really close due to their 14-year age difference. Since Xander and Matthew are only five years apart, she hopes they continue to strengthen their already established bond.

When Xander started driving and got a cell phone, he reached out to Natasha more. Currently, their relationship is driven more by him. She recently went to one of his ski competitions, which happened to be near her house. She said it was more awkward for her than for him because she did not want to breach his boundaries. But he was confident and comfortably introduced her to his teammates as his birth mom. In her mind, she thought, "Ohhhhh, you're comfortable with that. *Alrighty then!*"

"That's the biggest reason why I wanted an open adoption – because I wanted that communication to be there."

Since Xander's adoption, many people have opened up to Natasha about their stories – some never talked about it to anyone before her. Being a birth mother makes her approachable in the eyes of others, and she welcomes their stories. She said, "It's weird. People are very open with me. Every single one is individual. There's not one that's the same."

Over the years, Natasha and May have become friends, calling each other on and off between their busy schedules. Currently, they have little contact, but the agency had prepared Natasha for the trend of birth and adoptive moms to split. Birth grandparents tend to have more contact with the adoptive families. That proved to be true in this case as well. Natasha's mother has a bigger relationship with May and Xander than she does.

Natasha does not doubt that she chose the correct path for Xander. He looks just like his parents. She said, "You would never know he's adopted. He was just right where he was supposed to be … nothing to explain it besides God leading the way of what was supposed to happen."

~ Advice Through Natasha's Lens ~

<u>For birth mothers:</u> "Don't second guess things if you feel that it's right. Then you do what *you* feel is right. You can't let other people tell you what is right and not right when it comes to adoption. You have to listen to your own feelings for your baby. It would have been totally different if I listened to my mom about the couple I chose. I listened to myself. My mom was there to help question it."

"Always listen to your gut feeling because you will be right ... Everybody has their own story of the 'why.' The 'why' is always different."

<u>For adoptive parents:</u> "The more open you are with your kids, whether [they are] adopted or from you [biologically], the better off your kid is going to be in the future. They're not going to feel lost. Xander feels very comfortable in his place. He is who he is. And he is okay with that. It shows. It was because of how open everyone is."

[Tears.]

"It's okay if you have regrets once in a while. too. Love leads all. That's for sure."

My Thoughts, My Lens

It is my belief that most adoptees would welcome a relationship with their birth mothers if they could all turn out like Xander's story. I know I would. Not only do I applaud Natasha for choosing a stable life for her son, but I also am impressed with May's willingness to *share* her son. I detailed how many adoptive mothers feel threatened by birth mothers in the intro to *Through the Lens of Adoptive Families* section in this book. I understand there are legitimate reasons for closed adoptions. But in this case, open adoption was the right choice. Unfortunately, adoptions encased in secrecy and fear result in leaving a "hole" in the adoptee – I can attest to that. Many adoptees yearn for community and family. To Xander's benefit, Natasha and May's actions resulted in expanding his family to include everyone. Because they acted in his best interest through love and rational decision making, he will never have to experience the anguish of not knowing his backstory.

I can't even begin to put myself in Natasha's shoes, but I can say that I admire her perseverance. Her mental strength is extraordinary; growing a baby after enduring a solo pregnancy during the turbulence of her ex-boyfriend's murder is unfathomable to me. But by choosing open adoption, she found a way to have the blessing of her son's birth embrace everyone she loved. Excellent.

Katherine J. | Retired Engineering Project Planner

Colorado
Year of Adoption: 2003

Katherine is an introspective widow. While only in her 60s, the depth of her experience rivals that of someone much older. But unlike some seasoned women, she is still tenderhearted – neither charred nor leathery but soothing and encouraging. I enjoyed listening to Katherine as she articulated her thoughts and emotions about her birth grandchild's open adoption. The story of her daughter, Natasha P., precedes this chapter.

Katherine and her late husband, Sean, had both been married three times. They had similar paths in life before meeting each other. The first marriage gave them children. The second marriage was the rebound. The third marriage was the ringer. Sean was a godsend to both Katherine and her daughter. He was a father figure to Natasha. When she was 21 and told them she was pregnant, he got up, put his arm around her, and told her that they were there for her, whatever she decided to do. The three of them discussed her options. Although Katherine and Sean were disappointed (they thought they had educated Natasha on safe sex), Katherine said, "We just kinda said whoa ... you have some decisions to make." Natasha's friends told her she should get an abortion, and nobody would know what had happened. Natasha's response was, "*I'll* know what happened." Given the turmoil in Natasha's life due to the murder investigation of her ex-boyfriend (detailed in Natasha's story), Katherine ached for her daughter. Ultimately, Katherine was glad that Natasha decided not to get an abortion and welcomed her when she moved in before having her baby. I asked Katherine what she would have decided for Natasha if she had been a minor. She said it would have depended on the circumstances, who the father was, how mature they were, and their relationship. However, neither Katherine nor her husband would have advised an abortion for Natasha, even as a minor child:

"I don't think there's one answer that fits all because each person is so unique, and each situation is so unique."

Unfortunately, Katherine and Sean's extended families had two very different opinions, which added to the pressure and complicated the decision making. Sean's family were New Yorkers who didn't quite understand "this open adoption thing." Sean never knew his birth father, a womanizer with whom his mother was madly in love when she became pregnant. He went off to war and never came back – that is, he was physically alive but never came back to her. She ended up marrying a wonderful man who treated Sean as his own son. But he never adopted Sean because of his German culture. Since Sean's birth father was still alive, her husband did not think that it would be morally right to adopt him. Years later, Katherine's sister searched for Sean's birth father and found him. However, Sean never contacted him. Katherine is saving the information for his children should they ever want it. From Sean's perspective, being the eldest of seven children, he did not want to disrespect his stepfather by looking for his birth father. When Natasha became pregnant, Sean's family had many questions about why she went the adoption route. They were open to it and were very curious but had difficulty understanding the benefits of adoption.

On the other hand, Katherine's family lacked the curiosity of Sean's family and rarely acknowledged complex familial issues. For them, when Natasha had the baby, it was done. Over with. Move on. Katherine felt conflicted with having two families with contrasting opinions.

Katherine admired Natasha's strength and resolve as she watched her stay the course of adoption, unfazed by familial opinions. When it came time for Natasha to choose between three potential adoptive families, Katherine and Sean offered their opinion but did not pressure Natasha to agree with them. Natasha chose Peter and May who had been trying to have a family for several years, experiencing invitro, several painful miscarriages, and three failed adoptions. Before coming to an agreement with Natasha, they had already decided if the adoption with her didn't work out, that would be their last attempt.

In Katherine's mind, *that* was the divine part of their adoption story. She said, "It was hard to see my daughter go through that pain. Meeting Peter and May made it easier. And liking them." The culmination of hope and faith is peace.

[Tears.]

Katherine, Sean, and Natasha developed a natural relationship with Peter and May. The five of them visited a few times before the birth. Katherine focused on helping Natasha handle her pregnancy as though she was Peter and May's surrogate. Peter and May came to town the day before Natasha's scheduled C-section, and they all had dinner together – complete with a big ice cream dessert bar.

The next day, Katherine was in the delivery room with Natasha when Peter and May's baby boy was born.

At this point in the interview, as Katherine described the scene, she wistfully held up photographs. She said, "This is my little guy ... he was so beautiful. That was in the nursery ... May and I met in there. This is my daughter ... they named him Xander – they were there." The picture that touched me the most was the one in which Katherine's husband, Sean, was handing the little bundle of Xander to Peter's outstretched arms.

Because Natasha had a C-section, she was able to stay an extra day in the hospital. She, Katherine, and Sean took that time to get to know little Xander. Natasha was even able to nurse him. Peter and May stayed with her on the second day so they could transition him over.

Xander was the center of the collective love from both families.

Although there were many tears, Katherine said that the nurses and other hospital staff couldn't believe how open and loving the whole process was as they witnessed the heart-wrenching moment when Natasha handed over Xander during the adoption ceremony (described in Natasha's story).

Katherine showed me another picture and said, "This is our little family." In the photograph, everyone was smiling with looks of relief intertwined with melancholy joy. One of the staff members told Katherine that Xander's adoption was completely different from another distressing adoption taking place in the hospital at the same time; the mother was young and didn't want to give up her baby.

The hardest part for Katherine was wheeling her daughter out of the hospital with nothing in her arms.

[Tears.]

After a pause, Katherine said, "I'm surprised that I am still crying. I haven't talked about this in a while. I was very proud of her … very sad." After Katherine and Sean went home, she found him in their bedroom weeping as he said, "What have we done? We should have made her keep that sweet little boy." Katherine told him, "That was not our decision."

Following Xander's birth, Katherine felt that her role was to listen to Natasha's sorrow and joy. Katherine is a deeply emotional person and associates certain songs with moments in her life. She said,

> *"The first time I heard this song 'Breathe' by John Tesh was at church service during Natasha's pregnancy. I questioned God so much about the heartaches Natasha was going through and hurt for her deeply. The lyrics kept going through my head 'I'm desperate for you, I'm lost without you' and resonated so deeply."*

She continued to describe how she felt for Natasha,

> *"This song broke me to pieces when I heard it. Sean and I were driving home from a visit with Xander, May, and Peter. Trace Adkins released 'Then They Do' in 2003, the year Xander was born. I kept thinking of all that Natasha was going to miss with Xander. I forgot how deep the heartache was then."*

At the time of Xander's birth in Colorado, birth mothers could legally change their minds during the six months following delivery. After his birth, May was having nightmares that Natasha would change her mind, calling Katherine with her concerns. When Katherine asked Natasha if she was going to change her mind, her response was, "Why would I do that? Here are these people who have that baby in their lives, and I'm going to rip him out of their hands?" Katherine said,

> *"I will tell you this about my daughter … she is the bravest and most courageous woman I know because she never wavered in her decision. She grieved the decision she had to make."*

[More tears.]

Katherine considers herself to be the "connective tissue" in the family. May and Peter told Katherine and Sean that they would always be Xander's grandparents. They also kept in touch with Natasha even after the six-month period. The families have visited each other often and still have a loving relationship. Their adoption was "wide-open" and has continued that way for 17 years.

"We gained a whole family when Natasha chose adoption for Xander."

Five years after giving birth to Xander, Natasha had another boy named Matthew with her fiancé. Years later, when Katherine accompanied them on a trip to California, she had to miss Xander's Junior High graduation ceremony. She sent him a note, texted him, and called him to make sure he knew she was thinking of him. She wrote, "To my number one grandson" on a card. Xander told her he didn't think he was number one and that Matthew would be jealous. To remove all his doubt, she responded that he was her first grandson and *still* was her number one.

"He is special to me because, in this whole thing, there was so much love involved. Peter and May were all about love. He was created for love. He's got a very soft, soft part of my life."

Swaddled in love since birth, Xander, in turn has embraced his role as Mathew's protective big brother. For example, when Katherine bought Matthew a mountain bike (Xander's passion), Xander peppered her with questions about the bike to make sure she got Matthew the correct one. One of Katherine's favorite memories occurred at one of Xander's soccer games. When he saw Matthew, he ran over, scooped him up, and showed him off to his teammates. She said, "I thought I was going to lose it. I wanted to cry so bad." He introduced him to everyone as his little brother. Katherine and May agree that since both boys are only children, they're going to need each other as adults.

Katherine recalled a dinner conversation in which Xander had many questions for both Natasha and May. She said, "It was really beautiful." Without animosity, he asked things like, "Why didn't you stay with my birth father?" or "Why did you pick my parents?" Both women were there for him, unified in answering his questions. May takes her adoptive mother role seriously; she said she feels a great responsibility to be the best mom she can be for Katherine and Natasha and to make sure that Xander has a good life.

"And um, that's how open it is."

~ Advice Through Katherine's Lens ~

<u>For birth grandparents:</u> "I personally live a life that I try not to project what I would do to someone else. You know your daughter very well, your son very well, you're going to have influence. You have to focus on the fact there's a child coming to this world, and you have to support the birth mother in particular to give them the best experience and love. You're still connected. Don't be judgmental. Just be there. Love them through whatever decision is made. As grandparents, if you're so privileged to have an open adoption, you're the connective tissue. As hard as it is, you've just got to come from that place of compassion, *forgiveness* and love – because we were fortunate enough to gain a family. I don't think we would change it for the world, looking back."

I asked Katherine to expand on what she meant by *forgiveness*. She said she meant the forgiveness of the birth parents. She said birth grandparents could make their children feel bad about what they've done, but she doesn't think they should. It was a very powerful moment when Sean told Natasha, "Okay, this is what's happened to your life. It's not what you wanted, but now we're here to support you in whatever you decide to do." Support them, don't reject them. She said,

"Forgiveness is the greatest support you could give."

"In hindsight, it's easy to say everything was right and fell into place. At the time, you just have to trust the decision, trust in God. Lots of prayer. I remember being on my knees screaming, "Why God? Why? I've asked you to protect her." Katherine said that by releasing her anguish, she was able to assist Natasha, which allowed strength and character to build in both of them.

<u>For extended families:</u> "It's the same thing I find as a widow. People don't want to talk about it because they don't want to make you feel sad. But they

don't realize that *not talking about it* causes so much more anxiety that you're sad anyways. So, talking about it opens what is held so deep inside."

"Forgiveness of oneself helps. Humility. It's okay to be sad. There's that baby that is bringing joy to another family. That family can be your extended family. If we all looked at ourselves, we can all find something that can be forgiven."

My Thoughts, My Lens

When Katherine mentioned the Trace Adkins song, I pulled up the official music video on YouTube to watch *Then They Do*.[48] As he sang, I teared up watching the parents in the video wishing their children would grow up during frustrating moments – and *then they do*. I glimpsed what Katherine knew Natasha would never experience with Xander. The magnitude of the gift her daughter gave to Xander's parents stunned me. I never thought about it from that perspective. Now, I get it.

I have always been impressed (and, if I'm being honest, envious) of people who can overcome complex life challenges with grace and forgiveness. Katherine and Sean's ability to set aside their own emotions and opinions so that they could lovingly offer Natasha their full support was exceptional. In the end, their reward was that they did *not* lose a grandson but instead were able to *gain a family*. Because Xander was everyone's priority, he was set up for success. I love it when grown-ups behave like adults.

---

[48] "Then They Do." *YouTube,* Uploaded by Trace Adkins, 24 Feb. 2009, www.youtube.com/watch?v=RYkzRYhlw_U. Accessed 12 Apr. 2021.

Louisa B. | Stay-At-Home Mom

Iowa
Year of Adoption: 1988

Louisa B. reminded me of Disney's Cinderella with her tender heart, blonde hair, and radiant smile. I almost expected bluebirds and charming woodland animals to spontaneously materialize on her shoulders as we talked. Her soft voice and quiet presence enclosed her delicate heart like parentheses. Her tears flowed throughout the interview, hushed reminders that her past was ever-present.

When Louisa was 18, she became pregnant by an older college boy attending a nearby university. They were both from the same small 500-person town in Iowa, consisting of one café, three churches, one bar, and zero stoplights. Louisa went to a neighboring town for high school because hers did not have one, and even then, her senior class consisted of fewer than 60 students. After graduating, she worked in a restaurant and planned to go to college. She and the college boy were not dating in the traditional sense. She said, "We had a mutual attraction. We would hook up and were very irresponsible about being careful."

When he learned Louisa was pregnant, he made it clear he wanted nothing to do with either her or their child. His family was cruel to Louisa and denied that he could have been the father. "It was odd that this guy's family turned ugly. People liked me, and I had known the family for a couple of years." They were "vocal and violent" with their opinions of her, insisting that someone else was responsible. When she asked them if they were interested or wanted to know anything about the child, they did not and insisted she was making it up. Even to this day, they are still in denial. When they see her in public, they turn the other way. The calloused lack of support from his family made Louisa's pregnancy that much harder for her.

[Tears.]

329

Unfortunately, Louisa and her best friend also had a falling out. Louisa was devastated when she discovered that her friend was ashamed of her and had been gossiping about her. The betrayal ruined their friendship. Louisa felt she could no longer go to her church because her friend's family attended the same one. Everyone in the town knew she was pregnant but wouldn't talk to her about it. She was cut off from the support of friendship and the comfort of her church while dealing with the birth father's crazy family bent on revenge. When I asked Louisa what her close friends or relatives could have done to help, she said,

> "It would have been comforting to me to know that other people had said something to his family that it wasn't right. It would have been nice to know that other people were sticking up for me. Things are changing now. It's easier now. [Girls are] not as ostracized now [as they were] back then."

Luckily, though, Louisa's own family was very supportive. They promised to figure it out and offered to let Louisa live with them if she wanted to keep her baby. She ultimately chose adoption because she knew she would have to depend on her parents if she chose to be a single mother. She didn't want them to have to shoulder her responsibilities. Years later, Louisa's mom revealed that she secretly wanted her to keep the baby. It was extremely hard on her mom because "I gave away her first grandchild."

Louisa never wanted to be ashamed about her choice. She consciously decided always to be open about her adoption.

> "If I was open and never guilty or ashamed, then no one could ever try to manipulate me ... it helped me to grow up and realize that we all make mistakes. We just need to do the best we can and keep going."

Except for the morning sickness, Louisa had a wonderful pregnancy. She took care of herself by eating well and exercising every day. When she was six months along, she met with a lawyer to start the adoption process. He was friends with a couple who had already adopted one child and were looking to adopt another one. Louisa chose that family because she felt good about their background. They were college-educated, Christian, and had a nice home.

Louisa was due on New Year's Eve, but since her doctor had holiday plans, they tried to induce her before Christmas. Louisa's baby girl was not having it and didn't show up until a few days after the New Year. Her post-holiday arrival proved she was as considerate as her birth mom, not wanting to inconvenience anyone with her presence. She was actually the first baby born in the New Year at that small-town hospital. But because she would be adopted, she was not given the celebratory gifts that a first newborn of the year usually received. Louisa's mother was there for the entire 14-hour labor and welcomed the bruises on her hand as Louisa squeezed to relieve the pain. Other than that, the birth went well with no complications. Louisa was able to hold her baby for a few tender hours, dress her, take pictures, and cry.

[Tears.]

"It was beautiful and painful."

Louisa and her mom had presents for the baby. They named her Heather, not knowing if they would ever see her again. Louisa desperately wanted Heather to know that she loved her. At that moment, Louisa didn't know if she would ever have another baby and wondered if she was giving away her only child. However, she wanted to give Heather the best and, in her mind, do the most loving thing she could for her. Since the adoption was closed, she didn't see the adoptive couple when they came to the hospital, and they didn't see her. Both parties knew the other was in the same building, but they did not have a face to face. The only thing Louisa insisted on was that they exchange letters once a year with updates. The lawyer ferried letters back and forth for 18 years. There were a few years that the family missed, but when they were reconnected, Heather's mom apologized profusely. They had moved, and the lawyer didn't have their new address. Those letters were extremely comforting to Louisa. Heather's adoptive mother intuitively knew which milestones and details that Louisa needed to hear. One year they sent her a snip of Heather's hair – a soft little curl. They also sent her pictures and updates on her progress.

Over the years, life quietly continued for Louisa. She got married and had two more children, a girl and a boy. She wrote letters about her family's activities, with details about Heather's biological half-siblings and grandparents. Louisa let Heather know that she was thinking about her and was grateful for her adoptive parents. Heather's parents saved all of Louisa's letters in a safe deposit box and gave them to her on her 18th birthday.

The letters to Louisa from Heather's adoptive mother did not include the name they chose for the baby. In Louisa's mind, her baby's name was Heather – and referred to her as such in her letters. Louisa named her second daughter Jessica, but unbeknownst to her, Heather had been renamed Jessica by her adoptive parents. When they received Louisa's letter announcing Jessica's birth, they "freaked out" because they thought she had somehow found them. The lawyer assured them that it was just a coincidence because they had different middle names. The letters continued between the two families. In the final letter before Jessica's 18th birthday, her adoptive mom wrote, "I think you'll like her name."

A few months after Jessica turned 18, Louisa received a card with a young girl's handwriting. At first, she was puzzled. But when she opened it, she realized it who it was from. Inside the card was a letter and Jessica's full name. Louisa called her kids in so they could read the letter together. They already knew all about Jessica; she never kept Jessica's existence a hushed guilty secret. In the letter, Jessica invited them to stay at her house and attend her high school graduation. Louisa and her family accepted the invitation. Before they met, Louisa and Jessica talked on the phone a few times. When the day came, they were both very emotional.

[Tears.]

Louisa said, "I wasn't sure if she would let me hug her. She did. We hugged, and it was very friendly and sweet." Louisa was appreciative of how Jessica's family was very giving and caring. Jessica was amongst the top students in her class and gave a speech with the other valedictorians and salutatorians. Louisa was extremely proud of her.

Jessica's family was lovely – her adoptive mother in particular was welcoming and considerate of Louisa's excitement and emotions. During their visit, they talked more with each other than Louisa and Jessica did. Jessica's mother freely shared their experiences, and Louisa was grateful to be able to get to know the lovely compassionate woman she had been corresponding with over the years. She told Louisa how they were waiting on "pins and needles" for Jessica's birth. She described how the doctors and nurses carefully scrutinized her and her husband to see if they deserved to have Louisa's baby. (Louisa remembered that the hospital staff was protective over her; one nurse had even invited her to her home, to make sure she was doing okay.) Jessica's mother opened up, sharing her worries and fears, for which Louisa was grateful – she said,

"She shared her child."

In addition to sharing her experience, Jessica's mother enjoyed learning odd little things about her daughter that weren't normal to their family. For example, when she made Louisa an omelet and asked what she wanted in it, she nodded and smiled when Louisa listed the same veggies that Jessica liked. Over the years, after their initial meeting, Jessica's mother would ask Louisa odd questions, such as, "Do you always have chicken stock on hand?"

Louisa does … and so does Jessica.

Louisa believes, "The hand of God was in this from the beginning to the end." Jessica always knew she was adopted. Her mother shared that, even as a little girl, Jessica would worry about Louisa. During her senior year, she created a little booklet of poetry and essays. She wrote one about getting to meet her birth mother someday and discovering where she got her smile.

Since their reunion, every year, Jessica has remembered Louisa on Mother's Day and her birthday. She has also made an effort to visit several times and get to know her half-siblings. When Jessica first visited, they went to Louisa's high school reunion as a family.

Louisa laughed as she described showing up with two daughters named Jessica.

It reminded her of the 1980s Newhart sitcom when Larry introduced his brothers with a twang saying, "This – my brother Darryl, and this – my other brother Darryl."[49]

---

[49] "Newhart: Season 2(1/6) Larry And His Brother Darryl And His Other Brother Darryl." *YouTube*, uploaded by Shout! Factory, 3 Feb. 2014. www.youtube.com/watch?v=79vMe31CuIQ. Accessed 20 May 2021.

Louisa is very proud of Jessica. She graduated from college, has a successful career, and adopted a child, too. When I asked Louisa if she could compare raising Jessica with her other two children, she said,

> *"I don't have all the minutiae – memories with her [like] the two I raised. I didn't see her walk or her first tooth or her first scar. I didn't go through her teenage heartaches. I couldn't, of course. So, I don't feel I did her a disservice or feel that I should have been there for her. I gave her to a family that provided all that and more—seeing how great she's turned out and how wonderful they've been to me ... I know I did the right thing. It was the right decision. She's probably a better person for it. I'm proud of her, and I do love her. But it's not the same as my other two because I think if she had seen me in my good, bad, and ugly (and vice versa), then it would be that much more."*

[Tears.]

Giving birth to Jessica impacted Louisa's decisions throughout her life. She had a profound fear of losing her younger children when they were little. She said, "It was because I had a baby. And then I *didn't* have a baby." Psychologically, she feared not being able to keep her subsequent children. Her son was diagnosed with leukemia at four months old and has spent a lifetime battling bone tumors and strokes. Over time, the fear of losing her children dissipated. Her son is still alive but has undergone bone marrow transplants, medication, radiation, and numerous surgeries. He once told Louisa that he wished they had let him die. But she wanted to give him the opportunity of life. She said, "I mean, you don't just give up on your kid."

Jessica's birth also propelled Louisa to become a consummate wife and mother. She efficiently ran the household as a stay-at-home mom. She became very involved in her children's lives – making sure her kids read early, teaching them to tie their shoes early, volunteering at the school, ensuring the teachers and principals knew her, joining the PTA, etc. Louisa couldn't afford ballet or piano lessons, but she gave her children her entire self. Jessica's birth guided Louisa's purpose in life, a series of selfless events that continued to the present and undoubtedly will persist into the future.

~ Advice Through Louisa's Lens ~

<u>For birth mothers:</u> "I have encouraged many people to consider adoption. I understand the reservations of not knowing if you're giving your child to a better situation. I try to show things can turn out great."

"For women who have given up children for adoption … it's hard to say because I don't know what kind of support [they have]. My religion and relationship with God were important. Support of family was important, [yet] many people do not have it. Be in tune with your world, whether you believe in God or something else. Know you did the best you could."

I asked Louisa if she thought she did the best she could. She replied, "Yes." A few beats later, she asked me if I thought *my* birth mom did the best that she could.

I was taken aback.

I answered, "Yes, I suppose she did. Thank you for asking me that. I'm not sure I have ever thought about it."

Louisa replied, "With all of the wonderful things that happened with the adoption, how can anyone think there wasn't a blessing with this situation? It continues to unfold … I am grateful for the experience. It has made me better and [has helped] other people. When I share this story with people, they are deeply touched, and the blessings continue."

My Thoughts, My Lens

For several days after the interview, I pondered Louisa's question and wondered why I was quick to answer "Yes." It was difficult to remove my emotion from the "equation" when trying to parse out why I immediately said my own birth mother did the best she could … because, over my lifetime, I was angry about my adoption.

From a purely logical approach (sans all, ugh … emotion): choosing adoption would have to be counter-intuitive for a mother. As a mom of two daughters, I have learned that the need to protect and nurture a child is undeniable. So, to make a conscious choice to remove the child from the "equation" would be to acknowledge that the child's life of "wholeness" takes precedence over the birth mother's natural instinct.

From a purely emotional space: choosing adoption would have to be harder than cutting off one's own leg – with a fork. Again, I say this as a mother of two – my girls are my soul, and if they were to be cut out of my life, my remaining existence would be as lifeless as a piece of coal.

I started yoga exercises this year for my tight neck and shoulders. An online yoga YouTuber mentioned, "Often neck pain is not seeing more than one side to something … take this opportunity to choose to let go of anything that's not serving you. Just release it."[50] The combination of practicing yoga and daring to think about the pain my birth mother surely endured caused my neck pain to subside (enough for me to discontinue weekly visits to my chiropractor). By giving me a chance at "wholeness" and intuitively knowing that a portion of her own soul would die when she chose adoption, she made the ultimate sacrifice – *a primal act of protectiveness.*

---

[50] "Yoga for Neck and Shoulder Relief – Yoga With Adriene." *YouTube*, uploaded by Yoga With Adriene, 18 Jun. 2017. www.youtube.com/watch?v=SedzswEwpPw. Accessed 20 May 2021.

Therefore, I'll have to stand by my quick response to Louisa and confirm: YES. I believe my birth mother did the best she could.

Through the Lens of The Author: My Story

Suni Z. | Retired Accounting & Finance Manager

Dongducheon, South Korea
Year of Birth: 1969

While I already shared parts of my own story throughout this book, I decided to share the remainder here to complete the gaps in my personal journey.

As an army brat, I've moved 34 times in my life (initially not my choice, but later in life, I moved out of habit). With each move, I was painfully aware that I was not "physically" part of any ethnic community. As a kid, I had many friends – both Black and White – but had only a few Asian and Brown friends. I believe I avoided my Asian counterparts because they were a subconscious reminder of my adoption.

Overall, I had a good childhood. My parents adopted me when my dad was stationed in South Korea. He was tasked with bringing fresh water from the army base to a nearby orphanage. He had taken up photography as a hobby and would snail mail photographs of Korean children to my mother who was living in Florida. When he suggested adoption, she bought a plane ticket and flew to South Korea. My mom stayed in a room rented from a Korean family while my adoption paperwork was processed through the Korean adoption agency. My parents were very loving, protective, and extremely strict – military style. Although Jewish by birth, my mom chose to worship in the Christian church, not in a synagogue. At one point she was zealous about Pentecostal Christianity. My dad was zealous about creating familial normalcy. As an only child, the upside was that I got 100% of their affection. The downside of being an only child was that I struggled to learn the art of forgiveness. In my observation, children with siblings seem to understand the inherent nature of forgiveness. They also have a natural sense of belonging, whereas I always yearned to be part of community (as I detailed at the end of Jack S.'s story).

341

My mother's Jewish family wholeheartedly accepted me with no reservations. From them, I learned the importance of education, hard work, female mental strength, and the healing properties of matzo ball soup. My dad's family members were self-proclaimed rednecks (of the hillbilly variety). Growing up, my mom and dad used to joke about how "red" his neck was. When I was a child, I thought they were referring to his skin color because he has some Cherokee roots, and his neck is tinged with red undertones that are pronounced when he tans. My dad's mother was from the southeastern part of Kentucky, and his father was from the southwestern part of Virginia. Their families were hardworking coal miners. About 70% of my dad's family accepted me as their "own." The ones who did claim me are fabulous; from them, I learned about affection, generosity, the importance of slow-cooked grits, and the joy of biscuits made from scratch. But I had both subtle and "jack-slapping" reminders that I was not biologically tied to my dad's family.

When I was in college, I went for a weekend to visit a few of my grandfather's relatives in Wise, Virginia, a small town of about 3,000 people in the mountainous part of the state near the border of Kentucky and West Virginia. (The movie *Big Stone Gap* with Ashley Judd provides a good visual for Wise.) My great aunt was wonderfully kind, as a starving college student, she stuffed me with country cooking and about ten Twinkies throughout the weekend. When we went to the tiny country church the Sunday morning before leaving, I met some of my third and fourth cousins who had no clue who I was. When I tried to engage them in conversation, I talked about how my grandfather was their grandparents' brother, and they looked at me like I had lost my mind. That moment was emotionally polarizing; I had just enjoyed the company of a sweet old woman, but then in the same timeframe, I was reminded that my Asian appearance was too much for the ethnically sheltered to grasp. I was brokenhearted and went back to school with delicious butter beans and cornbread, but they were tasteless when I ate them later. At least those relatives were polite enough not to say anything ignorant to my face. Unfortunately, other relatives from my dad's family educated me about the evil that occurs when hatred and racism are nurtured. One of my cousins once told me I looked like the N-word at the end of a sun-filled Florida summer with no sunscreen. Another cousin was disgusted with my father because he thought my father had married a Black woman (when he saw me for the first time, he thought I was half Black/half White). I was speechless, not understanding why he thought it was a bad thing to be half Black. As the rest of my father's relatives laughed, awkwardly shook their heads with amusement, and howled at his ignorance, I pretended to think it was funny, inwardly crushed by the reminder that I was not a genuine Miller.

My awareness of my ethnic displacement was originally molded in the second grade when my family moved to Mannheim, Germany. Like John H., who mentioned a similar experience in his story, German teenage boys hurled the classic "slanty-eye" insults at me. But unlike John H., it did not stop there. I was also one of their favorite punching bags. For two years, my family lived "on the economy" in a German high-rise apartment building. We were one of two American Army families in that complex; most military families lived on the Army and Air Force bases. The other American family was Black, and I was friends with the three siblings – twins (one year younger than me) and an older sister (two years older than me). Some of the adult Germans in our complex had an obsessive fascination with my Black friends' hair. They literally put their hands on my friends' heads and felt their hair with impunity – just digging in their scalps as though they were kneading bread.

Our parents didn't understand that when they sent us out to play or to the bus stop, we were the target of the cruel German teenage boys who felt it was their duty to show us we did not belong. When the adults were not around, the teenage boys would grab my friends' hair by the fist-full and pull them down to the ground. They punched, kicked, and spit on us. Because we were elementary schoolers, we didn't have the physical strength to protect ourselves, so we took the abuse, planting nuggets of hate in our hearts. I was always wary of the depraved teenage boys lurking behind corners. They were in my mind every time we walked to and from the bus stop at the top of the hill (a few blocks from our apartment building). On one occasion, we were ambushed, and three teenage boys held me down while a fourth one shoved his hand up my dress between my legs. My friends had no idea what to do, so they just stood by and helplessly watched until the boys were satisfied that my shrieks of horror were genuine. I think we were all so shocked – we never talked about it to anyone else, much less to each other. That was the moment when the sorrow I had about being adopted transformed into full-blown rage. A few months later, another American family with two very sweet half-Asian, half-White elementary school-aged daughters moved into our building. I am ashamed to admit that I teamed up with my friends to beat them up, exacting our displaced revenge.

I was finally part of a team.

I'm sure some psychologist would have a field day picking apart why I would beat the hell out of the innocent half-Asian girls. I think it's pretty apparent that my self-hatred spilled over into my actions.

After about a year of abuse by the German teenagers, my friends' family was transferred out, and another Army family moved into their vacated apartment. They had a beefy redheaded son who was much taller than the average sixth-grader. When we walked to the bus stop or played badminton in the courtyard, I was never ambushed by the German teenagers. It was a relief to have an unwitting bodyguard. He was a good kid and very patient with me when I had my meltdowns. I remember getting angry for losing at badminton and whacking him as hard as I could on his head with the metal rim of my racket. It definitely hurt him because he doubled over and held the back of his head for about 15 seconds. When he composed himself, he stood up and calmly told me that I shouldn't have done that. I've learned through my adoption research that it is not uncommon for adoptees to lash out. I suppose on some level, I was testing his loyalty. I didn't deserve his kindness, but in looking back, I am grateful (and lucky) that he had the composure and maturity to be so understanding with me.

While the experiences I had as an elementary schooler ignited my rage over my adoption, it did not color my overall view of Germany. I have many fond memories of Germans. I had a very kind and patient teenage babysitter with blonde hair and buck teeth who seemed to know only three English words: "you bad girl." My parents were friends with other German families who treated me kindly. I was relieved when my family moved from Mannheim to other German cities because then we lived on the American Army bases. The other Army brats became my family over the two tours of duty – one in elementary school and the other in high school. Counterintuitively, our transient military community was tight-knit. We had to make friends very quickly because we all moved often.

Unfortunately, my parents didn't understand that immersing a non-White child in an ethnically homogenous environment outside of the military bases led to trouble. But I didn't tell them about many of my experiences, so how could they have known? My father used to get exasperated with me when I would obsess about being the only non-White member of the family. He would try to comfort me by saying it didn't matter that I was a different "color" than White. I have no doubt that he loved me very much. However, while my skin color didn't matter to *him*, he couldn't see that it mattered *to me* – because it *certainly* mattered to other people. I'm guessing most non-White adoptees who grow up in predominantly White neighborhoods do not experience the extreme abuse that I did as a little girl – however, many of them unquestionably feel out of place.

Deborah D. Gray said (quoted by Rachel Garlinghouse),

> *"There is a comfortable anonymity to blending into one's surroundings. Children and adults feel a constant, low level of stress by being the only person of a particular race in their school, on their street, or in the grocery store. Even if they are 'accepted,' the word itself points out the difference factor. Someone else has the choice of accepting or not accepting. In their making the choice, often the naturalness of an everyday interaction is changed."*[51]

People are going to see what they want to see, though. When I was younger, I had a difficult time reconciling my Asian exterior with my White interior.

I do feel bad for enlightened White people when they are grouped in with the ignorant – my husband is disappointed when non-White people automatically assume that he is a racist just because he is White. I want to believe that most humans try to coexist peacefully and are not racist at their core. As a non-White person, when I am the recipient of microaggressions or outright aggressive acts, it is those memories that often stand out for me, effectively blurring all of the positive experiences I've had over my lifetime. My parents worked hard to give me a safe and loving home. Most of my upbringing was decent. But when I go down the uncomfortable path of dark childhood memories, I need to force myself to remember there are many

---

[51] Gray, Deborah D. *Attaching in Adoption*. As quoted in Garlinghouse, Rachel. *Come Rain or Shine, A White Parent's Guide to Adopting and Parenting Black Children*. CreateSpace, 2013, p. 139.

more accepting humans in the world than blind ones. These days I make a concerted effort to see that most people are good.

Racism, again, hit me in the face when I enrolled in a new private high school in Virginia my senior year, during which I made friends quickly (as I had learned to do as an Army brat). The school was not affiliated with the military. Unfortunately, at first, I wasn't aware that a few of the girls in my new group were racist against Black people. As we got into the semester, I became aware of it but ignored it because, as a new student, I was glad to have a cadre, too naive to understand the concept of "guilt by association."

That proved to be a big mistake.

I should have been more selective in choosing my friends because three Black girls decided that I would be their target. They were abusive and unabashedly nasty towards me – threatening to beat me and screaming obscene Asian insults whenever they could. Frankly, they scared the hell out of me, and I was careful to avoid being alone with them. I used to obsess and cry in anger, confused as to why they would act so hatefully when in my mind, they certainly knew what it was like to be on the receiving end of prejudice. I understood their rage but was confounded as to why *I* was their target. When I finally had an opportunity to ask the least aggressive of the trio why they hated me so much. (We were at a graduation party – she had been drinking and was in a good mood.) She told me it was because of the prejudiced friends I had.

What?

At the time, that confused me even more. I bristled and self-righteously rationalized that they didn't know me or who my friends were before senior year, nor were they privy to the time when I was four years old, and my normally uber-calm mother uncharacteristically flipped out and pounded into my brain the horrendous nature of the N-word (Thank you, Mom). For years, I churned – sad and angry that they couldn't see my heart – over and over, it gnawed at me. I couldn't understand how they could be blind to the fact that their actions against me were exactly the same prejudicial actions they were railing against. *Now*, I understand. It was a hard lesson for me to learn that *friend choice matters* (as evidenced by my experience detailed at the end of Jack S's story). But in hindsight, I now know that they could not see clearly because their own pain clouded their vision.

346

And then … I realized I had done the same thing.

I debated on whether to share the following because the admission leaves me feeling vulnerable. However, after tearfully discussing it with one of my dearest friends, she told me that a good book is one in which the author leaves something "on the table." She is right. I've asked so many people to be vulnerable with me for this book, so it is only fair that I do the same. When I told my youngest daughter about my regret, she said the vulnerability was good for me.

Here it is: I am very ashamed to admit that I wasn't always an ally of the LGBTQ community. Growing up, I was confined by the Bible-thumping belief that homosexuality is a sin, which I completely believed. I was also enveloped in a 20th century military community where it was perfectly acceptable (and even applauded) for my generation to denigrate anyone who wasn't straight. I offer this up as an explanation and *not* as an excuse. For years, in my mind, I foolishly placed myself in a loftier position than non-heterosexuals. By stepping on them with my thoughts and careless comments, I fed my own bruised ego. Ugh, it distresses me now at how indiscriminately I perpetuated the prejudice. My first nudge towards awakening was when I became friends with my husband's college roommate, who came out during his junior year and introduced us to his friends. We had some good times, and I learned that humans are humans.

All are worthy of love.

Deplorably, it took another 20 years to completely purge my irresponsible opinions of the LGBTQ community. I regret that it took so long and wish I could have been more cognizant of the harmful effect of my blind ignorance much sooner. It wasn't until the past decade that I believe I have completely shed the last vestiges of prejudice. With the help of my daughters and their young friends, they correct me when I misstep and gladly answer questions I have about gender roles and sexuality. I love Generation Z – they embrace a broader scope of our human differences without the myopic lens that many in my generation held for years.

I think when someone is hurting, choosing hate is a convenient way to dull the pain – or as my mom says – "hurt people hurt people."

I now see that the rage I had about my adoption affected my outlook on humans. I wish I could adequately express how truly sorry I am; I hope that

347

my subsequent actions have demonstrated that it is 100% possible for someone to change.

My oldest daughter's best friend is a lovely gay man whom I have come to *adore*. Recently he has been harassed and threatened regularly by one of his neighbors. It broke my heart when he said that he shouldn't have to continuously defend his rights or worry if he wants to hold his boyfriend's hand in public. The visible pain on his face as he told me about his story captured the collective pain of all humans.

Now I understand that the three Black girls who hated me my senior year were also in pain. I hope they have since found healing and freedom from their grief. My wish for the German teenage boys, who are now older men (if they are still living), is that somewhere along the way, they were able to drop the hatred they carried and were able to make room in their hearts for love.

For years, in my journey to find acceptance, the resentment I carried about my adoption and the shame I had about my race were so intertwined that when one reared up, I blindly fought both – while in the process, I looked down on the LGBTQ community to keep my head above the surface.

Futile.

I pray that by sharing this side of me, my story brings hope to those who feel ostracized. Remember, I was seemingly predestined to embrace bigotry because of my upbringing. I am proof that it *is* possible to change. Therefore, I believe that it is also possible for the stigma and shame of adoption to change. Just like my husband's roommate opened my eyes to my closed mind simply by being himself, I believe that we as an adoption community have the power to normalize the existence of adoption simply by *openly being ourselves*.

I hope that birth parents who feel judged will take comfort.

I hope that adoptive parents will believe they are the "real deal."

I hope that all adoptees (both domestic and international) will have faith that someday, all humans will view adoptees as legitimate members of their adoptive families.

I hope that those who are holding on to prejudice will feel safe enough to release their hatred.

I hope that everyone will take a step closer to love.

I hope.

I had to learn how to "bravely hope" by taking a page from a dear friend's playbook. For decades, he buried the abuse he endured as a child so that on the surface, he appeared to have a flat-line demeanor. But the gurgling poison of his memories beneath his exterior slowly ate away at his roots to the point that he started to die on the inside. Because he refused even to take a small glimpse at his past (and certainly refused therapy), he unintentionally hurt those in his path … closing himself off to everyone. It wasn't until he was on the precipice of losing his family that he agreed to go to therapy. Serendipitously, he found the proper professional for him, a perfect mix of assertiveness, acerbic wit, and intelligence. It wasn't until his therapist pulled the complete story of his past out of him that he was able to shed the layers of scales he had built as armor over the years.

The key was that he had to first examine his pain *thoroughly* to be able to leave it in the past. From that point, he was able to grow in love.

Much to my surprise, following my friend's example, writing this book has been my therapy. Story by story, slowly, steadily … as I compared them to my own, I felt a little bit lighter. Somehow, listening to both the tumultuous and peaceful adoption stories validated my own feelings. For those of you still suffering from despair over your adoptions, I encourage you to look at your own stories and allow the fire of pain to burn its hottest.

Allowing myself to look directly at my pain enabled me to unclench as the fire died down.

We once grew tomatoes in our firepit. That year, the tomatoes were a venerable saliva-squirting party-in-the-mouth. And I'm not normally that crazy about raw tomatoes. New life flourished out of the ashes.

Unacknowledged pain has power.

By acknowledging our past, it will no longer have control over us.

The last thing I want to say is this: I hope that the love that caught me by surprise after intensively examining my own pain is able to find you, too.

Afterword

"Try to learn to breathe deeply, really to taste food when you eat, and when you sleep really to sleep. Try as much as possible to be wholly alive with all your might, and when you laugh, laugh like hell. And when you get angry, get good and angry. Try to be alive. You will be dead soon enough."

-Ernest Hemingway

To my family, Kurt, Anna, Melodie, Maggie, Steph, and Nermal: you are my heart. You have taught me that love is worth the trials of life.

I am grateful for all of the participants in this book. Through the Lens of Ourselves, I can breathe. I can taste. I can see. I can feel. However, according to my daughters, I am going deaf. In listening to the adoption stories of everyone in the preceding chapters, somewhere in the back of my mind, I was paranoid that I would miss a key word such as "not." As the adoptees, adoptive families, and birth families revealed their vulnerabilities, I became very aware of the gift they were giving me, and I wanted to protect them. By sharing the genuineness of their raw feelings and experiences, I was compelled to treasure their stories and bundle them with the same care that I swaddled my daughters as babies. While I did my best to be as accurate as possible, any discrepancies that slipped through are 100% my doing.

First of all, a heartfelt thanks to the interviewees of this book. Without you, this book would not exist. Your eagerness and honesty carried me through the year of COVID-19, racial tensions, political mayhem, and uncertainty. You propelled me to feel, churn, and ultimately grow into a place of love and self-acceptance.

An immeasurable thanks to all of my friends, relatives and coworkers who made introductions and vouched for me with the interviewees. I will only list your first names here to keep the privacy of the interviewees intact ... but you *know* who you are: Anna, Anthony, Brad, Craig, Emily, Karen, Kim, Julie, KT, Margot, Michael, Michele, Rachel, Phil, Sara, Sue, and Tammy.

351

A special thanks to Gail Spector, my wise aunt, coach, and counselor. Thank you for always being on my side, answering every question, and your endless supply of advice. Over the years, and especially this past year, you have generously given me nuggets of wisdom and propped me up when I was the most insecure. I love you dearly and will forever be grateful that you came with the package of my adoptive family.

Thank you, Sarah Mayor, for editing my manuscript without judgment. Your comments on clarity and TMI were spot on. Your professionalism, sense of humor, and tenacity helped to transform my book into a product to which I am proud to attach my name. I had a blast working with you.

Thank you, Brigitte Issel, for your developmental edit. Your insight to social awareness and political correctness expanded my thought process. By providing a reader's perspective, you helped me reach a deeper understanding of all players in the adoption triad. Thank you for supporting me.

Thank you, Joanne Campo, for your brilliance in designing the book cover. You created a visual masterpiece of what was in my heart. The sunset will always remind me of my beloved grandmother and now the world will see her beauty because of you.

Thank you, Melissa St. James, for your constant enthusiasm over my project and for the plethora of beach photographs. I appreciate that you comprehensively and freely shared your academic perspective. Thank you for the final T-crossing and I-dotting – as well as listening to me as I rode the roller coaster of doubt and confidence. Your patience is astounding.

Thank you, Katie Timmons, for making me cry (you know why). You are the bee's knees to my elbows. Thank you for cheering me on and believing in me when I needed it the most. I can't believe we have known each other for 35 years. Our parallel lives have unfolded as they were *supposed* to happen.

Thank you, Kim Maturo-Hilt, for telling me that I *had* to write this book when it was only a percolating concept and not yet a reality. Thank you for your website design prowess, you are an IT goddess.

Thank you, Ken Spector, for recommending Lisa See's historical fiction, *The Island of Sea Women*. Thanks to your thoughtful email from out of the blue, the pages of her book propelled me to find *my* story.

Thank you to everyone who selflessly gave me the time to impart your knowledge: Cliff Edwards, for taking the time out of your busy schedule to offer your wisdom about forgiveness and life goals. Paul Spector, for supporting me through logic and helping me understand the intricacies of digital marketing. Jim Hilt, for educating this 20th century throwback about 21st century social media. Jill Murphy, for helping me understand the sequence of publishing through your birth mother story. Connie Thompson, for pointing me in the right direction and offering big picture advice. Sue Goodman, for introducing me to Connie.

To Kurt, **my favorite person in the world**, my husband of nearly 30 years, my sense of humor sensei, my SFD editor: I'm not sure how you managed to keep up on my tandem second-guessing hamster wheel without having a heart attack (or how you resisted the urge to push me off). It was worth it. Thank you for sticking with me. I am looking forward to jogging the next 30 years with you.

Most of all, thank you, Mom and Dad. My life is exactly as it should be. A hemisphere couldn't keep us apart. Thank you for your boundless love. I cherish that you have always been my biggest fans. I love you in this world and into the next.

Suggested Reading

- Brown, Brené, PhD, LMSW. *Rising Strong: The Reckoning. The Rumble. The Revolution.* Spiegel & Grau, an imprint of Random House, a division of Penguin Random House LLC, 2015.

- Eldridge, Sherrie. *Twenty Things Adopted Kids Wish Their Adoptive Parents Knew.* Bantam Dell, a division of Random House, Inc., 1999.

- Fessler, Ann. *The Girls Who Went Away.* Penguin Group, 2006.

- Garlinghouse, Rachel. *Come Rain or Shine, A White Parent's Guide to Adopting and Parenting Black Children.* CreateSpace, 2013.

- Glaser, Gabrielle. *American Baby: A Mother, a Child, and the Shadow History of Adoption.* Viking, 2021.

- Gray, Deborah D. *Attaching in Adoption: Practical Tools for Today's Parents.* Jessica Kingsley Pub, Reprint Edition 16 Jan. 2012.

- Han, Hyun Sook. *Many Lives Intertwined.* Yeong & Yeong Book Company, 2004.

- Irving, Debby. *Waking Up White and Finding Myself in the Story of Race.* Elephant Room Press, 2014.

- Ki-young, Hyun. *Sun-i Samch'on.* Asia Publishers, 2012.

- Lifton, Betty Jean. *Journey of the Adopted Self: A Quest for Wholeness.* Basic Books, Reprint Edition, 1995.

- Maangchi with Martha Rose Shulman, *Maangchi's Big Book of Korean Cooking.* Houghton Mifflin Harcourt Publishing Company, 2019.

- Murphy, Jill M. *Finding Motherhood.* CreateSpace, 2015.

- See, Lisa. *The Island of Sea Women.* Schribner, An Imprint of Simon & Schuster, Inc., 2019.

- Verrier, Nancy Newton. *The Primal Wound: Understanding the Adopted Child.* Gateway Press, Inc., 1993.

- Wolff, Jana. *Secret Thoughts of an Adoptive Mother.* Andrews and McMeel, a Universal Press Syndicate Company, 1997.

Made in the USA
Monee, IL
09 June 2021